BRAZILIAN JIU-JITSU
FIGHTING STRATEGIES

BRAZILIAN JIU-JITSU FIGHTING STRATEGIES

Romero "Jacare" Cavalcanti
Mark Van Schuyver, PhD
PALADIN PRESS · BOULDER, COLORADO

Other books by Mark Van Schuyver:

Fighting Strategies of Muay Thai:
    Secrets of Thailand's Boxing Camps (with Kru Pedro Solana Villalobos)

Brazilian Jiu-Jitsu Fighting Strategies
by Romero

Copyright © 2006 by Mark Van Schuyver
and Romero

ISBN 13: 978-1-58160-548-8
Printed in the United States of America

Published by Paladin Press, a division of
Paladin Enterprises, Inc.
Gunbarrel Tech Center
7077 Winchester Circle
Boulder, Colorado 80301 USA
+1.303.443.7250

Direct inquiries and/or orders to the above address.

PALADIN, PALADIN PRESS, and the
are trademarks belonging to Paladin Enterprises and
registered in United States Patent and Trademark Office.

All rights reserved. Except for use in a review, no
portion of this book may be reproduced in any form
without the express written permission of the publisher.

Neither the author nor the publisher assumes
any responsibility for the use or misuse of
information contained in this book.

Visit our Web site at www.paladin-press.com

Table of Contents

Introduction 1

Chapter 1: Brazilian Jiu-Jitsu 3

Chapter 2: Standing 21

Chapter 3: Closed Guard 45

Chapter 4: Open Guard 65

Chapter 5: Half Guard 85

Chapter 6: Side Control 103

Chapter 7: North-to-South Control 123

Chapter 8: Knee-in-the-Belly 139

Chapter 9: Mount 155

Chapter 10: Back 173

Chapter 11: Diagnosis 189

References 203

DEDICATION

This book is dedicated to the late Rolls Gracie.

You set a good example for me, for all of us. You influenced a whole generation. I think I will never meet a person like you again. Thank you very much for being my instructor, mentor, and friend. From the bottom of my heart, God bless you, Rolls.
—Professor Romero "Jacare" Cavalcanti

ACKNOWLEDGMENTS

The authors would like to thank Melissa Taylor for taking the photos featured in this book. Special thanks to Dr. Billye Van Schuyver for editing our final draft. Our sincere thanks to Ben Sutherland for the many hours of work that he spent editing the photos and supporting the project. And thanks also to Alliance manager Stephen Smith for gathering information and archival photos for the book.

The authors would like to thank those who agreed to be interviewed and/or photographed for this project, including Pat Harvey, Chris Moriarty, Roberto Traven, Flavia Traven, Bull Shaw, Felipe Neto, Fabio Gurgel, Abdul Mutakabbir, Ryan Ellison, Fernando Gurgel, Eduardo Carvalho, and D.J. Farmer.

The authors would like to express their respect and support of all those who teach, practice, and promote the art of Brazilian jiu-jitsu. We wish you much success.

Finally, the authors offer their heartfelt thanks to their beloved wives, Elaine Rito-Cavalcanti and Dessa Van Schuyver. This project would never have been completed without their support.

PREFACE

Many books have been written that describe the techniques of Brazilian jiu-jitsu; however, no book, to our knowledge, has ever been written that exposes the *strategies* behind the successful use of those techniques. This is the first book on the market to provide a detailed overview of the techniques, tactics, and strategies used by today's best gi and no-gi grapplers and no-holds-barred (NHB) fighters.

From this book you will learn how to:

- conduct a strategic diagnosis of your overall strengths and weaknesses against the overall strengths and weaknesses of your opponent
- identify your opponent's preferred fighting style and construct a strategy to take advantage of his weakest links
- compare your opponent's technical skills and fighter attributes with your own

Brazilian Jiu-Jitsu Fighting Strategies will give you the insight and the tools that you need to move beyond the mediocre approach followed by the masses and join with the elite fighters of the world. In other words, the information contained in this book will enable you to make the jump from technician to strategist, from fighter to *thinking* fighter.

The authors of *Brazilian Jiu-Jitsu Fighting Strategies*, Master Romero "Jacare" Cavalcanti and Dr. Mark Van Schuyver, are uniquely qualified to produce this volume—Cavalcanti because of years of training at the Gracie School in Brazil, his impressive competition record, his rank as 6th-degree black belt, his vast knowledge of the art, his extensive experience as a winning coach, and his worldwide fame as a leader in the art; Van Schuyver because of his extensive and highly successful career as a martial arts writer, including three books and dozens of articles, and because of his considerable knowledge of Brazilian jiu-jitsu gained from many years of intensive study with Cavalcanti.

Authors' note: For the sake of simplicity, we use the pronoun "he" and its derivatives in this book when referring to all jiu-jitsu practitioners.

INTRODUCTION

From this book you will learn:

- core gi, no-gi, and no-holds-barred (NHB) techniques of Brazilian jiu-jitsu
- tactical options for each of the core techniques
- strategies for working your overall game in a way that maximizes your strengths and minimizes your weaknesses
- a methodology for conducting a strategic analysis of your own skills in comparison to those of your opponents
- how to attack, counterattack, defend, and outsmart your opponent from each of the 18 ground fighting conditions.

Chapter 1 sets the stage with a brief history of the art of Brazilian jiu-jitsu, a discussion of its primary strategy, and a description of its foundational principles, including the principles of leverage as they are applied in the art. Chapter 1 also lays the groundwork for moving from a tactical approach to a strategic approach to fighting.

Chapters 2–10 contain comprehensive descriptions of many of the offensive and defensive techniques and tactics necessary for gi, no-gi, and NHB fighting from the following conditions: standing, closed guard, open guard, half guard, side control, north-to-south, knee-in-the-belly, mount, and back.

In addition, these chapters conclude with interviews with Cavalcanti's top black- or brown-belt instructors on the topic of strategy:

- Chapter 2: Dr. Pat Harvey, an Alliance black-belt instructor, Brazilian jiu-jitsu and NHB competitor, and NHB trainer.
- Chapter 3: Chris Moriarty, an Alliance top gi and no-gi jiu-jitsu competitor.
- Chapter 4: Roberto "Spider" Traven, the world-famous Alliance jiu-jitsu champion, NHB champion, and black-belt instructor and his wife, sports nutritionist Flavia Traven.
- Chapter 5: Bull Shaw, an Alliance black-belt instructor and jiu-jitsu and NHB champion.
- Chapter 6: Felipe Neto, an Alliance Brazilian jiu-jitsu and NHB black-belt champion.
- Chapter 7: Fabio Gurgel, an Alliance black-belt instructor, jiu-jitsu champion, UFC contender, and NHB champion.
- Chapter 8: Abdul Mutakabbir, an Alliance black-belt instructor and multiyear tournament champion.
- Chapter 9: Ryan Ellison, an Alliance top jiu-jitsu competitor and NHB champion.
- Chapter 10: Fernando Gurgel, an Alliance black-belt champion jiu-jitsu competitor and instructor.

In Chapter 11 you will learn how to diagnose your opponent's fighting style and devise a comprehensive strategy to suit. This chapter ties everything together, enabling you to continue your ground fight training in a way that will allow you to take advantage of your natural strengths and abilities while simultaneously minimizing your weaknesses. Chapter 11 also contains the key elements that you need to complete your transformation from technician to strategist.

Chapter 1

Brazilian Jiu-Jitsu

Now the general who wins a battle makes many calculations in his temple ere the battle is fought. The general who loses a battle makes but few calculations beforehand. Thus do many calculations lead to victory, and few calculations to defeat: how much more no calculation at all! It is by attention to this point that I can foresee who is likely to win or lose.
—**Sun Tzu**, *The Art of War*

This is a book about Brazilian jiu-jitsu, one of the world's greatest martial arts. From this book you will not only learn techniques and tactics of gi, no-gi, and NHB (no-holds-barred) jiu-jitsu but also how to formulate a comprehensive strategy for winning. Whether you are a beginner or an accomplished veteran of the art, when you finish reading this book, your life as a martial artist will be forever changed. Apply what you learn and you will find yourself transformed from follower to leader, from private to general, from technician to strategist.

In this chapter you will learn the primary strategy of Brazilian jiu-jitsu and see the evidence that shows the effectiveness of the art. You will also learn how jiu-jitsu fighters apply the principles of leverage in virtually every submission technique. In this chapter you will discover the 18 conditions common to ground fighting and the classifications of Brazilian jiu-jitsu. You will discover how different personality types manifest themselves in different fighting styles, and you will read a brief history of the art itself. This chapter also explains the difference in techniques, tactics, and strategy, and it sets the tone for the comprehensive overview and analysis of the art that follows in chapters 2–11.

FIGHTING TECHNIQUES OF BRAZILIAN JIU-JITSU

Brazilian jiu-jitsu is massively successful because of two things: It always works, and it is always evolving. This is so because practitioners of the art are continuously fighting and competing at all levels and, therefore, they are always learning. Since the formulation of this system by Carlos Gracie Sr. in

Figure 1-1. Romero "Jacare" Cavalcanti.

the 1920s, Brazilian jiu-jitsu fighters have been accepting challenges to fight in the ring, on the mat, on the beach, and pretty much anywhere that it is possible for them to test their stuff.

What makes it work? How has this art withstood countless challenges for the better part of a century? To understand this, you must first have a grasp of the primary strategy that makes ground fighting, and Brazilian jiu-jitsu in particular, so amazingly effective.

The Primary Strategy

Brazilian jiu-jitsu is a derivative of Japanese jiu-jitsu. Unlike most of the traditional Japanese jiu-jitsu and judo systems, Brazilian jiu-jitsu places great emphasis on ground fighting techniques, called *ne waza* in Japan. The primary strategy behind this system is to *take the opponent to the ground and force him to fight you there*. The theory behind this is simple and it has been proven to work on the street, in the NHB ring, and on the mat time and again. It goes like this: If you are skilled at fighting on the ground and your attacker is not, your attacker will be virtually at your mercy once you have him on the ground. Furthermore, the theory goes, it is extremely difficult for any opponent to stay on his feet when confronted by a skilled ground fighter.

If you are unfamiliar with ground fighting, you may be asking yourself this question: "Why should I bother to learn ground fighting?" You may be thinking, "My stand-up skills are so strong that I'll never end up on the ground. After all, how likely is it that I will be attacked by a trained ground fighter on the street? Why should I worry about it?" Well, think long and hard before you decide to leave ground fighting out of your portfolio of skills. Think about all the fights that you were personally involved in, witnessed, or heard about firsthand. Did these fights end up on the ground? We're betting the answer is yes, because many experts, including Rorion Gracie, estimate that more than 80 percent of all street fights end up on the ground.

We consider it to be an obvious fact that most street fights go to the ground, and it is certainly a fact that most NHB matches are fought at least partly on the mat. Given that virtually everyone knows this is true, it astonishes us that so many instructors in the traditional martial arts invest little or no time in ground application.

The Importance of Leverage

Give me a place to stand and a lever long enough and I will move the world.
—Archimedes, 220 BC

Virtually every technique in Brazilian jiu-jitsu makes use of leverage. To excel in jiu-jitsu you must, therefore, understand what leverage really is and how it works within the context of the art.

Most students of jiu-jitsu learn one technique after another but never bother to learn how and why the techniques work. This is called being a technique-dependent learner, which limits your skill level to the number of techniques you can memorize. It's akin to the old saying, "Give a man a fish and you feed him today; teach a man how to fish and you feed him for a lifetime." Technique-dependent learners are being *given* the technique instead of being taught the principles behind the technique.

When you learn the principles of leverage, you will know how and why your techniques work or don't work. Learn the principles of leverage and you will be able to create your own submissions, and you will know why one technique trumps another in a given situation. Learn the principles of leverage and you will be able to defend against your opponents' submission attempts far more effectively because you will understand what is going on mechanically. Learn the principles of leverage and you will move beyond technique dependency to technique independency.

Principles of Leverage

Leverage is the act of using a small amount of effort to move a large load. All levers have

Figure 1-2. Alliance competitor Andrew Uria wins with a Kimura submission.

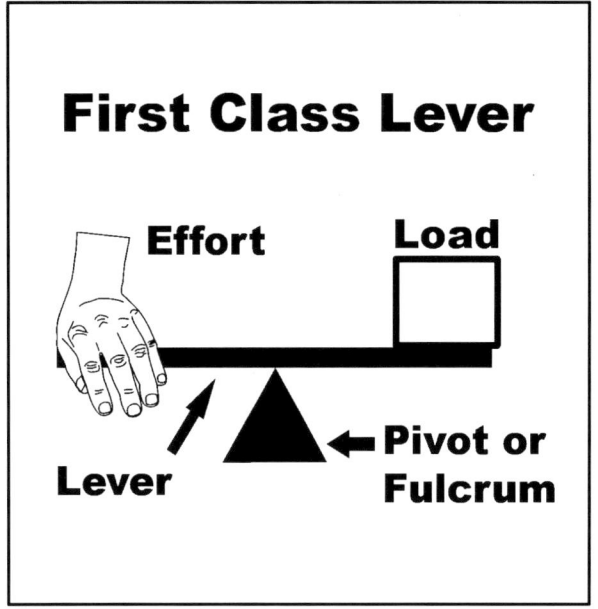

Illustration 1-1. Levers of the first class (fulcrum in the middle) magnify the effect of effort.

three components: the fulcrum, the load, and the effort. The fulcrum is the point about which the lever rotates; the load is the force applied by the lever system; and the effort is the force applied by the user of the lever system.[1] In the third century the famous Greek mathematician Archimedes was the first to describe the fundamental mechanics of leverage. He gave us this formula: *The effort times its distance from the fulcrum = the load times its distance from the fulcrum.*

There are three types of lever. The type of lever is determined in accordance with the position of the fulcrum in relation to the effort and load.[2] The three types of levers are:

Levers of the first class: The fulcrum lies between the effort and the load. Examples include a crowbar, seesaw, and scissors.

Levers of the second class: The fulcrum is at one end, the effort at the other end, and the load is between the effort and the fulcrum. Examples include a wheelbarrow and a nutcracker.

Levers of the third class: The fulcrum is at one end, the load at the other end, and the effort is between the load and the fulcrum. Examples include tweezers, tongs, brooms, and fishing poles.[3]

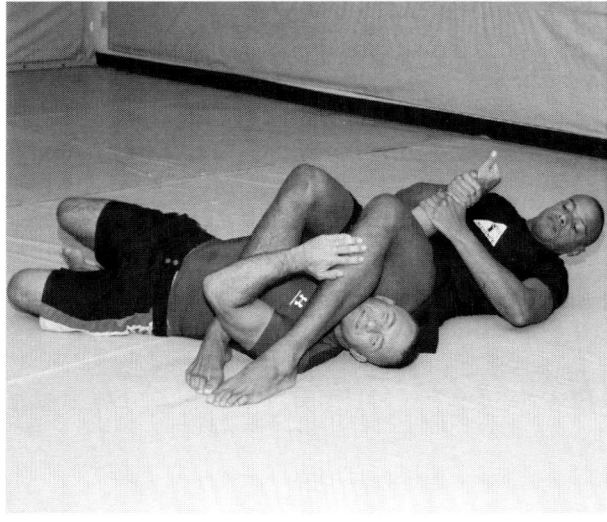

Figure 1-3. The arm bar applies lever of the first class principles.

Brazilian jiu-jitsu techniques apply principles derived from all three types of lever. Illustrations of levers of the first, second, and third type are shown below. Photos of Brazilian jiu-jitsu techniques that make use of principles from lever types one, two, and three are also shown.

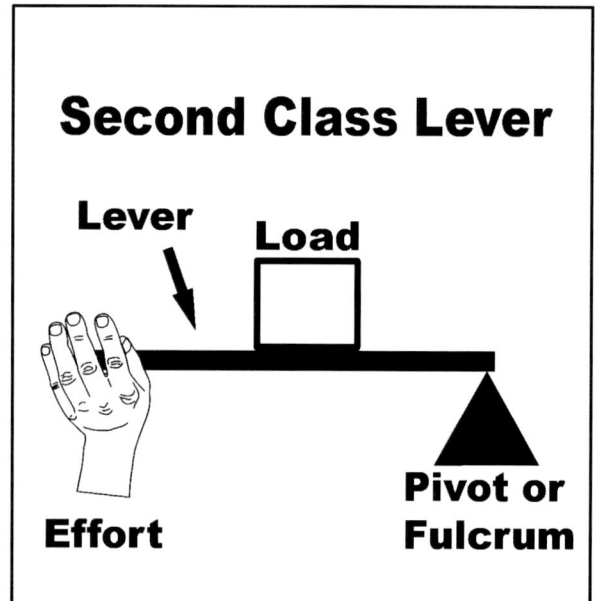

Illustration 1-2. Levers of the second class (load in the middle) magnify the effort.

Figure 1-4. This side mount escape employs principles of levers of the second class.

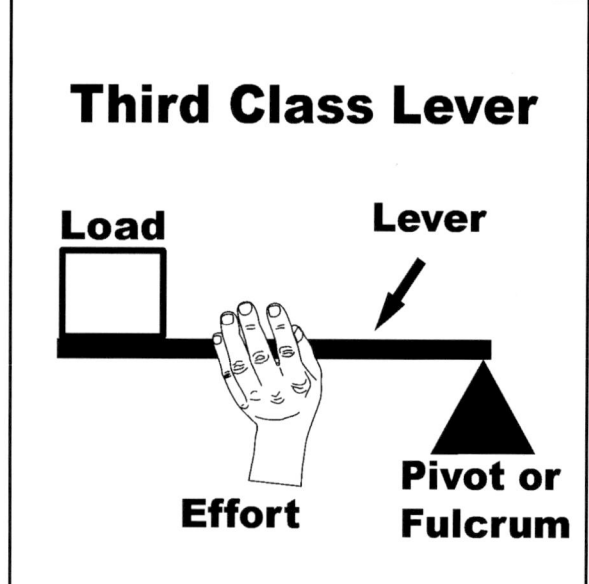

Illustration 1-3. Levers of the third class (effort in the middle) magnify distance.

Figure 1-5. Squeezing the knees together to restrict an opponent's movement, as shown in this close-quarter open guard position, makes use of lever of the third type principles.

Brazilian jiu-jitsu fighters apply the principles of leverage to execute submissions. This is done by isolating one part of an opponent's anatomy, such as an arm or neck, and then applying pressure from a superior position. A jiu-jitsu fighter might, for example, isolate an opponent's arm and apply the full power of his arms, back, and legs against that opponent's elbow joint to create an arm bar.

Brazilian jiu-jitsu fighters also seek to apply leverage to execute sweeps, throws, and takedowns. This is done by applying leverage at the precise moment it will have maximum effect—the moment of maximum opportunity. A fighter might, for example, attempt to use a scissor sweep, which is based on lever of the first type principles, at a moment in which his opponent is slightly imbalanced. This is the moment in which the opponent is already leaning toward the "tipping point," i.e., the point at which he could easily lose balance and fall or be swept. At these moments of imbalance (or poor balance), a minimum amount of leverage will tip an opponent over.

The use of leverage in fighting is a great equalizer because, except for power lifters and giants, hardly anyone's elbow, knee, ankle, wrist, shoulder, or neck is stronger than the leveraged force of someone else's arms, back, and legs in combination. Every fighter, no matter how big and how powerful, will present "moments of opportunity" in which he can easily be taken down by minimal leverage correctly applied. Thus, the principles of leverage, in proper application, make it possible for a smaller and weaker person to defeat a much larger and stronger opponent.

Of course, stronger fighters are able to use sheer muscle to accomplish more action with less leverage than weaker fighters can. Weaker fighters must find ways to generate the maximum amount of leverage in order to compensate for their lack of strength. A fighter, whether weak or strong, who continually maximizes the use of leverage is typically referred to as a "technical fighter."

The sophisticated application of leverage

Figure 1-6. Cavalcanti (seated) demonstrates a single-leg takedown with Pat Harvey.

for which Brazilian jiu-jitsu is famous was largely the contribution of jiu-jitsu Grandmaster and Gracie family patriarch Helio Gracie. Grandmaster Helio, who is in his nineties and still going strong as of this writing, was the Gracie family champion for many years in the last century. This is surprising because Helio is a fairly small man. As a child, he was unusually weak and had significant health problems. According to the family's official Web site, "Helio was always a very physically frail child. He would run up a flight of stairs and have fainting spells. Nobody could figure out why."[4]

To overcome his physical limitations Helio introduced innovative new ways to use leverage into the art of jiu-jitsu. It was this modification of traditional techniques that allowed him to defeat much larger opponents while simultaneously advancing the art itself. "[Helio] soon realized that some of the techniques he had memorized from watching Carlos teach were not very easy for him to execute. He then started to adapt those moves to his frail body's abilities, improving the leverage in the execution of some of those techniques," the site states.[5]

These two elements, using superior sources of strength against inferior strength (i.e., isolation) and using leverage to amplify power and take advantage of moments of opportunity are what make jiu-jitsu a martial art that works for almost everyone, including smaller, weaker, and older practitioners. Strength and size are certainly a factor in any fight, but as Grandmaster Helio Gracie proved again and again, a fighter trained in the ways of leverage and isolation can compensate for considerable variances in size and strength.

The 18 Ground Fighting Conditions

There are nine primary situations that are most common to Brazilian jiu-jitsu and ground fighting in general. Each of these nine situations is fluid and has many variations. They are:

1. Standing
2. Closed Guard
3. Open Guard
4. Half Guard
5. Side
6. North-to-South
7. Knee-In-the-Belly
8. Mount
9. Back

If you investigate the art more thoroughly, however, you will see that there are actually 18 common ground fighting conditions that the student of Brazilian jiu-jitsu must be concerned with, because each situation has two aspects. Thus, we have:

1. Standing Attacks
2. Standing Counters
3. Closed Guard, top
4. Closed Guard, bottom
5. Open Guard, top
6. Open Guard, bottom
7. Half Guard, top
8. Half Guard, bottom
9. Side Control, top
10. Side Control, bottom
11. North-to-South, top
12. North-to-South, bottom
13. Knee-in-the-Belly, top
14. Knee-in-the-Belly, bottom
15. Mount, top
16. Mount, bottom
17. Back, top
18. Back, bottom

Some of the 18 conditions describe dominant situations such as throwing your opponent to the ground or being mounted on your opponent's chest. Some describe defensive situations such as being under the mount or having an opponent on your back. Some are both offensive and defensive, such as working from the open guard and its many variations. The point is that the successful ground fighter must have more than a few throws and a handful of submission techniques. The successful fighter needs a methodology for attacking, defending, counterattacking, and outsmarting different opponents in a wide variety of situations. In other words, the successful fighter needs a strategic plan for how to work in all 18 conditions common to the game.

The Classifications of Brazilian Jiu-Jitsu

Brazilian jiu-jitsu approaches martial arts from four different domains, or classifications. The first three classifications are grappling with the gi, grappling without the gi, and NHB fighting without the gi. Rule variations for these three classifications exist, such as submission grappling with no time limits and no points, submission grappling with time limits, submission grappling with limited striking, and more.

The first two classifications, grappling with the gi and grappling without the gi, are sometimes referred to as "sport jiu-jitsu." Most sport events follow rules that allow submissions and give points for control (e.g., two points for takedown, three points for passing the guard, and two points for placing the knee-in-the-belly). The third classification, NHB fighting without the gi, is also known by several other names. These include no-rules, vale tudo, and mixed martial arts (MMA). (Not covered in this book is a fourth classification of the art known generally as "self-defense." The self-defense classification of Brazilian jiu-jitsu includes a massive array of specialized techniques and tactics used for defending one's self on the street. These include one-on-one empty-hand self-defense techniques, techniques for defending against multiple attackers, and techniques for defending against weapon attacks barehanded.)

To be a well-rounded jiu-jitsu fighter, it is important to train in all four classifications. Training with the gi, for example, teaches the student how to deal with clothing during a fight. This is important because clothing can be used as a weapon on the street.

In addition, it appears that training with the gi will add something to your no-gi game. According to Royler Gracie, there is significant evidence that training hours spent wearing the gi translate into improved performance in no-gi matches. "The overwhelming success of Brazilian jiu-jitsu fighters in competitions such as the ADCC, Grapplers Quest, Arnold's, and NAGA is the best proof for training with a gi. From 1998 to 2001, 75 percent of the ADCC winners were from jiu-jitsu backgrounds," Royler states.[6]

Training without the gi is equally important because it teaches you to react more quickly and to use positional holds for leverage rather than relying on cloth. This will also give you the skills necessary for dealing with attackers wearing sleeveless shirts, shorts, swimsuits, or some other type of flimsy attire.

NHB training is also essential in jiu-jitsu fighting because it adds the element of striking from a standing position and from a grounded position to the ground fighter's game. As Carlson Gracie said, "No martial art can maintain its claim as a real-life fighting art without being able to prove its efficiency in the field of no-holds-barred."[7]

Remember, striking from a prone position is entirely different than striking from a standing position. Power, leverage, angle, reach, and other elements of the striking game change radically when you are on the ground.

Techniques, Tactics, and Strategies

Dictionary.com defines techniques, tactics, and strategy in the following language:

Techniques: The systematic procedure by which a complex or scientific task is accomplished.

Tactics: The military science that deals with securing objectives set by strategy, especially the technique of deploying and directing troops, ships, and aircraft in effective maneuvers against an enemy.

Strategy: The science and art of military command as applied to the overall planning and conduct of large-scale combat operations.

Novice jiu-jitsu practitioners typically concern themselves with techniques exclusively. There are hundreds of submissions and sweeps in the art of Brazilian jiu-jitsu, but while these techniques are important to be sure, techniques alone are not sufficient.

Intermediate jiu-jitsu fighters include tactics in their bag of jiu-jitsu tricks. For them,

Figure 1-7. Stephen Smith works a sweep from the guard.

knowing techniques is just the beginning. They recognize the importance of being able to combine techniques for attacking, counterattacking, and defending. They are skilled at executing well-timed maneuvers to gain advantage or avoid danger.

Advanced jiu-jitsu practitioners know lots of techniques and are able to formulate tactics before the fight and on the fly. Advanced players also realize that techniques and tactics don't work in the same way against different opponents. They know that each fight and each fighter will provide unique challenges. Advanced fighters understand that a point advantage or disadvantage can alter the dynamics of a match. Advanced competitors know the value of planning ahead and, therefore, much of their training time is devoted to strategy.

If I always appear prepared, it is because before entering on an undertaking, I have meditated for long and have foreseen what may occur. It is not genius which reveals to me suddenly and secretly what I should do in circumstances unexpected by others; it is thought and preparation.
—Napoleon Bonaparte

It might be helpful for you to consider the concepts of techniques, tactics, and strategy by way of a simplified military analogy. Generals create the plans for battle (strategy). Lieutenants devise appropriate maneuvers on the field of battle (tactics). Privates execute orders, such as shooting the enemy (techniques). Advanced jiu-jitsu players are like generals who shoot. They plan, they maneuver, and they execute. Advanced jiu-jitsu fighters are equally concerned with strategy, tactics, and techniques. From this book you will learn all three.

Assessing Personality Types

Psychologists tell us that there are several different personality types and that understanding these different types can help us communicate better and be more successful in life, sports, and in business. One of the most useful personality assessment tools used in the business world today is the DISC (dominance, influence, steadiness, compliance) model, which is based on the work of Dr. William Moulton Marston. He developed the Bisocial Theory of Emotion and Personality, and in 1926 published the results of his research—and the DISC test—in his book, *The Emotions of Normal People*.[8]

Through his research Marston identified four distinctly different personality styles or temperaments. These personality styles are:

- Dominance: assertive and domineering
- Influence: fast-paced and highly social
- Steadiness: amiable, conscientious, and passive
- Compliance: careful, with a tendency toward perfectionism

These four main personality styles manifest themselves in the mannerisms of martial artists from all arts and have been described in slightly different ways by a number of authors and practitioners, including Muay Thai fighter/trainer Pedro Villalobos, boxing writer Monte Cox, boxing expert R. Stockton, and karate legend Karyn Turner, who says, "After fighting, coaching, and witnessing hundreds of matches I am still convinced that there are only four main types of fighters . . . As simple as it sounds, if you can beat these four fighters you can beat almost anybody in the world. Ninety-seven percent of all competitors use one of the four styles of fighting almost exclusively."[9]

In Brazilian jiu-jitsu these four personality styles can best be described as:

- Aggressive: Attacks and charges constantly at full power.
- Deceptive: Uses timing, fakes, and quick movements assertively to gain advantage.
- Defensive: Defends constantly, stalls a lot, avoids submissions, escapes danger, and attacks rarely and only when it is safe to do so.
- Interceptive: Sets traps and uses counterattacks frequently.

In general, the aggressive and deceptive fighters are more proactive, and the defensive and interceptive fighters are more reactive. Deceptive and interceptive fighters are, by and large, more dynamic in their approach to fighting. We believe that every fighter has a natural tendency toward one or two of the styles described above. Every fighter also has the potential to adapt his way of fighting to any one of the four styles or some combination.

Understanding the four types of fighters and being able to adapt your style to accommodate for each type is an important element of strategy. We will cover this in detail in Chapter 11.

To Become a Champion

What does it take to become a gi, no-gi, or NHB jiu-jitsu champion? How many hours of training must you commit each day, week, and year? Relson Gracie said, "In order to be world champion, you've got to be like a Brazilian; train morning and afternoon, five days a week to be at top level, and you've got to have a good teacher for sure."

The exact number of hours required to become a champion is a matter of opinion, but everyone agrees that it takes a lot of heart, a ton of hard work, lots of mat time, and plenty of competition experience. An understanding of the techniques, tactics, and strategies of the game is vital.

Mastery of the mental aspect of training is also critical. The point of this is to emphasize that the mental element of the jiu-jitsu game is just as important as the physical element. In one study, two men practiced free throws each night for a month, while a third only visualized shooting the ball. The first man visualized and practiced free throws, while the second man just shot the ball without visualizing. At the end of the month the most improved player was the one who both visualized and shot free throws. Coming in second was the man who simply visualized, and coming in last was the one who shot without visualizing.[10] To be great—really great—you must give 100 percent of yourself, body and mind.

A BRIEF HISTORY OF BRAZILIAN JIU-JITSU

Jiu-jitsu, literally "gentle art," was born in Japan and evolved over a period of many centuries. Many versions and variations of jiu-jitsu

Figure 1-8. Roberto Traven (top) and Dave Berry battle in the UFC in 1996.

Figure 1-9. From left, Luis Eduardo, Fabio Gurgel, Elijah Gardner, and Cavalcanti.

were practiced during Japan's long feudal period. The systematic practice of jiu-jitsu began in Japan's Edo period, the years between 1603 and 1868.[11] In 1882 the art experienced a major evolutionary breakthrough when Jigoro Kano formulated a new style of jiu-jitsu that he called Kodokan judo. Kano wasn't the first to use the name *judo*; it had been in use at the jiu-jitsu schools where he studied before he made the word famous in the late 1800s.[12]

After many years of study with a variety of masters, Kano observed that each teacher presented his system as a collection of techniques rather than explaining the underlying principle that made the techniques work.[13] Eventually, Kano identified the principle by himself and later came to call it the principle of maximum efficiency. "With this principle in mind, I again reviewed all the methods of attack and defense I had learned, retaining only those that were in accordance with the principle . . . The resulting body of techniques, which I named judo to distinguish it from its predecessor, is what I taught at the Kodokan."[14]

Kano's Kodokan judo represented a radically new approach to the ancient art of jiu-jitsu. It was new in part because it was based on the principle of maximum efficiency and in part because it was among the first styles to be practiced with rules that enabled trainees to spar and to compete without excessive injuries. Kano was a martial art revolutionary, and his new jiu-jitsu sparked a major change in the way that martial arts were trained. His contribution to jiu-jitsu was huge and his influence on all the martial arts was enormous.

Kano's jiu-jitsu was an amalgam of existing styles and techniques. Originally he put great emphasis on throws and takedowns. Later he added a well-rounded regime of ground fighting techniques, including more joint locking techniques, choking techniques, holding techniques, and ground techniques. Author Gene Simco says, "With friends from other jiu-jitsu systems, among them being Fusen Ryu practitioners, Kano formulated the Ne Waza (ground techniques) of Kodokan Judo."[15]

In 1897, Mitsuyo Maeda (sometimes cited as Esai Maeda), who later became known as Count Koma (or Konde Koma in Portuguese), began training with Kano. In 1904 Maeda traveled to the United States with another of his instructors, Tsunejiro Tomita. Tomita and Maeda went to West Point and demonstrated their art. They also traveled to the White House and performed demonstrations of Kano's Kodokan judo for President Theodore Roosevelt.

The Gracie Family

Later, Maeda went to San Palo, Brazil, on a mission to help establish a Japanese colony. It was here that Maeda met Gastao Gracie. Gastao helped Maeda establish the colony and, to return the favor, Maeda taught Kano's new form of jiu-jitsu, Kodokan judo, to Gastao Gracie's son, Carlos. (There is some question about the name that Maeda used to refer to his martial art. No one seems to know for sure, but in a 1994 interview with Nishi Yoshinori, Helio Gracie said that he believed Maeda referred to his art as jiu-jitsu rather than judo.)

So it came to pass that young Carlos Gracie learned Master Kano's new form of jiu-jitsu/judo from Maeda beginning in 1916, when he was 15 years of age, continuing until he was 21. It is important to note that this training took place at a time when it was considered improper, and perhaps even illegal, for a Japanese martial arts instructor to teach a non-Japanese person.

When Maeda left Brazil and returned to Japan, there were no other instructors available for Carlos to turn to. From that day forward, young Carlos Gracie was completely on his own. This turned out to be an event of major significance. Kid Peligro, who has coauthored several books with members of the Gracie family, says, "With no one to rely on but himself, Carlos began to develop the art in a way that never would have been allowed by the tradition-bound Japanese. He also found that others wanted to learn this effective martial art, and he began to teach private lessons from his house. These proved so popular that he soon opened a school, the first Brazilian jiu-jitsu academy in the world."[16]

Carlos was a fighter. He continually tested himself and his art in no-rules matches. He took on all comers regardless of size or weight. He spread the word everywhere and actually took out a newspaper ad challenging anyone to step into the ring with him. According to the Gracie Web site, "Even though he was a mere 135 pounds, his style was so effective that Carlos Gracie was never defeated and he became a legend in Brazil."

Carlos taught jiu-jitsu to many family members, including his brothers, Jorge, Gastao, Osvaldo, and Helio. In time, each of the brothers became a champion of the art in his own right. It was Helio, however, who gained national fame through a series of high-profile fights. One of these famous fights took place in July 1951 when a 5th-degree black belt judo fighter named Kado accepted Helio's challenge. Helio dominated the fight and eventually choked Kado into unconsciousness. Helio Gracie was declared the winner and became a national hero of Brazil.[17]

The defeated Kado had traveled to Brazil as part of a three-man team. His teammates included a famous and very powerful judo fighter named Masahiko Kimura and another judo black belt named Yamaguchi. A short time after his victory over Kado, Helio, who had been the Brazilian champion for the previous 20 years, challenged the team again. Yamaguchi declined, but the infamous Kimura accepted. After a long and grueling battle in front of 20,000 fans, Kimura broke the 34-year-old Helio's elbow with an ude-garami arm lock that is now widely known as "The Kimura." According to Chen, "Even with the broken elbow, Gracie still refused to give up, so his corner 'threw in the towel.' Kimura was declared the winner by TKO. Although Kimura won the actual fight, it was acknowledged that Gracie had great fighting spirit and will. Kimura later applauded Gracie's tremendous will to win."[18]

Although not a victory, Helio's brave fight with Kimura served to advance his reputation even more. The Gracie family's jiu-jitsu gained greater notoriety, and the Gracie name became even more famous in Brazil.

Later, Carlos Gracie taught jiu-jitsu to his son, Carlos Jr., who in turn trained his children. When Helio eventually retired from vale tudo competition, it was Carlos Jr.'s son, Carlson Gracie, who became the family champion.

Figure 1-10. From left to right, Carlos Gracie Jr., Rorion Gracie, Helio Gracie, Richard Bressler, Cavalcanti, and Rickson Gracie in California in 1980 after a morning training at Rorion's garage.

Figure 1-11. From left, Helio Gracie, Ursula Cavalcanti, and Romero "Jacare" Cavalcanti.

Figure 1-12. Cavalcanti, left, with Carlson Gracie.

Carlson opened a school of his own in Copacabana, which is a district of Rio de Janeiro. Carlson won many high-profile matches and, in so doing, did much to advance the reputation of jiu-jitsu in Brazil. Carlson was also responsible for opening jiu-jitsu up to the public, thus causing the art to flourish at an exponential rate.

Promoting Brazilian Jiu-Jitsu

In 1993 the Gracie family introduced the United States and the larger world audience to Brazilian jiu-jitsu by way of the UFC (Ultimate Fighting Championship). According to author Roberto Pedreira, it was Rorion Gracie who originally conceived the idea of marketing jiu-jitsu in America by using a no-rules fight featuring Brazilian jiu-jitsu. "Rorion's cousin Carlson had been one of the top champions of the vale tudo (no-holds-barred) ring. Rorion himself and most of his brothers and cousins had also participated in vale tudos. Rorion simply promoted one in the United States. He called it The Ultimate Fighting Championship."[19]

Before the first UFC in 1993, it was common for traditional stand-up-style martial artists in the West to argue that their students need not worry about the ground because their superior stand-up techniques would ensure that they would never end up there. They were very wrong. The martial arts world got a wake-up call when Royce Gracie, who weighed only 180 pounds, entered the fenced fighting arena now known as the octagon and demonstrated the amazing effectiveness of Brazilian jiu-jitsu. He shocked the world by showing that a skilled ground fighter can almost always take a stand-up-only fighter to the ground and keep him on the ground whether he wants to go there or not.

Royce Gracie used his ground fighting skills to defeat many larger and stronger opponents in UFC competition. He won three of the first four UFC contests, beating kung-fu fighters, boxers, kick boxers, wrestlers, and other martial arts champions. His amazing victories sparked a revolution in the martial arts. "Unlike the American no-holds-barred contests of today, Royce had to fight several times in each tournament. There were no weight classes and Royce was usually the lightest, sometimes being outweighed by 80 lbs. or more. There were very few rules: no eye gouging, no biting, and no time limits," says Simco.[20]

Since that time, virtually all of the NHB competitors include extensive groundwork in their training routines. These days it is common for fighters to combine elements from Brazilian jiu-jitsu, Western wrestling, Muay Thai boxing, and other proven styles when training for NHB matches. Today, these blended styles are collectively known as mixed martial arts (MMA), but in effect this is just a continuation of the vale tudo (NHB) tradition advanced by Carlos Gracie Sr. in Brazil back in the 1920s. "During the mid-1900s while Vale Tudo (free-style fighting) was developing in Brazil, there were experts of Judo, wrestling, capoeira, and boxing, mixing together in these no-rules contests," Simco said.[21]

Figure 1-13. Rolls Gracie.

Rolls Gracie

Rolls Gracie, the person to whom this book is dedicated, was the son of Carlos Gracie and Claudia Zandomenico. Rolls was born on March 28, 1951. He died in a hang gliding accident on June 6, 1982, at age 31. In his brief life Rolls made major contributions to the art of Brazilian jiu-jitsu.

As a child Rolls trained privately with Helio and became extremely proficient in the use of leverage and technical execution. In other words, Rolls learned the unique skills that had enabled Helio to overcome much larger opponents. When Helio moved to Rui Barbosa, Rolls stayed in Copacabana and continued his training at Carlson's academy. "[Rolls] was one of those students that was always looking for the essence, the full knowledge of everything," says Carlson. ". . . To me he was the best fighter in the family." [22]

After some time, Rolls established a following. Eventually, he opened a "school within the school" where he taught the highly technical, leverage-rich style of jiu-jitsu that he learned from Helio. Despite branching off, the brothers continued to share the location.

The innovations that Rolls Gracie made to the art of Brazilian jiu-jitsu were due in part to his open-mindedness. He was a continuous learner and was always seeking to push the limits of the art and introduce new elements. One of his contributions was the advancement and evolution of the open guard as a fighting condition.[23] Another of his contributions was in the area of leg locks and ankle locks. Yet another area where Rolls expanded and added to the art was in throws and wrestling-style takedowns.

To improve his throwing game, Rolls spent more than a year perfecting his stand-up skills by training with judo instructor Osvaldo Alves. Soon after, Rolls became notorious for his takedowns. "He was famous for his uchimata. He would take his opponents down with the uchimata then arm lock them or put the knee on the stomach to choke for the submission," according to Peligro.[24]

Rolls was also a competition wrestler, and on many occasions he swapped techniques with one of the world's top wrestling coaches, Bob Anderson. Anderson is famous for coaching many champions in his career, including Rulon Gardner, Dan Henderson, Randy Couture, and Darrell Gohlars. Rolls and Anderson "quickly developed a strong bond and spent hours adapting wrestling moves to jiu-jitsu and vice-versa . . . From their friendship and exchanges came several move variations now standard to Brazilian jiu-jitsu, including the now famous 'Americana' lock," according to Peligro.[25]

Rolls Gracie was a powerful force in competition. A true champion, he won many Brazilian jiu-jitsu events, NHB fights, Sambo matches, and wresting matches. Peligro says, "He would enter every tournament there was, whether it was Brazilian jiu-jitsu, Judo, Sambo, or Wrestling. He especially liked Sambo, a Russian martial art that involves many knee and foot submissions that Brazilian jiu-jitsu lacked at the time."[26]

Rolls also won a considerable number of street fights and high-profile school challenges. Some of his school challenge fights are documented in the *Gracie in Action* video. One of his victories, against a karate instructor, was televised on Brazilian TV.

Rolls Gracie was a man of action to be sure, and he finished many fights, yet he was a truly good and generous person. Through his teaching and his example, Rolls influenced many of today's best—and best-known—jiu-jitsu fighters and coaches. "Rolls later passed his personal developments on to his brothers and cousins, giving the younger generations a great push forward. His influence on Rickson and Royler is unmistakable. He also taught Carlos Jr., Rillion, and Crolin," according to Peligro.[27]

Before his death, Rolls Gracie promoted six individuals to the rank of black belt. One of those fortunate few is the coauthor of this book, Romero "Jacare" Cavalcanti. The following list shows, in alphabetical order, the lineage of black belt promotions from Helio to Rolls to Cavalcanti:

HELIO GRACIE'S BLACK BELTS

Armando Wriedt
Carlos Henrique Elias
Flavio Behring
Francisco Mansor
Guillherme Valente
Pedro Hemeterio Araujo de Castro
Pedro S. Valente
Pedro Valente Sr.
Relson Gracie
Rickson Gracie
Robin Gracie
Rolker Gracie
Rolls Gracie
Rorion Gracie
Royce Gracie
Royler Gracie

ROLLS GRACIE'S BLACK BELTS

Mario Talarico
Marcio Macarrao
Mauricio Motta Gomes
Nicin Azulay
Paulo Conde
Romero "Jacare" Cavalcanti [28]

In 1985, three years after Rolls was killed, Cavalcanti and his top students created the now world-famous Alliance Team. Since that time, Alliance fighters have been a major force in the jiu-jitsu scene.

ROMERO "JACARE" CAVALCANTI AND THE ALLIANCE TEAM

The formation of the Alliance Team took place at a time when the art was in transition. In 1994 Cavalcanti, coauthor of this book, and his top students—Roberto Traven, Fabio Gurgel, Fernando Gurgel, Alexandre Paiva, Leonardo Castelo Branco, and Vinicius Campelo—collaborated with the intention of becoming a force in competition and a force for the advancement of the art.

The mission of the Alliance Team was, and is today, to carry on the legacy of Rolls Gracie. Today, the Alliance Team is home to a large number of the world's top jiu-jitsu competitors and coaches, many of whom were trained by Cavalcanti himself, including Fabio Gurgel, Rodrigo "Comprido" Medeiros, Felipe Neto, Ratinho Terere, Roberto Traven, Ryan Ellison, Leo and Rico Vieira, Marcello Garcia, Ricardo Medeiros, Chris Moriarty, Fernando Soluco, Fabio Clemente, Ricardo

Miller, Paulo Sergio Santos Sarruco, Marcelo Mendes, Leandro Borgo, and GiGi.

After several years and much success with the Alliance Team in Brazil, Cavalcanti moved to the United States. He taught for a short time in Miami then moved to Atlanta. Today he owns and operates two Alliance Martial Arts Centers in the Atlanta metro area. He oversees eight satellite schools and many affiliate schools at various locations in the United States, Brazil, Canada, Australia, Finland, Germany, and Venezuela.

Cavalcanti is the hand-to-hand combat consultant/instructor for the U.S. Army Rangers at Fort Benning, Georgia. He is also the founder of the Brazilian Jiu-Jitsu Federation, the president of the Georgia State BJJ/Submission Wrestling Federation, head coach of the international Alliance Team, and a referee for the Brazilian Jiu-Jitsu Federation. In 2004 the International Fighting Federation elected him Coach of the Year, and in 2005 he was inducted into the Grappling Hall of Fame.

Cavalcanti is widely regarded as one of the top Brazilian jiu-jitsu instructors in the world today. After many years of teaching, Cavalcanti has promoted 29 black belts. These individuals are listed below in alphabetical order.

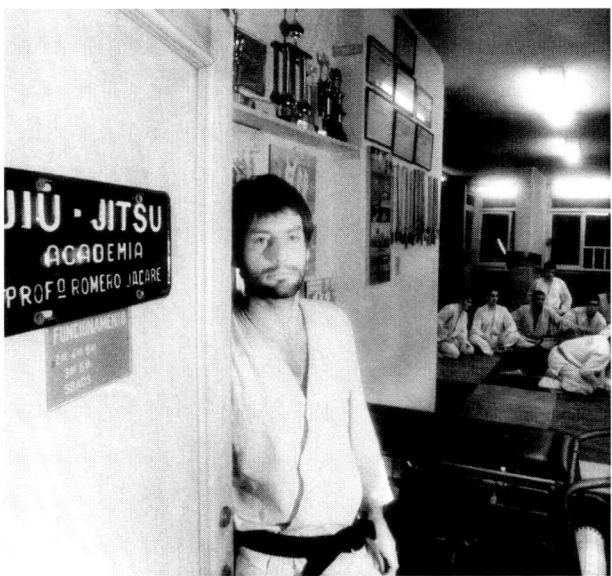
Figure 1-14. Cavalcanti at his first academy in Brazil.

Figure 1-15. Cavalcanti holding Bud World Cup team trophy.

Figure 1-16. Cavalcanti, front left, with students.

ROMERO "JACARE" CAVALCANTI'S BLACK BELTS

Abdul Mutakabbir
Alexandre Paiva
Alfredo "Pouca Telha" Araujo
Allen Mohler
Anderson "Sarruco" Xavier
Bull Shaw
Carlos "Pinduca" Carvalho
Claudio "Toti" Lino
Eduardo "Jamelao" Conceicao
Fabio Gurgel
Felipe "Zicro" Neto
J.D. Shelley
Jose Luis "Sucuri" Togno
Leonardo Alcantara "Leozinho" Vieira
Luis Felipe "Mentirinha" Costa
Magrao Gurgel
Marcelo "Telo" Mendes
Michele da Mata
Octavio Henrique "Ratinho" Couto da Silva, Jr.
Pat Harvey
Paulo "Portuga" Bodas
Paulo Sergio Santos
Pericles Laudier
Ricardinho Vieira
Ricardo "Franjinha" Miller
Roberto "Spider" Traven
Roberto Werneck
Rodrigo "Comprido" Medeiros
Roger Patrick Brooking

STATE OF THE ART

Brazilian jiu-jitsu in all of its classifications—gi, no-gi, NHB, and self-defense—is

Brazilian Jiu-Jitsu   19

Figure 1-17. NHB fighter Darren Roberts moments after victory.

evolving faster today than at any time in its history. New techniques, tactics, and strategies are invented for each of the four classifications every day. This rapid evolution is due to a number of factors, including the vastly increased number of practitioners and qualified schools and the fact that low, middle, and very high profile gi, no-gi, and NHB competitions are increasing in popularity. There are also more amateur, semipro, and professional competitors training and testing their jiu-jitsu skills today than ever before. The influx of techniques from other styles such as Muay Thai boxing, Western wrestling, and Sambo is also at an all-time high. The leaders of the art continue to honor and encourage innovation, experimentation, and progressive changes.

At this moment, the art of Brazilian jiu-jitsu is absolutely electrified with a spirit of experimentation and innovation. Brazilian jiu-jitsu continues to be a dominant player in the global martial arts scene while simultaneously experiencing dramatic, exponential evolutionary

Figure 1-18. Cavalcanti teaching U.S. Army Rangers.

change. With so much energy and innovation at work, Brazilian jiu-jitsu is well positioned to maintain its place as one of the world's premier martial arts through the foreseeable future.

ENDNOTES

1. Brian MacKenzie. "Levers." Sports Coach. http://www.brianmac.demon.co.uk/levers.htm (accessed 2005).
2. "ASME Tools of Discovery." American Society of Mechanical Engineers. http://www.asme.org/education/precollege/discovery/page13.htm (page discontinued).
3. Brian MacKenzie. "Levers." Sports Coach. http://www.brianmac.demon.co.uk/levers.htm (accessed 2005).
4. Gracie.com. Official Domain of Gracie USA. http://www.gracie.com/ (accessed 2005).
5. Ibid.
6. Royler Gracie and Kid Peligro. *Brazilian Jiu-Jitsu: Submission Grappling Techniques.* Montpelier, VT: Invisible Cities Press, 2003, p. 6.
7. Carlson Gracie and Julio Fernandez. *Brazilian Jiu-Jitsu: for Experts Only: Classic Jiu-Jitsu Techniques from the Master.* Montpelier, VT: Invisible Cities Press, 2004, p. 6.
8. Personality Assessment Solutions, Ltd. ThePeople@TestsontheNet.com. "The Ubiquitous DISC Test and Lies." http://www.testsonthenet.com/disc/ww-info.htm.
9. Karyn Turner and Mark Van Schuyver. *Secrets of Championship Karate.* Contemporary Books, 1991.
10. Montanha. *The Brazilian Jiu-Jitsu Mind Set: To Submit Your Opponent from Any Position.* Walnut Creek, CA: Montanha Press, 2004.
11. Kano, Jigoro. *Kodukan Judo.* Tokyo: Kodansha International Ltd., Bunkyo-ku. 1986.
12. Gene Simco. *Brazilian Jiu-Jitsu: The Master Text.* Poughkeepsie, NY: Jiu-Jitsu Net, 2001.
13. Kano, Jigoro. *Kodukan Judo.* Tokyo: Kodansha International Ltd., Bunkyo-ku. 1986.
14. Ibid.
15. Gene Simco. *Brazilian Jiu-Jitsu: The Master Text.* Poughkeepsie, NY: Jiu-Jitsu Net, 2001.
16. Kid Peligro. *The Gracie Way: An Illustrated History of the Gracie Family.* Montpelier, VT: Invisible Cities Press, 2003.
17. Chen, Jim. "Masahiko Kimura (1917–1993): The Man Who Defeated Helio Gracie." The Original Judo Information Site. http://judoinfo.com/kimura3.htm (accessed 2001).
18. Ibid.
19. Roberto A. Pedreira. "Then Came Rorion." Global Training Report: Academy Reports. http://www.geocities.com/global_training_report/rorion.htm (accessed 2000).
20. Gene Simco. *Brazilian Jiu-Jitsu: The Master Text.* Poughkeepsie, NY: Jiu-Jitsu Net, 2001.
21. Ibid.
22. Kid Peligro. *The Gracie Way: An Illustrated History of the Gracie Family.* Montpelier, VT: Invisible Cities Press, 2003.
23. Ibid.
24. Ibid.
25. Ibid.
26. Ibid.
27. Ibid.

Chapter 2

Standing

Most Brazilian jiu-jitsu fighters prefer to fight on the ground. Needless to say, getting an opponent to the ground and keeping him on the ground requires a good bit of skill. To accomplish this, modern-day Brazilian jiu-jitsu incorporates dozens of throws and trips from its parent style, Japanese jiu-jitsu. The art also includes a wide variety of takedowns developed by Brazilian jiu-jitsu practitioners or assimilated from Western wrestling, Russian sambo, modern judo, and other grappling arts.

This chapter contains techniques and tactical options for fighting in the stand-up condition. At the end of this chapter you will read the first of nine interviews on strategy. In this chapter we hear from Brazilian jiu-jitsu black belt, veteran competitor, and experienced NHB fighter and trainer Dr. Patrick Harvey.

STANDING ATTACK WITH THE GI

In sport jiu-jitsu, the rules for throws and takedowns are more relaxed than those used in modern judo. Most Brazilian jiu-jitsu fighters are very concerned about taking the fight to the ground quickly and less concerned with how the fight gets there, whereas judo players do just the opposite. It is rare to see a gi or no-gi jiu-jitsu competitor rely on his stand-up game as a primary fighting strategy. According to Alliance veteran Chris Moriarty, "To make your whole game stand-up in jiu-jitsu is dangerous . . . It is not like judo with someone standing you back up if there is no quick action." (For more from Chris Moriarty, see the interview at the end of Chapter 3.)

Unlike in judo, in jiu-jitsu matches there is no rule against the way that the competitors stand, so jiu-jitsu fighters tends to adjust their posture to avoid a variety of different throws and takedowns. It is common, for example, to see jiu-jitsu fighters lean forward and thrust their hips back.

The methods used by different jiu-jitsu fighters to take an opponent to the ground vary greatly. For example, one fighter may seek to avoid the stand-up game altogether by dropping to the ground and pulling his opponent into the guard, while another fighter may attack with a traditional judo throw, a shooting technique, or some other type of takedown.

The following is a description of one of the most common techniques that jiu-jitsu competitors use to take their opponents to the mat during tournaments—the foot-reap throw. This core technique is competition tested and, like all of the techniques shown in this book, will work equally well in a tournament or on the street.

Core Technique: Foot-Reap Throw

The foot-reap throw works best in gi competition. To make it work, you must grab your opponent's lapel and prevent him from grab-

22 Brazilian Jiu-Jitsu Fighting Strategies

Figure 2-1. Control your opponent's gi and wrist.

Figure 2-2. Step inside his right leg with your left and drop to your knee.

Figure 2-3. Pull downward on his gi and arm.

Figure 2-4. Control your opponent and go on top.

bing yours. This technique requires precise timing. See Figures 2-1 through 2-4.

You must drop to one knee to make the foot-reap throw work. Do not fall into the habit of dropping all of your weight onto your knee with a thud. This is a bad habit that is easy to cultivate when training on mats. Remember, there are no mats on the street. Learn to drop your weight to your knee very lightly and smoothly. Practice on the mat and test your knee-landing skills periodically on a hard surface.

Tactical Options

Now that you know one of the fundamental techniques for taking an opponent down, you should devise a set of tactical options that you can employ instantly without thought. Your tactical options, or maneuvers, give you the ability to adapt to the situation. This is absolutely critical to your success in a fight because conditions are constantly changing.

Use your tactical options to adapt and overcome as in the examples that follow. As a general rule, you should master at least two tactical options to support each of your core techniques. Some fighters maintain a repertoire of dozens of tactical options, each related to a core technique or fundamental position.

Large Outer-Reap Throw

If you are unable to get the foot-reap throw, you can immediately attempt a large outer-reap throw (called osoto gari in Japanese). To execute this traditional jiu-jitsu/judo throw, grab your opponent's left lapel with your right hand while grabbing his right sleeve near the elbow with your left hand. Step toward your opponent at a diagonal, moving to your left, and extend your right leg forward. Swing your right leg backward and into the back of your opponent's right leg. As you do this, push on your opponent's torso with your right hand and pull on his sleeve with your left. This pushing action must take place just as your leg makes contact. (Figure 2-5) Twist your body to the left as you execute the throw.

Be aware that your right arm must be protected from arm bar and triangle counterattacks at the conclusion of the large outer-reap throw. At the moment that your opponent lands, he is vulnerable to attack, but you will also be open to counterattack. Avoid the counterattack by going for an arm bar yourself or by putting your knee in your opponent's belly to keep him pinned to the mat. You can also secure your advantage by dropping your weight onto your opponent to assume side control.

Figure 2-5. Executing the large outer-reap throw.

Figure 2-6. The one-arm shoulder throw.

One-Arm Shoulder Throw

Hip throws are also traditional to both jiu-jitsu and judo, and there are many variations of the hip throw. One of the most effective versions of the hip throw is the one-arm shoulder throw (called ippon seoinage in Japanese). This throw comes in several varieties. To execute one of the most effective versions of this throw, grab your opponent's right lapel with your left hand and jerk him forward. Reach under your opponent's right arm with your right arm as he comes toward you. Turn your back to your opponent (Figure 2-6) and press your body close to his. Turn your head to your left and use your legs to lift your opponent. Bend at your waist to take him over your shoulder and onto the mat.

Hip throws are powered by your legs, not by your arms and back. You must bend your knees and place your hips and back against your opponent's body before executing the throw. When you bend forward, the power from your legs takes your opponent over the fulcrum point that is your hips. Your arms and back do not do the lifting.

Hip throws, like all throws and takedowns, require precise timing. If you miss an attempt, you must quickly recalibrate your position and turn back to face your opponent. It is extremely unwise to keep your back to your opponent for any extended period of time as it opens you to a number of counterattacks.

STANDING ATTACK WITHOUT THE GI

When we refer to techniques without the gi, or no-gi competitions, we are referring to jiu-jitsu sport matches in which the gi is not worn and striking is not allowed. No-gi competitors typically wear tight-fitting short- or long-sleeved athletic shirts and athletic shorts. Just as with gi competition, no-gi matches are won by submission or by the accumulation of points depending on the rules of the event.

Grappling without the gi alters the dynamics of the jiu-jitsu game because it eliminates the friction that occurs between gis, and it takes away all of the hold points provided by clothing. With less friction between the grapplers, the no-gi matches tend to move faster than gi matches. There are a few submission techniques that are possible without the gi that are difficult or impossible to do with the gi because the gi adds a layer of protection against certain types of chokes and cranks. In total, however, there are considerably fewer submission techniques possible without the gi than there are with it because there are no sleeves, collars, lapels, shirttails, belts, or pants to use as weapons.

Standing 25

Figure 2-7. To execute a double-leg lift-and-slam takedown, first maneuver yourself as close as possible to your opponent without letting him grab you.

Figure 2-8. Drive forward on one knee and hold behind your opponent's knees.

Figure 2-9. Drive forward.

Figure 2-10. Lift your opponent onto your shoulder.

Figure 2-11. Slam him onto the mat.

Core Technique: Double-Leg Lift-and-Slam Takedown

The double-leg takedown derives from various wrestling traditions and has been thoroughly assimilated by Brazilian jiu-jitsu stylists across the globe. Over the past few years, the double-leg takedown has evolved from a football-style tackle to a more refined series of movements as in the example described here. Keep in mind that the double-leg lift-and-slam technique described in Figures 2-7 through 2-11 is only one of many variations on this proven standard.

It is very important that you keep your head up as you make contact with your opponent's body. Otherwise you will be vulnerable to a guillotine counterattack.

Tactical Options

Without the gi, many of the traditional judo throws and takedowns are not possible. Takedowns that rely on clinching and shooting techniques are the norm. The tactical takedown options for no-gi that follow are relatively easy to do and highly practical.

Single-Leg Takedown

Like the double-leg takedown, the single-leg takedown also comes to Brazilian jiu-jitsu from wrestling. There are many variations on this move, most of which require a capture and complete isolation of one of your opponent's legs. This technique flows naturally with the double-leg takedown described above. If you miss one, then go for the other.

To perform a single-leg takedown, begin by lowering your body and dropping your forward knee gently to the floor as you drive forward toward your opponent's nearest leg. Reach around your opponent's forward knee and clap your hands together. Move to position yourself behind your opponent and place your left shoulder behind his right knee. (Figure 2-12) Reach between your opponent's legs with your left hand and trap his left leg near the

Figure 2-12. The single-leg takedown.

Figure 2-13. The arm drag.

ankle. Use your arms and shoulder in concert with your legs to drive your opponent to the ground and to his back.

Once you have captured and isolated one of your opponent's legs, you should take your opponent down and assume back control or side control as quickly as possible. You will be in a good position to press the attack once you've fully isolated one of your opponent's legs but, of course, there are counters to this and every takedown. You must advance your attack quickly. You won't have all day to act.

Arm Drag

If your opponent resists the tactical options described above you can take advantage of the moment and go for an arm drag. The arm drag is deceptive and very reliable. In tournament after tournament, top Brazilian jiu-jitsu competitors such as Alliance Team member Marcello Garcia have proven that this simple technique is highly effective. Like all takedown moves the arm drag depends on position and demands perfect timing.

To execute an arm drag from a standing position you must first grab your opponent's wrist, then his elbow. (Figure 2-13) Then pull your opponent forward with a sudden and decisive movement. Drop to the mat at the same time that you pull and move your hips to the side as you land. When your opponent lands, he will be in an unstable, forward falling posture. Take advantage of this moment and climb to your opponent's back. Immediately sink your hooks to stabilize your position. Submit your opponent with a rear naked choke.

The arm drag won't work in slow motion. You must drag your opponent a fraction of a second before he is aware that this is what you are up to. Like most techniques, the arm drag relies on two things: proper positioning and perfect timing.

STANDING ATTACK FOR NHB

The stand-up striking techniques used in today's NHB jiu-jitsu fights include kicks and knee, elbow, and fist strikes. Many of these techniques were assimilated from Muay Thai boxing. NHB stand-up striking techniques are used offensively and defensively. In NHB fighting, however, as with sport competition, the Brazilian jiu-jitsu stylist will almost always try to take the battle to the mat.

Core Technique: Double-Leg Lift-and-Slam Takedown

The double-leg lift-and-slam technique is a bread-and-butter takedown for NHB fighting. It works best against an opponent that is near your same weight. Follow the steps in Figures 2-14 through 2-18 to execute the double-leg lift-and-slam takedown.

You must establish control the instant that your opponent hits the ground. The knee-in the-belly is a good option. With luck, your opponent will have his breath knocked out, and you will have an advantage in the scramble.

Figure 2-14. To execute a double-leg lift-and-slam takedown for NHB, jab and take a long step forward with your left leg to close the distance

28   Brazilian Jiu-Jitsu Fighting Strategies

Figure 2-15. Reach around your opponent's waist with your left arm and grab behind your opponent's left knee with your right hand.

Figure 2-16. Drive your hips forward and use your legs to lift your opponent off the ground.

Figure 2-17. Lean forward to throw.

Figure 2-18. Slam your opponent onto the mat.

Tactical Options

NHB fighters who specialize in ground fighting must grab their opponents and take them down as quickly and efficiently as possible. The tactical options that follow employ this strategy. Takedowns in NHB matches are dangerous to be sure; to pull off a takedown in a no-rules match means that you must be able to pass through the gauntlet of punches, kicks, knees, and elbows just to get into range. Every NHB/mixed martial arts fighter—even those that specialize in ground grappling—must be competent in closing this gap.

Clinch Takedown

The clinch takedown is one of the most commonly used takedowns in NHB competition. To the untrained eye it may appear that one fighter just grabs the other and jerks; in reality, the clinch takedown requires considerable finesse. It is a natural progression from the core technique, the double-leg takedown described above.

Figure 2-20. Back clinch to the submit/takedown.

Figure 2-19. The clinch takedown.

To execute a clinch takedown you must first close the distance, taking care to defend against punches, kicks, knees, and elbows. Once in range, reach around your opponent's torso with both arms and clasp your hands together. Then drive forward until your opponent's balance breaks and he falls. (Figure 2-19) Follow your opponent to the mat, while all the time maintaining your clinching grip. Then quickly assume a side control or mounted position.

Properly held, the clinch position exposes you to minimum danger from counterattack. You must, however, be on the watch for knee strikes while holding the clinch. Use your inside arm to defend against knee strikes as necessary. Keep your head tight against your opponent, because a flexible opponent will be able to strike your head with his knee. The clinch position opens the door to many takedown options, such as the next one.

Back Clinch to the Submit/Takedown

This technique is extremely effective. You should, however, expect fierce resistance, as all jiu-jitsu fighters know that they are most vulnerable when an opponent is on their back. This is true in the standing position as well as on the ground.

To execute a standing back clinch takedown you should drive under your opponent's arms and clinch. Then swim under your opponent's arm and move behind him. As soon as possible, climb to your opponent's back, place your hooks, and execute a rear naked choke. Continue to apply the pressure until your opponent taps or falls. (Figure 2-20)

When you grab your opponent's back, he may try to roll, drop to the side, fall backward, or dive forward. If this happens, hang on tight, tuck your neck, keep your hooks in place, and do not cross your ankles. Chances are you will be able to take advantage of this back-controlling position regardless of how much your opponent flops around.

Remember, it is OK to cross your ankles while on your opponent's back so long as he is standing. When on the ground, however, you must never cross your ankles while in the back control position, or you will be vulnerable to an ankle lock counterattack.

STANDING DEFENSE WITH THE GI

Fights are won and lost from powerful takedown techniques. Not only can you get injured if you don't know how to defend, you can land in a very bad position, as Alliance competitor Aqil Abdush-Shakur learned in one of his first tournament experiences.

> *I went for a single-leg takedown. I had the guy's ankle locked between my legs and I had a good grip on his leg. I was in control, so I thought, and I was about to shoot forward to grab his other leg and take him down when he grabbed my belt, turned his hips out, and slammed me on the mat. Instantly I was tapping from an arm bar and trying to catch my breath and see through the stars!*
> —Aqil Abdush-Shakur

Defending against takedown techniques is a critical part of the game. Standing counter techniques are too important to overlook. Advance your game by adding the following counterattacks to your bag of tricks.

Figure 2-21. Hold your opponent's gi in preparation for a takedown.

Core Technique: Hip-Throw Defense

Hip throws are effective techniques when attempted by an opponent who is well skilled in their use. As with most techniques, the best defense is to avoid the attack altogether. You can do this by keeping your opponent from getting a grip on your lapel. If, however, your opponent gets a good grip and snaps you forward, you must react quickly, or you are going for a quick ride to the mat. You can defend even after your opponent has turned his back in preparation for the throw by following the steps in the photos.

Tactical Option

Take advantage of your momentum by going to your opponent's back or by executing a clinch takedown. Don't hesitate. If you do, your opponent will have time to recalibrate and attack again.

Reaping-Throw Counter

If your opponent attempts a reaping throw (Figures 2-22 and 2-23), you can counter by holding his leg and going with the throw. Use your hold on your opponent's leg to keep rolling to end up in a superior position. This counter is very effective but only works if done with perfect timing.

Figure 2-22. Push your hips forward to stop the attack.

Figure 2-23. Drive your opponent over your left leg to complete the counterattack.

STANDING DEFENSE WITHOUT THE GI

Standing defenses are important in all of the classifications of jiu-jitsu. In no-gi matches the stand-up game tends to be very fast, so shooting and clinching are favored.

Figure 2-24. Observe that your opponent is about to shoot for a single-leg takedown.

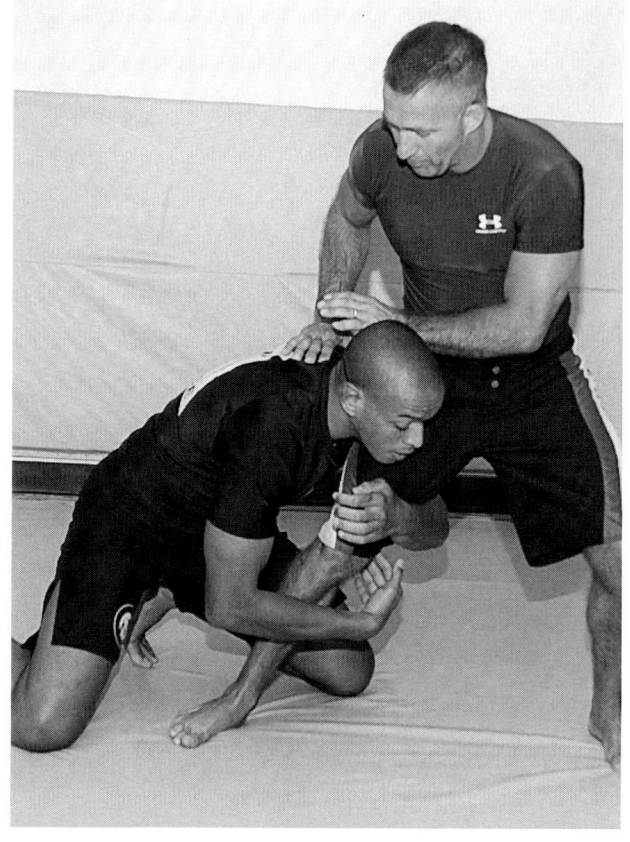

Figure 2-25. Push down on your opponent's shoulder with both hands.

Figure 2-26. Sit on your opponent's shoulder and press down with both hands.

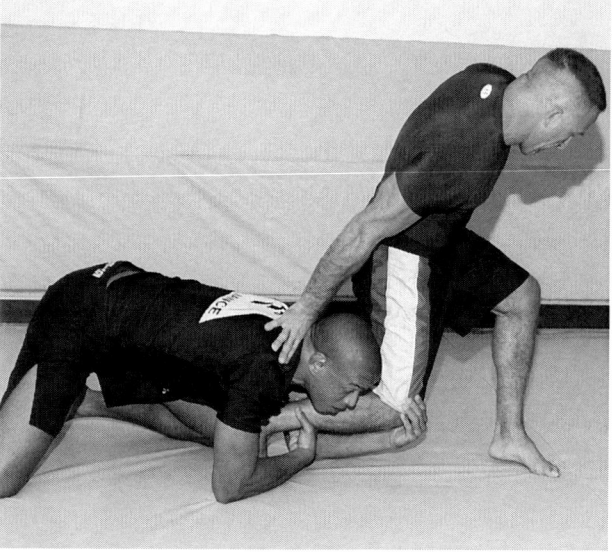

Figure 2-27. Turn your hips to the left.

Figure 2-28. Jerk your foot free.

Core Technique:
Single-Leg Takedown Defense

The single-leg takedown is one of the most effective takedown techniques used with or without the gi. Once an opponent has a hold on your leg, you must respond by sprawling. If you sprawl quickly, you have an excellent chance to defend and launch a counterattack. The scenario shown in Figures 2-24 through 2-28 assumes that you are standing with your right leg forward when your opponent goes for a single-leg takedown.

Timing is critical with this and all defensive moves. Your defense is dependent on the speed, direction, and height of your opponent's attack. To make this work you must drop your weight onto your opponent's shoulder the instant that he isolates your right leg; otherwise, you will almost certainly be taken down.

Tactical Options

Your opponent is not limited to one option when he drives forward in an attempt to take you down. He can go for many varieties of the clinch, the double-leg takedown, or the single-leg takedown. Your counters must, therefore, be fluid and adaptable.

Figure 2-29. Sprawl to defend against a double-leg takedown.

Double-Leg Takedown Defense

Your opponent can easily switch up on you and convert an attempted single-leg takedown into a double-leg takedown. Apply the following countermeasures if he is successful in grabbing both of your legs in preparation for a double-leg takedown: Begin by hooking your arm under your opponent's shoulder and neck. Perform this action just as you sprawl backward. Your goal is to keep your opponent from grabbing your legs, but if he is successful, you should continue to push your legs backward, forcing the sprawl. As soon as your legs are free, move immediately to your opponent's back. (Figure 2-29)

Arm-Drag Counter

The arm drag is a simple and surprisingly effective technique. One of the best counters is to go with the drag rather than resist it. (Figure 2-30) If you go with the arm drag, you can execute a number of counterattacks. You can, for example, move forward with the arm drag but at an angle that allows you to move to your opponent's back.

Remember, your opponent isn't arm-dragging you for your health—he is attempting to pull you to the ground and execute a submission. Your counterattack must occur while you are on balance and before you get pulled down.

STANDING DEFENSE FOR NHB

The main difference in counter techniques used for NHB vs. gi and no-gi competitions is the fact that striking is allowed and can occur at any time. One of the most basic counters to any attempted takedown is, therefore, a barrage of kicks, punches, knees, and elbows. The following counters describe situations in which your opponent has penetrated your striking defenses and has you in grappling range.

Figure 2-30. Counter the arm drag.

Standing 35

Figure 2-31. Face off with your opponent.

Figure 2-32. Push against your opponent's left shoulder as he shoots.

Figure 2-33. Sprawl your legs back before your opponent secures a grip around your legs.

Figure 2-34. Throw your left knee into your opponent's face as he advances.

Core Technique: Single-Leg Takedown Defense

In this situation your opponent drops to one knee and shoots forward and clinches one of your legs. Once your opponent has one of your legs clinched and isolated he is in position to execute a single-leg takedown. You can avoid this takedown by following the steps shown in Figures 2-31 through 2-34.

You must sprawl before your opponent locks his arms around your legs or you will be taken down in an instant. Should you fail in your attempt to counter and find yourself being taken over, you must scramble for position the instant you hit the mat.

Tactical Options

Once the range for kicks has been breached, you may be able to hold your opponent at bay with punches and knee strikes. Once the punching range is breached, however, you will usually find yourself in a contest for the clinch. This doesn't mean that you don't have to worry about strikes at very close range, but the greatest danger at this distance is from being taken down, landing hard, and ending up in a compromised ground position.

Figure 2-36. Countering a clinch takedown.

Figure 2-35. A guillotine submission is applied as a counter to a double-leg takedown.

Double-Leg Takedown Defense

When your opponent charges in and attempts to take you down with a double-leg maneuver, you can turn the tables by sprawling your legs back and simultaneously hooking your arm over his neck in a guillotine grip. When you have the grip, you should fall back immediately to assume a guard position. From here, you can execute the guillotine submission. (Figure 2-35) Be sure to push forward with your hips to increase the power of your guillotine as you finish.

This counterattack allows you to take advantage of your opponent's forward momentum. It works particularly well on an opponent who shoots in with his head perpendicular to the mat, as this provides you with the optimal angle for snatching the guillotine.

Clinch Takedown Counter

If your opponent secures a clinch with his arms underhooking yours, you are in for a fall unless you act quickly. You can counter by reaching over your opponent's arm with your right and scooping up his leg with your left arm. Then pick your opponent up into the air and slam him onto the mat. (Figure 2-36) Follow up by placing your knee into your opponent's belly and dropping punches with your right fist.

STRATEGIES FOR STANDING

Following are four different strategies, one for confronting each of the four fighter types in the stand-up condition. Recall that the four types of fighter are:

- Aggressive: attacks constantly with lots of power
- Deceptive: uses timing, fakes, and quick movement to gain advantage
- Defensive: defends and stalls until his opponent gets tired
- Interceptive: sets traps and uses a counter-attacks to defeat his opponent

The examples that follow are good strategies, but they are not the *only* strategies. Study these examples and then formulate your own. Customize your strategies to suit your strengths and weaknesses in relation to your opponent.

Fighting an Aggressive Opponent

Unless you are a lot stronger than your opponent, it is wise not to go head-to-head with him when standing. This is especially true if you are up against an aggressive fighter. Aggressive fighters seek to dominate every aspect of the game starting with takedowns and other stand-up techniques. Their strategy is to attack with full force at a relentless pace and generally overpower their opposition.

You can avoid and redirect an aggressive opponent's strength by using an interceptive strategy. To visualize how this might play out, imagine yourself up against an aggressive fighter in a sport jiu-jitsu tournament match. Assume that you've seen this person fight earlier in the day. You know that this opponent is an aggressive fighter and you have seen that he has a favorite attack pattern for the stand-up part of the match. The pattern that you observed is as follows: He charges, grabs the gi with his right hand, and goes straight for the large outer-reap throw (osoto gari). When this opponent misses the throw, he immediately drops to the ground for a single-leg or double-leg takedown.

Knowing this, you can formulate an interceptive strategy that contains a trap, or counterattack, for each of your opponent's favorite techniques. Your strategy might look like this: Begin by faking weakness and insecurity. Do this by hunching your shoulders slightly and by not looking your opponent in the eye. Move slowly, circling to your right, walk with hesitating steps to indicate that you are an easy target to attack. When it is safe to do so, cross your legs when you step to indicate inexperience. Lower your arms to make it look like it will be easy to grab your lapel. When your opponent charges at you and reaches for your lapel, grab his wrist with your right hand and step quickly to your left. Take advantage of your opponent's forward momentum and clinch him at the waist from the side. Lift your opponent into the air and take him down immediately.

If you miss this counterattack once or twice, it is likely that your opponent will get wise and charge in with one of his other favored attacks (in this example it would be the single-leg or double-leg takedown). Knowing this, you can use your hand to make it hard for him to grab your lapel, while also altering your stance to intentionally expose one of your legs as an easy target for a single-leg takedown. Be prepared to sprawl immediately and counterattack by moving to your opponent's back.

Fighting a Deceptive Opponent

A combination of defensive and aggressive strategies works well against a deceptive opponent in the stand-up part of the fight. Keep in mind that deceptive fighters rely on fakes and on speed. Knowing this, your strategy might be as follows: Begin by moving very slowly. Use your body language to indicate that you are not going to attack. Watch your opponent's hips and be wary of fakes followed by fast attacks. Play defense until you determine a pattern in your deceptive opponent's approach. Do this until you feel that he is becoming overconfident, and then explode into a series of aggressive takedown attempts. Keep charging and forcing him to defend until you find a weakness. Exploit the opening and take him down immediately, if possible. If you miss the opening, return to a defensive strategy and repeat.

The essence of this strategy is to use a defensive attitude to force the deceptive fighter to reveal his game and spend energy while exposing yourself to minimal risk. Then, when the weakness or pattern is identified, you force your opponent to go into defensive mode while you charge in and take advantage of his weakness.

Fighting a Defensive Opponent

Remember that a defensive opponent rarely attacks and is generally less concerned with winning and more concerned with surviving the fight. His strength is in avoiding and escaping. If you wait for him to attack, nothing will happen. If you charge in, the odds are very good that he will drop to the guard. If, however, you employ an interceptive strategy, you might be able to exploit this fact and score points with a takedown as in the following example: Move very slowly to put the defensive fighter at ease. Use your body language to indicate that you are not going to attack. Fake a double-leg takedown by charging forward and lowering your body. When your opponent responds by moving his hips back, grab his sleeves and roll backward into a guard position. Hook your left foot outside your opponent's right knee. Place your right hook inside his left knee. Pull your opponent's arms above your head and lift him over your head as you rock backward. Follow him over and assume a mounted position

This strategy is based on deception, speed, and timing. Since the most common response for a defensive fighter is to pull a guard, any fake that you do must cause him to have the opposite response, as in the example above.

Fighting an Interceptive Opponent

Interceptive fighters are defensive fighters. They are trap setters who specialize in counteroffensive techniques. To win the takedown against such a fighter it is best to force him to play a different game as shown in the following strategy. In this example, you will employ a defensive strategy first, followed by an interceptive strategy. Begin by moving very slowly. Use your body language to indicate that you are not going to attack. Subtly offer a number of openings to provoke the interceptive fighter to attack you. When your opponent attacks you, observe his pattern of techniques, and then fight fire with fire by switching to an interceptive fighting style. Employ interceptive counterattacks for each of your opponent's takedown attempts

Even the most defensive of the interceptive types will eventually attack if you don't press the attack. Force the interceptive stylist to go on the offensive and you will put him at a disadvantage.

INTERVIEW:
DR. PATRICK HARVEY ON STRATEGY

The following is an interview with Dr. Pat Harvey, an Alliance black belt, NHB competition veteran, Brazilian jiu-jitsu instructor, and NHB fight trainer. A five-time Pan Am tournament medalist, Dr. Harvey shares his strategy for success in jiu-jitsu.

Question: How would you describe your jiu-jitsu competition strategy?

Harvey: When I first started, all I did was attack. Then I had a couple of injuries and I couldn't attack all the time. I had to learn to counter and to fight defensively. I realized that it is not enough to be aggressive and attack all the time. I don't think that you can become a really good fighter if you don't know how to counterfight.

If you are new to training, and you are not very strong, you will find yourself defending and countering for a long time. Some people do that and become really good defensive fighters. They become defensive stylists. The problem is that now that everybody knows jiu-jitsu, it's hard to compete at a top level, say, in the open level as a defensive fighter. It used to be, way back when, that you could be a defensive fighter and become a world champion. Now many competitors, including me, are using both offensive and defensive strategies.

Q: How do you prepare for a fight?

Harvey: About 12 weeks before a tournament I change my training. I pick out what I consider to be my weakest areas. I work on those weaknesses over and over again. Let's say, for example, that I am working on defending the side mount. I will give that position to my training partners all the time, over and over. I won't wait for them to create the condition. I will pull them on top of me.

I prefer to attack from on top, so 12 weeks out I begin to train defensively a lot. I do this because that is not my best game. It's not that I am going to go into the tournament and fight defensively—this is the training I do in case I

Figure 2-37. Pat Harvey (right) demonstrates a rear naked choke on Roberto Traven.

need it. It greatly increases my confidence level when I do this.

Let's say I am training defensively and fighting from my guard over and over. For the first four weeks some people will beat me because this is not my game. You've got to be able to take a little of this from your sparring partners; if you can't handle getting beaten, then you should not compete. You can't train the best part of your game exclusively where you are winning and tapping out everybody all the time. If you do that, you are not going to win anything big. If you do that, when you go to a tournament, you will get into that bad situation that you didn't train and you will get stuck there.

Early in the 12-week cycle I pick out several moves for each position and practice them together. I never plan just one move; I always chain several moves together and practice them in sequence. This way I don't have to consciously remember every move when I am competing. I only have to remember the first move in the chain then the others will come to my mind instantly. I link a minimum of three moves together for every position, although I have linked as many as eight.

When I am preparing for a tournament I hardly work my strong areas at all; I don't even worry about my strong areas. It's the stuff that I am not as good at that I train the most.

Q: How do you keep track of your progress through the 12-week cycle?

Harvey: The whole time that I train for the tournament, I write things down. I write about how the moves that I tried worked or didn't. The main thing is that I always have a plan for what I am going to do.

At some point in the 12 weeks my weaker areas get stronger. Under constant pressure like this my brain finds a way to get better. Working deliberately from a disadvantage gives me real-time feedback. This is kind of like receiving electric shocks. Pretty soon I find the ways out of those situations I keep putting myself into.

Q: What else do you do to prepare?

Harvey: Before a tournament I do a lot of takedown training. Takedowns are one of the areas that we (Brazilian jiu-jitsu fighters) do the least of in regular practice. I don't try to work on a bunch of takedowns before a tournament, maybe two. But when I say two, I mean every derivation of those two. I drill those few takedowns over and over. By tournament time I want my takedowns to be at a level where I don't have to think about them.

Another important part of my strategy for any tournament is not getting hurt before the event. So I keep close track of the amount of training I do. I don't overtrain.

I stop lifting weights two weeks out. I replace the weight training with more and more mat time and lots of stretching.

If I feel a twinge, I stop. I don't push through it. I remind myself that I am training at a very high intensity and it is better not to push and just pick it up the next day. This is especially important near the end of the 12 weeks.

Just before I go to train, I review my plan in my notebook. I look over the three or four moves that I have selected to do when I am in each situation. You have to realize there are a lot of situations to work—open guard, half guard, turtle—almost everything and every derivation. Three moves for every situation add up to a lot of moves.

For 12 weeks before the tournament I work on my weakest areas, but when I get to the tournament I fight with my strongest. My goal is to take the guy down and go on top. If I do end up on bottom I don't freak out. As soon as I go on bottom I go into those weak-area moves that I've been working on and most often I wind up back on top. I don't even have to think about it because I've been drilling those moves so hard for 12 weeks.

Training my weak areas gives me confidence. I know in the back of my mind that if I do get on bottom, I will be OK. This makes me even more aggressive when I am on top.

Q: What is your strategy regarding points?

Harvey: I want to tap the guy out but I want to make sure I get my points up first. Part of my strategy is to try and be five points ahead before I tap the guy out. I do this unless it is near the end of the time.

Q: Why do you do that?

Harvey: Because if I am only two points ahead and he winds up sweeping me and passes my guard, he will get five points. He will be two points ahead with 10 seconds left. If I wait until I am five points ahead and I mess up a submission attempt, it will still be fine.

Q: How do you keep up with the points during the heat of the competition?

Harvey: You need to have somebody backing you up. Part of my strategy is to have a corner man working for me and to listen to him during every match. In the last Pan Am that I was in, my game plan went great. I was listening to my corner man all along and won my weight class. So I moved up to the absolute. I didn't expect to win but I wound up in the finals. I got off strategy because I stopped paying attention to my corner man. I went in there and fought this guy that was much bigger. I was fighting really well, but I was under the impression that I was losing. Since I thought I was losing, right in the last 30 seconds I took a really hairy chance to pass his guard and I got swept. I wound up losing. My corner man, Ed Kennedy, said, "Why did you do that?" I told him I might as well try something because I was behind in points and I wanted to win. He said, "You were ahead, Pat. You had it won." So you see, in the absolute I didn't follow my game plan; I quit listening to my corner. This was purely a strategy mistake. I should have won two gold medals instead of one. It showed me how important the little details of strategy are. It reminded me that my strategy does work, but I have to follow it in detail from 12 weeks out all the way till I step onto the mat. It doesn't guarantee that you will win, but it makes it a lot more likely.

Q: When you go to a tournament, you know that you will be going up against a number of different opponents. Does your strategy include ways for dealing with these different styles of fighting?

Harvey: I prepare for different types of fighters by working with different training partners. I don't want to roll with the same guy all the time. I will try to work with guys that I do poorly against in particular situations and figure out why. For example, if there is a guy in my training circle who is passing my guard, I will train this situation with him over and over. Hopefully after three or four weeks I will have figured out how to stop him.

When I am up against a faster guy or a stronger guy, it does require me to change how I am going to do stuff. For example, I try to get the very strong guys tired before I go for submissions. I try to cook them, hold them in.

For really fast guys, I try to use their gis to tie them up and slow them down. I hold them still first, then attack them. You don't want to fight the fast guys in transition because that is their game. No matter what type of fighter I am up against I want to keep him in my game.

Q: What is your game?

Harvey: My game is aggressive and very, very tight. I like to stay on top. I want to be really, really close. I want my chest to their chest or my chest to their back. My goal is to constantly draw them in close.

Q: Which sort of fighter do you have the hardest time with?

Harvey: The really lanky guys that keep me pushed away give me the hardest time. This is one of the types of fighters that I like to work with over and over again in the weeks before a tournament.

Q: Do you change your game when up against a lanky fighter?

Harvey: Yes, I do switch my game somewhat. I have my three or more moves (for every position) but I will emphasize the moves that I think will work best against this guy. Say, for example, that he has long arms and legs and a long open guard. I might try a foot lock or go for a knee bar before I attempt to pass his guard.

Q: What about an opponent that is not as strong as you are or that you think is not in as good condition?

Harvey: When I roll with somebody, I always listen to his breathing. One of my goals is to get the guy breathing harder than I am breathing. I will not try to submit him before I hear that. I will try to hold the guy and inhibit the guy's breathing. It can happen that you get ready to submit a guy and he will do this huge blast of energy and by the time he gets out of your submission you are the one who is blowing really hard. So, I try to get on top and attack him with a mild choke, I mean, an attack that forces him to defend but where I'm not really trying hard to choke him. I do this to force him to fight out of my choke without spending a lot of energy myself. I want him to use his whole body and lots of energy to defend. Once he starts blowing up [breathing hard] then I start to attack in earnest.

Part of my strategy is to always be aware of how full my gas tank is and how full his tank is. This is important, especially when you get older. When you are young, you can attack, attack, attack. When you are older, you need to run your opponent down a little bit then attack him.

Sometimes you see both fighters pause for a breather during the fight at the same time. This happens more with older fighters. My strategy is to be in better shape than my opponents. When I see the other guy pause to recharge, I take advantage and attack.

Q: You describe yourself as an aggressive fighter who likes to go on top and stay very tight. If you were matched against someone with exactly the same talents, how would you adapt your game?

Harvey: I would try to open one door and, if it is locked, go to another door. At a black-belt level you need to be versatile. I would try things according to my game and test him out. I would vary things a bit but try not to get away from my game.

Q: What if the guy was 35 percent stronger and heavier than you but had the same game?

Harvey: In that case I would need to adapt because I would lose if I went head to head. If I had no choice, I would go to my secondary area.

But I am not going to do anything really weird, and I am not going to try any new moves. I would feel him out and adapt.

You have to learn what's going on. Every opponent is different. For example, some people are really good against their same style and really poor against other styles. You can find some guys that can beat everybody who does a top game because they are so good at turning people on their back, but they can't fight a good defensive fighter. That is why I train for three months ahead of time in all those different areas. It is too late to wait until the fight. I have a first choice, second choice, and third choice for how to fight depending on how it goes.

My goal is to control the entire fight. Of course there are times when I can't control the fight. If I am losing on points, for example, I shift gears and go all out for a submission. I get really aggressive and take extra chances near the end of the fight if I am losing anyway. At this point, I will try to submit the guy from every single angle there is.

When I get on the bottom and get tired, I look for opportunistic ways to submit. If the guy puts me in an *uma plata*, for example, I might try to wrap his ankle around my head for an ankle lock. That's when I pull out that bag of tricks, sometimes strategy goes out the window and I just try to win. I never give up. When I get in a desperate situation, I start pulling stuff out of the blue. Sometimes it works but if not, what difference does it make since I was going to lose anyway?

Q: So you have a sort of a backup, desperation strategy?

Harvey: Yes, but I never start with my desperation strategy. I won't try something out in a tournament just because I think it is a tricky move. I tried that approach once and ended up losing in the first round. My strategy is to start with my tried-and-true. My goal is to dominate and control and then in the end, if it is not working, I pull the tricks out of the bag. These tricks come to me while I am lying there on the bottom, breathing hard. I look around and maybe there is an ankle out there I say to myself, "OK, if I just move over a little bit and totally go for it . . ." I do this when I am really in a bad spot. I say to myself, "I will breathe after the match is over, I am going for it and if I pass out, I just pass out."

Q: What do you do after a tournament to learn from your experiences?

Harvey: When I win, I forget about it right away. I take it easy. When I lose, I remember everything. When I lose, I go back home and train like crazy. It's a shame, but I get more bothered by losing than I get joy from winning.

Q: You have trained and been the corner man for a lot of successful NHB fighters. How do you coach guys who have different strengths from yours?

Harvey: Almost all the guys that I coach, I

fight with. While I am fighting with them, I can see what is working against me. I don't tell them to do what works for me—I tell them to do what works against me. This is a bummer sometimes because after you tell them that, they do it against you next time and you have to learn some new way to adapt to it.

Every time I do a move on one of these guys, I see in the back of my mind what he should do to get out. When you are the trainer, you have to tell them. I like to catch them about three times to give them the negative reinforcement. If the guy is making a mistake, he needs to know that this is a bad thing. You can't say, "I could have caught you"; you have to actually catch them. You need to put it on them first and then tell them how to get out of it. If I do this and the guy doesn't listen to me, I catch him again and do it harder. I keep doing this until he learns.

Q: Could you compare the styles of a couple of the top NHB fighters that you have trained?

Harvey: One of our best middleweight guys has good technique, but he relies a lot on his athleticism, on his cardio in particular. He puts pressure on you to make you try to counter and then he backs out and comes at you from a different direction. He does this over and over again. After he has done this for about five minutes, you know what he is going to do. You know how to defend it but you are exhausted and he gets you. He wears you out by attacking you.

Another of our top guys is a lightweight fighter who is really, really good. He waits until you make a mistake, then he gets very aggressive. He is a defensive guy. He waits for you to mess up and then attacks. He is a true counterfighter. When you make a mistake, he will attack you and he can do it from any angle. He also has good cardio. The difference is that he lets you wear yourself out by letting you attack him rather than by attacking you.

Q: How do you counsel these two different fighters?

Harvey: I tell them to play to their strengths. I tell the middleweight to go after his opponent aggressively, take him down, get on top, and punch. I tell the lighter guy to let his opponent come after him and then take him down when he does. I also encourage the lightweight to use his guard because he is truly a dangerous guard fighter. He's beaten a whole bunch of guys from his guard.

Q: How do you coach your fighters to approach a specific opponent?

Harvey: We don't always know the opponent. We have to ask around. Usually the information we get is general stuff. We get information by category, like whether the guy is a wrestler or a striker, whether he is a Brazilian jiu-jitsu guy, or a combination of all of the above. At this level we don't usually get films.

Q: How do you coach your guys to approach fighters from some of those different categories?

Harvey: If we don't know anything about the opponent, we have our fighter just train his all-around game. If we know that the guy is a wrestler, we are going to train our fighter to crouch a little bit lower and punch the tar out of the guy. This is something we will train over and over again. We will have some of our guys who are good wrestlers work with our fighter. We will get them to try to take our fighter down over and over while our guy stays in there with boxing gloves on and does two things: punches and sprawls.

If our fighter tries to play the wrestler's game and go for takedowns, he's going to wind up getting turned over. So in this case we would train to overcome what we know is that particular opponent's strength.

Q: What is the greatest weakness of a wrestler?

Harvey: The greatest weakness of a wrestler is being on his back. His second greatest weakness is getting caught in arm bars and triangles.

Most wrestlers are good at takedowns and

punching but not so skilled in submission fighting. Our guy will try to take advantage of this and try to get the wrestler on his back. Our guy will also go for sweeps, arm bars, triangles, chokes, and other submissions. Our guy will have to worry about getting punched by the wrestler but normally he won't have to worry much about submission attempts. This means our fighter can go for submissions that he normally wouldn't attempt on another Brazilian jiu-jitsu guy.

Q: What if your opponent is a jiu-jitsu guy?

Harvey: If the opponent is a Brazilian jiu-jitsu guy, we are going to find some of our best defensive grapplers and have them train with our fighter. We will ask these guys to attack the fighter with arm bars, triangles, and other submissions. The fighter in training will try to ground and pound these training partners, without getting submitted, until he passes their guards.

Even though our guy might be a better Brazilian jiu-jitsu guy than his opponent, we still train him as if he is going against the best jiu-jitsu guy around. If the opponent is a jiu-jitsu fighter, we will try to find out what the guy is good at and we train against that over and over.

Q: Can you give me an example of a time when you prepared for a specific fighter that you had seen fight before?

Harvey: I'm thinking of a Muay Thai guy that we had seen fight before. We knew that he had really good elbow and knee strikes. So we trained our fighter not to go in for a straight double leg. We trained him to avoid knee strikes by shooting to the side and going for the single leg. This way he could avoid the knee strikes and take the guy down safely. Our goal was to get our fighter to put the Muay Thai guy on his back, where he had no knee and elbow strikes. Most Muay Thai guys are in a lot of trouble when they get on their back, so in this case we trained our guy, who was normally a guard fighter, to go on top. In this instance, we changed our fighter's game for that particular opponent.

If the guy had been a wrestler, we would have trained our guy to work from the guard and go for arm bars. If he had been facing a jiu-jitsu fighter, we would have to know whether the opponent was a top guy or a bottom guy, whether he could strike, and so on.

Q: What if you were training a fighter who was a strong aggressive-style grappler and his opponent was also a strong aggressive-style grappler? Would you have your guy change his game in this circumstance?

Harvey: Only rarely would we have our guy completely change his game. We are not going to take a top guy and make him a bottom guy just because the other guy is a top guy. There is a reason that he has a game.

Most people have a couple of good moves; hopefully, you can find out what your opponent's best moves are in advance. Generally speaking we adapt aspects of our fighter's game; we don't drastically change his game.

Chapter 3

Closed Guard

The "guard" refers to any condition in which one fighter's legs are placed forward relative to his opponent. There are three primary guard positions that are most common in the grappling game: the open guard, the half guard, and the closed guard. Each has a top and a bottom condition, meaning that you can have someone in *your* guard (you are in the bottom position), or someone can have you in *his* guard (you are in the top position).

The closed guard is formed when one fighter wraps his legs around the other's waist and locks his ankles together. To the untrained eye the fighter on the bottom appears to be at a disadvantage. In reality, the fighter on the bottom has more submission and sweeping options than does the fighter on top. The fighter on the top, therefore, is typically considered to be at a disadvantage in matches where striking is not allowed.

This chapter contains techniques and tactical options for fighting from and fighting against the closed guard. At the end of the chapter is an interview with top Alliance jiu-jitsu competitor Chris Moriarty.

CLOSED GUARD TOP WITH THE GI

The closed guard position is particularly difficult to deal with for the person on top because the legs of the person on the bottom are wrapped around his waist and crossed at the ankles. This position provides enormous leverage for the person on the bottom. Since the fighter in the top position has very limited setoff attack options and is in constant danger of being swept or submitted by the fighter on the bottom, his best option is to get out of the situation altogether. This is called "breaking the guard," and it is a major skill all to itself.

Several guard breaks are discussed below. Each of these guard breaks assumes that your opponent is wearing a gi and that the sport jiu-jitsu rules, or submission-only rules, are in effect (i.e., no striking).

Figure 3-1. Sit on your knees and grab your opponent's lapels with your right hand at a point near his sternum.

45

Figure 3-2. Hold your opponent's hips to the floor with your left hand and break his guard as you stand up.

Core Technique: Standard Guard Break

The "standard guard break" is one of the safest ways to break the closed guard. It can be used on any opponent, large or small. This break, like all of the breaks described in this book, relies on leverage, not on strength.

When you perform the standard guard break, be sure to keep your weight on your left hand, not on your right. The right hand is in place to prevent your opponent from sitting up. (Figure 3-1)

It is very important to note that you do not use arm strength to break your opponent's guard with this technique. Strength for the break comes from your legs. Your left hand provides a leverage focal point, and your diagonal step backward gives you the angle necessary to break free by applying leverage against the weakest part of your opponent's hold. Again, power for the break comes from your legs. (Figure 3-2)

Tactical Options

If you fail to break the guard using the core technique described above, you can accomplish this task by flowing into any one of the following tactical options, the knee-in-the-tailbone guard break, or the single-sleeve guard break. These tactical options are interchangeable; in other words, you can start with either option as needed.

Knee-in-the-Tailbone Guard Break

The knee-in-the-tailbone break works well against an opponent who is determined to remain in the closed and locked guard position. It requires some flexibility but relies almost entirely on leverage, not on power. Follow these steps to execute the knee-in-the-tailbone guard break: Form a stable base by sitting on your knees with knees wide. Grab both of your

Figure 3-3. Executing a knee-in-the-tailbone guard break.

You must take care to defend against arm attacks at the moment in which your opponent's guard breaks. Do this by bringing your elbows in as soon as you feel your opponent's ankles break apart.

Single-Sleeve Guard Break

This is one of the most reliable closed guard breaking techniques. It is also one of the safest ways to break the closed guard. To do it, first form a stable base by sitting on your ankles with knees wide. Grab your opponent's right sleeve with your left hand and pull upward. Quickly place your left foot near your opponent's right hip and stand. Pull upward on your opponent's sleeve, push your hips forward, and keep lifting until your opponent's shoulders are off the mat. (Figure 3-4) Place your right hand on your opponent's left knee and push downward. Shake until your opponent's guard breaks, then immediately pass his guard.

It is critical that you lift your opponent's shoulders off the floor when you stand up with the sleeve hold. Your opponent may attempt to hold your right leg with his free hand and sweep you. By keeping your opponent's shoulders off the floor you will deny him the leverage needed to sweep.

Figure 3-4. Executing the single-sleeve guard break.

opponent's lapels and jam them under his armpits. Pin your opponent down by keeping your weight on your grips as you stand up. Sit down, allowing your right knee to penetrate the small gap between your opponent's tailbone and your hips. (Figure 3-3) Control your opponent's legs as his guard breaks.

CLOSED GUARD TOP WITHOUT THE GI

Breaking the guard in a no-gi contest is challenging because it is against the rules to grab clothing for leverage. If your opponent is determined to hold you in his guard and attack you from this position, you may end up wasting a great deal of energy defending. Your best option is to break the guard and break it quickly.

Figure 3-5. Place your hands in your opponent's armpits.

Figure 3-6. Stand up and put your right knee forward.

Figure 3-7. Sit on your left shin, keeping your right knee up to break the guard.

Figure 3-8. Drive your right knee over your opponent's thigh.

Closed Guard

Figure 3-9. Pass the guard and assume side control.

Figure 3-10. Reach behind to break the guard.

Core Technique: Insert Knee to Break Guard

This is an extremely effective technique for breaking the closed guard in a no-gi match. To execute this move, study Figures 3-5 through 3-9.

Tactical Options

When you are inside your opponent's closed guard, you are at risk for a huge variety of attacks and sweeps. If your opponent prevents you from executing your core guard breaking technique, move immediately to one of the many tactical options, such as the reach-behind-to-break option and the press-hips-to-break option shown below.

Reach Behind to Break the Guard

To execute this break, grab your opponent's left wrist with your right hand. Then stand up fast. Next, reach behind your back with your left arm. Use your left hand to force your opponent's ankles to unlock. (Figure 3-10)

It is absolutely essential that you watch the position of your right arm when you reach

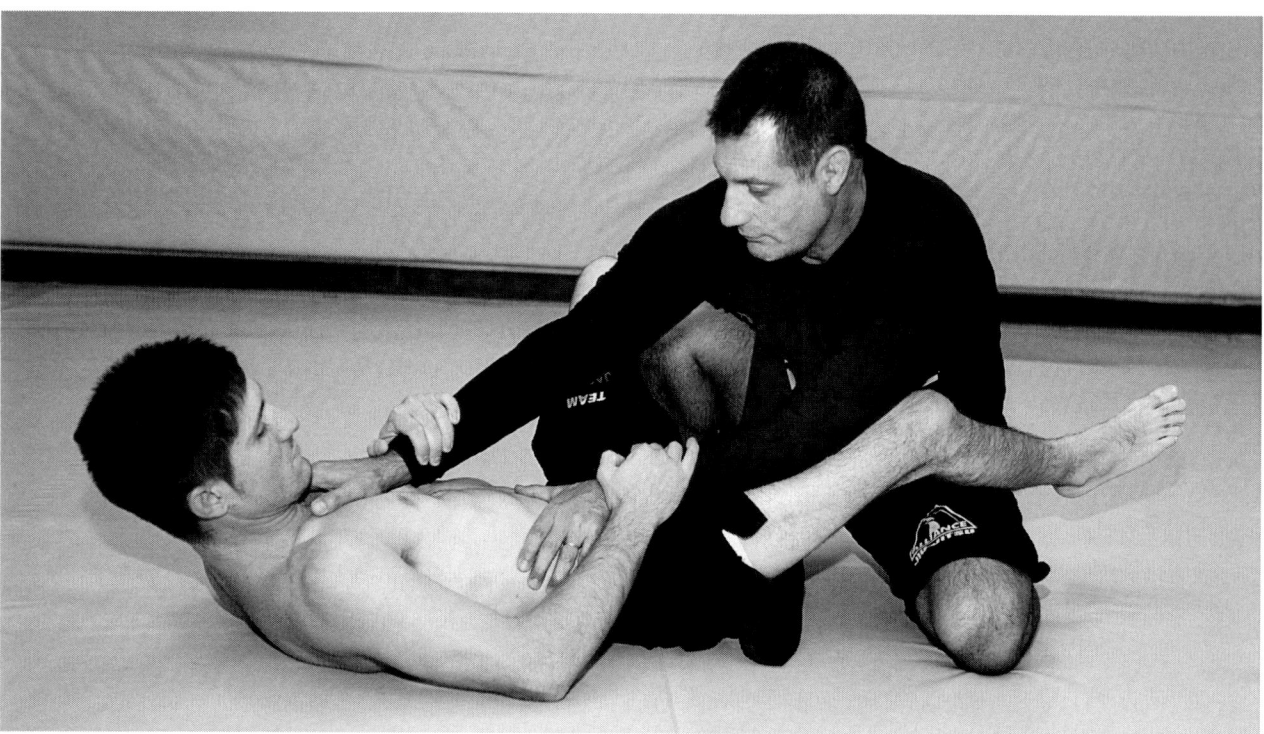

Figure 3-11. Press your opponent's hips and neck and push backward to break the guard.

between your opponent's ankles in this technique. A good guard fighter will snatch an arm bar or triangle in less than the blink of an eye if you give him half a chance.

Press Hips to Break the Guard

This technique works well when you run up against an opponent who holds you firmly in his closed guard. First, place both of your hands in the hollow of your opponent's hips. Be sure to keep your elbows inside of your opponent's thighs. Move your left knee back and to the side, and push down and forward on your opponent's hips. Move your hips backward until your opponent uncrosses his ankles. (Figure 3-11)

It is very important that you angle your hips as you execute this tactical option. This is accomplished when you move your left knee back and to the side. Angling your hips amplifies your leverage and makes it much harder for your opponent to maintain his closed guard position.

CLOSED GUARD TOP FOR NHB

The guard game changes dramatically when punches are allowed. The fighter on top is no longer at such a disadvantage. In general, the two sides of this game are fairly equal. It is with this position that many no-holds-barred battles get locked up. It can become a stalemate, twilight zone where neither fighter can gain advantage. In most of today's NHB contests, fighters are only allowed to stay in the closed guard position for a short period before the referee makes them break and start back from a standing position.

Figure 3-12. Sit on your ankles and control your opponent's arms.

Figure 3-13. Stand up quickly in one movement, place your left hand on your opponent's throat, and punch downward into his face.

Figure 3-14. Thrust your hips forward when he uncrosses his ankles.

Figure 3-15. Push your opponent's legs to the right and pass his guard.

Figure 3-16. Assume side control.

Core Technique: Punch

Though difficult, it is possible to punch a trained opponent from inside his closed guard. But since your reach and leverage are limited, real damage is hard to accomplish from this position. Because of this, your primary goal should be to use punches as a way to pass the closed guard. If the opponent is untrained or not used to fighting with punches, then his guard can be passed quickly with a punching assault.

Follow the steps in Figures 3-12 through 3-16 to punch your way out of the closed guard.

Falling prey to the arm bar and the triangle are the big dangers for the fighter on top. Each time you attempt to punch your opponent, you place your arm at risk for attack. You must be constantly aware of this danger and prepared to defend by bringing your elbows back quickly.

Tactical Option

If your "pound and ground" punching assault does not cause your opponent to release

Figure 3-17. Leveraged punching.

Closed Guard

Figure 3-18. Establish the closed guard and grab both of your opponent's sleeves.

Figure 3-19. Cup your opponent's right elbow in your left palm and pull his arm across your centerline.

his closed guard, you can proceed with a variety of tactical options, including leveraged punching. Leveraged punching is described below. If leveraged punching does not work, you can opt for a can opener or other tactical option.

Leveraged Punching

The leveraged punching technique is primarily used as a way to pass the guard. To break the guard using a leveraged punch, simply sit on your ankles and control your opponent's arms. When ready, reach forward and hook your left hand behind your opponent's neck and punch him in the face with your right hand. (Figure 3-17) When your opponent releases his ankle grip, press your hips forward and pass the guard.

CLOSED GUARD BOTTOM WITH THE GI

There are countless techniques that can be executed from the closed guard. Descriptions of four of the most common and most effective follow below. Remember, it is not the technique but rather how you set the technique up that determines complexity.

Core Technique: Arm Bar

By now you are no doubt beginning to see that the arm bar can be captured from almost

Figure 3-20. Execute the arm bar.

any position. It is one of the most effective and ubiquitous of all ground attack techniques. To execute the arm bar from the closed guard control position, follow the steps shown in Figures 3-18 through 3-20.

To make the arm bar work smoothly you should hook your legs over your opponent's back. This action causes the weight of your legs to drop onto your opponent's back, thus greatly increasing the stability of your attack.

Tactical Options

The gi can be a liability for your opponent when you have him in your closed guard. Many grip points will be available to you, including the collar, lapel, sleeves, cuffs, and shirttails. You can alternate your grip points to add leverage to the techniques described below.

Figure 3-22. The uma plata, or shoulder lock with leg submission.

Figure 3-21. The triangle choke.

Triangle Choke

The triangle choke, like all attacks, requires some skill. Begin with a fake or other distraction, then follow these procedures to execute a triangle choke from the closed guard. Grab and control your opponent's left wrist with your left hand. Uncross your ankles and move your weight onto your left hip. Shoot your right foot over your opponent's left shoulder and place it on his back. Swing your left leg over and form a figure-four lock with your right ankle inside the crease of your left knee. Pull your opponent's right arm far across his chest. Pull down on your opponent's head with both hands and squeeze your legs to finalize the submission. (Figure 3-21)

In order to get the pressure of the triangle onto your opponent's neck, you must turn your body counterclockwise to assume a more-or-less perpendicular positional relationship. Otherwise the power of your attack will be wasted against his shoulders.

Uma Plata

You can capture the uma plata, or shoulder lock with leg submission, from the half guard, but first you must isolate your opponent's left arm. Do this by holding your opponent's wrist and elbow at the same time. Then release your ankles and swing your right leg over your opponent's left shoulder. You can gain space for this by pushing your opponent's head away as you swing your leg over his shoulder.

Once your foot is clear, create a figure-four position with your legs by placing your right foot inside your left knee. Scoot your hips away and force your opponent to fall forward. Keep your opponent's arm pinned against your hips as you lean forward. Finalize the uma plata submission by bending your knees to your left and placing your weight onto your opponent's shoulder. (Figure 3-22)

CLOSED GUARD BOTTOM WITHOUT THE GI

Without the gi you lose the advantage of the leverage that grip points provide. Your opponent also loses this advantage and the net result is that you have a significant leverage advantage when you hold your opponent in your closed guard without the gi. Remember, he has few options to attack you while held in this fashion. You, on the other hand, have a wide variety of attack and sweep options. Let's take a look at a few of them, beginning with the Kimura.

Figure 3-23. Capture your opponent's right wrist with your left hand.

Figure 3-24. Hold your left wrist with your right hand.

Figure 3-25. Unlock your ankles and scoot your hips back.

Figure 3-26. Execute the Kimura lock.

Core Technique: Kimura

The Kimura is a powerful submission technique that works by placing extreme pressure on the shoulder. Perform the Kimura from the closed guard in the manner described in Figures 3-23 through 3-26.

To make the Kimura submission work you must press your opponent's arm up and behind his back. If your opponent is able to prevent you from bending his arm back, you should abandon the Kimura and go for another option.

Tactical Options

In no-gi matches you can afford to stay in the closed guard for long periods of time if you choose. Remember, you have superior leverage and many attack and sweep options when you hold your opponent in your closed guard. Since the rules provide that your opponent cannot hit you, you need not rush.

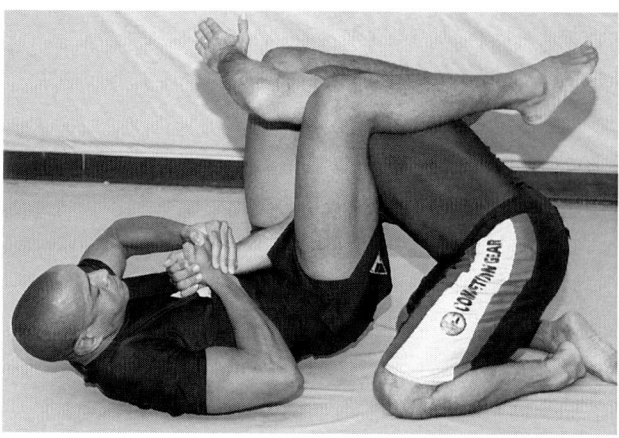

Figure 3-28. The arm bar.

Figure 3-27. The triangle choke.

Triangle Choke

Capture the triangle by pressing your opponent's right arm across your body as you slide your left leg over his neck. Lift your hips as you do this. Hook your left leg over your right ankle. (Figure 3-27) Execute the triangle submission. You will gain power and leverage if you drive your body into a perpendicular position as you engage the triangle. You can do this by holding under your opponent's leg with your arm. Be sure to pull down on your opponent's head as you squeeze for the submission.

Arm Bar

Push your opponent's right arm across your chest. Place your left foot on your opponent's right hip. Lift your hips and swing your right leg over your opponent's back. Bend your leg to apply pressure, then swing your left leg over your opponent's head to execute the arm bar. (Figure 3-28)

CLOSED GUARD BOTTOM FOR NHB

As with most of the conditions common to the ground fighting specialist, the closed guard game changes dramatically when strikes are allowed. While you may have superior leverage when you hold your opponent in the closed guard, it is possible for your opponent to punch you or hit you with his elbows. It is critical, therefore, that you control your opponent's arms at all times while in this position.

In gi and no-gi sport competition, it is almost always against the rules to slam an opponent who holds you in his closed guard. This is not true in NHB fighting. You must, therefore, be on the watch for the slam. By slam we mean a situation in which your opponent stands up while you are holding on in the closed guard, then drops his weight forward and body slams you onto the mat.

Figure 3-29. Lock your ankles around your opponent's waist to secure the closed guard.

Figure 3-30. Control your opponent's arms and deflect if he tries to punch.

Figure 3-31. If your opponent attempts a can opener, reach across his neck with your right hand and reach under and control his left arm with your left.

Figure 3-32. Uncross your ankles and swing your left leg across your opponent's back.

Core Technique: Arm Bar

From the closed guard, begin by controlling both of your opponent's wrists. Do this by grabbing your opponent's wrist so that your thumbs point toward your chin. Hold your opponent's arms against your chest to prevent him from punching. Then follow the steps in Figures 3-29 through 3-33 to perform the arm bar.

Remember, your opponent can punch you from this position so you must control his arms at all times. Prevent your opponent from punching you during the transition to the arm

Figure 3-33. Swing your right leg over your opponent's neck and arch your back and lift your hips to execute the arm bar.

bar by squeezing him tightly to you. This will take away the space that your opponent needs to generate an effective punch.

Tactical Options

In no-rules fighting, as in other forms of jiu-jitsu, the triangle is one of the most effective techniques. It works well by itself, or as a tactical follow-up to a missed arm bar or uma plata.

Triangle Choke

To execute a triangle choke from the closed guard position, hold your opponent's right arm down and control his left wrist. Lift your body and capture a triangle grip with your legs. The triangle leg grip is sometimes called a figure-four because it is constructed by placing one ankle inside the knee of the other leg, thus making a shape similar to a four. Once in this position, push your opponent's arm across his body and move to your left. Tighten your triangle lock by squeezing your knees toward one another. Pull down on your opponent's head with your right hand to finish. (Figure 3-34)

Figure 3-34. The triangle choke.

Figure 3-35. The Kimura.

Kimura

When attacking from the closed guard, the arm bar, triangle, uma plata (shoulder lock), and the Kimura often present themselves. The Kimura is easily captured when an opponent places one of his arms on the mat. You can encourage this from the closed guard by pulling your opponent's body forward with your legs. The instant that your opponent's right palm touches the mat you should grab his wrist with your left and wrap your right arm over his arm. Connect the Kimura grip by grabbing your left wrist with your right. Uncross your feet, move your body to your left, and swing your left leg over your opponent's back. Lift your opponent's right arm up and push it behind his back to execute the Kimura submission. (Figure 3-35)

STRATEGIES FOR THE CLOSED GUARD

Following are four different strategies, one for confronting each of the four fighter types—aggressive, deceptive, defensive, and interceptive—in the closed guard condition. Remember that no single strategy works on all occasions. The strategies that follow are examples, not absolutes.

Fighting an Aggressive Opponent

When your opponent has you in his closed guard, your goal must be to break the guard as soon as possible. As a general rule it is best to stand up to break an opponent's guard. This is true for every type of fighter, aggressive, deceptive, defensive, or interceptive, and it is true for gi, no-gi, and NHB matches. If you stand, you will have far more leverage for breaking the guard than you do if you stay on your knees. If you do stay on your knees, you will have few attack options. Meanwhile, your opponent will have a long list of options for attacking you.

Escaping from an aggressive fighter who chooses to hold you in his closed guard often requires an aggressive response. Don't wait for your opponent to attempt a sweep or attack your arm. Stand up quickly and act aggressively and decisively to break the guard.

Fighting a Deceptive Opponent

The deceptive fighter who favors the closed guard is a dangerous animal. He will set you up by faking one attack and then going for another. For example, the deceptive fighter might open his guard and fake a scissor sweep then follow with an arm bar.

To avoid getting caught by these tricks you must move rapidly. Set the game in motion before your opponent has time to attack. Stand up fast and use your position and your leverage to break the closed guard as quickly as possible.

Fighting a Defensive Opponent

The closed guard position is heaven for the truly defensive fighter. A highly defensive opponent will often use the closed guard to stall the game and wear you down. He is unlikely to take many risks until you show real signs of fatigue.

To escape from a defensive fighter's guard you should stand immediately and proceed aggressively to break free. Otherwise you will waste tons of energy and lots of time in closed guard limbo.

Fighting an Interceptive Opponent

If you are up against an interceptive fighter who has a good closed guard game, you are in for a battle. This type of fighter is likely to give you one apparent opening for escaping the guard after another. Yet each "opening" will actually be a trap with a killer submission waiting at the end.

An interceptive guard fighter might, for example, open his legs and lower one knee. This action opens the door for you to pass over his thigh. When you make the move you realize that you've been set up for an over/under choke.

It is important for you to set the pace with the interceptive fighter. You must avoid the temptation of moving toward the apparent opening and likely trap. As a rule of thumb, do not wait for the interceptive fighter to set you up. Make your move to break the guard by standing up quickly and using leverage to free yourself.

INTERVIEW: CHRIS MORIARTY ON STRATEGY

The following interview contains the strategy used by top Alliance competitor Chris Moriarty. Moriarty is a Cavalcanti brown belt and has won many, many events. Some recent highlights from his record include Grapplers Quest US Nationals, over 175 pound Purple Belt Champion, 2005; Music City Grappling Open, Lightweight Pro Division Champion, 2005; Ultimate Man's Weekend, Light Heavyweight Purple Belt Champion and Advanced No-Gi Light Heavyweight Champion, 2005; Extreme Grappling Open, Heavyweight Invitational Division Champion and Absolute Brown Belt Champion, 2005; and American International Grappling Championships, Brown Belt Super-Fight Champion and Advanced No-Gi Light Heavyweight Champion, 2005.

In the interview that follows, Chris Moriarty addresses many of the nuances of the strategy that have made him so successful.

Question: How do you prepare yourself to go out for the first match of the day?

Moriarty: One of the things that always happens to me right before a match is that I get such a rush that my body kind of shuts down. My legs get weak and I feel like I have no power in my legs. So I put on warm clothing and I go outside and I do explosive things, exercises for my legs. I do this where no one can see me. I don't like to warm up in front of a lot of people and show them how seriously I am warming up.

I like to go out on the floor with an attitude that shows that I am not taking the match too seriously. I don't want to do things that get my opponent pumped up even more than he already is. If I behave in a way that gets him riled up, it will cause me to get riled up. When this happens, it's like you are fighting each other before the match begins. I don't want this to happen, so I always try to get my opponent to calm down. I do this by trying to look relaxed and calm even if I am not.

At the beginning, the match always seems surreal. My first match of the day always feels like I am not there because I am so nervous. So I like to close my guard, take a breath, and control the sleeves. I try to look like I am really going for something to get the guy to stop thinking about passing for a second and start worrying about defending. I do this so I can think about what my next step will be.

Q: How do you approach a match when you know that you are up against a power fighter?

Moriarty: If I see that the guy is really running at me, I will usually grip up with him. I always act like I am really aware of what I am doing on my feet, even if I am not. I give the impression that at any moment he could be in danger. But then, if the guy really pushes me, I will jump to the closed guard. I don't like to sit guard anymore because if the guy is really aggressive, when you sit guard, even if you have grips, the guy can get a grip on your pants and start throwing your legs around and you can find yourself in a scramble before you are ready.

Your heart rate can go through the roof

Figure 3-36. Chris Moriarty (top)

really fast when the match starts if you aren't careful. So I like to start the match, not as slowly as possible, but at a pace that I can control for a little while before I start turning it up. Often I will jump closed guard so I can dictate the pace on a guy like that. If I see that the guy is not really aware on his feet, then I will press the stand-up action more, but if the guy is really, really aggressive, I usually jump to the closed guard. I will control his sleeves, and then he will have no choice but to calm down. If he doesn't calm down, he will make mistakes.

Q: How would you describe your style of fighting? What is your game? What is your strategy?

Moriarty: My game is all about the transitions of jiu-jitsu. When I am grappling in class, I will see that the guy is kind of sitting up weird and I will think, "I'll bet I can pull my leg out right now and mount," and I will just try it. Or I might see that he is moving his arm a certain way and I'll just try an uma plata spontaneously. It is all about action during the transitions.

Q: How did you develop this game?

Moriarty: It is not a choice that I made; it is just the way my style developed. Some people I know started off as wrestlers and they never really got a grasp on submission. They will pass and get to the side and stay there and go for a few things, but they are never really comfortable enough to take risks and go for submissions.

I am very impatient. For example I don't like the side mount because it is boring. I cannot force myself to hold a position like that so I am always trying stuff. At the beginning of a match, my way is not always good. I miss a lot of submissions early on but after the guy slips out of the same submission a few times I find the counter to his defense.

I do the things that a lot of other people don't do. I watch other competitors a lot, and when I see something new that I like, I try it as soon as I can. For some reason I can replay things that I see in my mind very clearly. If it doesn't work the first few times I keep trying it. Eventually it will start working for me. It always does.

That is where I got my overhead sweeps. I have a bunch of unique sweeps that I do from my closed guard where I let the guy stand up and sweep him over my head. These unique techniques always work because nobody expects them. People say, "Stick to the basics," and I think that is important, but if you use things that are really off the wall, they often work because nobody expects that kind of stuff.

Q: Everyone says that you have a phenomenal guard. But what you are describing is not just a guard game; you are describing a game of playing the unexpected, of playing between the lines.

Moriarty: Yes. My game is all about the position changes. The submissions that I catch, most of them, are not set up in advance. They are spontaneous. I look at what the guy is trying to defend then I think about what he is not defending and I go for that. I am always taking risks and changing the position dynamically. I look at everything but don't focus on any one thing.

Q: You create position changes? Can you give an example of this?

Moriarty: When I would pass the guard, my opponents would always try to turn into me. I got sick of just always trying to force them onto their backs. It seemed to me that this was really inefficient. I decided to find a way to switch to something during the transition that would make passing easier for me to pass. To accomplish this I started doing a move that I saw Eddie Bravo do that they call the Ninja Roll. I started doing that and I was able to pass guys' guards over and over again. This works because everybody does the same jiu-jitsu so they have the same instincts. If you start to pass their guard, they turn and go to their knees, and so I set up stuff off of that. I anticipate what they are going to try to do to defend. I don't attack with what they are going to expect. I attack from the back door.

Q: People think of guard fighters as defensive fighters but you are not a defensive fighter, you are an offensive fighter who chooses to use the guard as one of your main weapons right?

Moriarty: Right.

Q: You are an offensive fighter but you are not a fighter that bowls people over with strength and power, you are a deceptive fighter, right?

Moriarty: Right.

Q: How would you approach a fighter who was highly skilled and had a style similar to yours?

Moriarty: If I had a lot of respect for this person and I thought he was really talented, I would probably pull closed guard. No-gi is different because it is hard to pull closed guard, but with the gi I like to pull closed guard because immediately the guy has to at least respect what I am doing. He has to think for a second and it gives me a second. I do this because, no matter what, he will have to be on defense when he is in my closed guard. Plus I lose no points.

Q: Do you worry about points?

Moriarty: I don't think about points at the beginning of a match; I think about gas. I think about how much energy this match is going to take me because by the end, no matter what, I am going to be exhausted if the guy is really tough. What you have to do is to pick your moments to explode.

Q: What is the difference between competing at the amateur level and the professional level?

Moriarty: There is a big difference in the amateur and professional. You have no idea how big the jump is. When you get really good and you are still fighting amateur level, the whole game is about what you want to do because your opponents are always a step behind you. When you start fighting professional, you realize you can't just push these guys around or you will gas yourself out.

Q: Other than jumping to the guard, what techniques do you use for stand-up?

Moriarty: I don't train stand-up to try to be really good at it, I train stand-up so that I have confidence. Before, when I didn't train any stand-up, I didn't have the option. That was scary because if the guy was really good at passing, I didn't even have the option of standing up with him. That was killing my confidence. Now that I know I have stand-up skills and the guy can't just easily take me down at will, he is going to have to work hard for it and maybe I will take him down. Now I can go on the mat and I don't care if the guy is good at takedowns and good at passing because I have the option; I can stand up with him now.

I like to do flying arm bars and flying triangles and stuff. I like to fake that I am really good at stand-up; you can fake it by the way you stand and the way you start to grip. Instead of reaching with your forward hand, for example, you reach with your back hand and feed it to your forward hand then start shaking the guy. If you do this sometimes you can make the guy think you are a lot better at stand-up than you really are. I've had guys break their grip and sit on me when I did this. If I feel that I can be successful at attacking the guy standing up, I will. But when the stakes are really high and the guy is really tough, I will put him into the closed guard.

Q: What do you do when you are up against a guard fighter?

Moriarty: I think that the way people pass traditionally is very flawed. You know, a lot of guys like to pass with double underhooks. I think that can be a mistake because it is a really hard position to pass that way and it takes a lot of endurance and a lot of strength. Plus there are not many options when you pass this way and you are at risk of getting caught in a counterattack.

My goal is to never let the guy on the bottom play his game. Usually when I am on top of somebody who is a really good guard player, I put one knee forward. I look at what he is doing; if he tries to control both of my sleeves, I keep one hand back so he can't. I had a match where a guy kept trying to do this, grab both sleeves, for the whole match, so I kept my hand back until the moment when I could grab his collar, grab his same side knee, and drive my head into his stomach and pass.

There are three main types of open guard: the half guard, the butterfly guard, and the long distance guard. The long distance guard comes in several varieties, including the spider guard and DelaRiva guard. For the spider guard and DelaRiva guard, your opponent must control both of your sleeves. So you should never let him have both of your sleeves.

Against a guy that plays butterfly guard you have to keep pressing. You have to keep your head inside, and you have to keep your weight down. Keep your chest forward on the guy and never let him have your arm.

With a guy that plays half guard you should to try to get your chest on his chest so he can't be on his side. The person who wins the swim and gets the underhook in half guard usually wins.

Q: So you play the same basic game against all types of fighters, right?

Moriarty: The general idea of my game remains the same. I am not a positionally dominant strength fighter. I am in and out and in and out the whole match.

Q: What do you do to build your skills other than attend classes?

Moriarty: Going back and training harder isn't always the answer. I watch videos all the time. Not instructional videos; I hate instructional videos. I watch match videos and I learn a lot that way.

I have gotten to a level recently where I don't lose that much in competition with the gi. I lose more in no-gi matches, but I haven't lost with the gi for a while. But with no-gi I get surprised every now and then because I am always fighting guys who are really good and after the match I think, "Wow, how did I let him get that far? What happened?" I know what to do from that position but it wouldn't work. So I watch match videos and I look for fighters who look like the guy that I had trouble with. Then I play the tape and I watch what he does. I just watch, and rewind, and watch. Pretty soon I figure out what I should have done with that guy. This is how I learn. I have made dramatic improvements doing this.

Q: How early do you begin to prepare for a major competition?

Moriarty: Three months' preparation time is optimal. I take tournaments on the fly and that isn't good, but it is necessary at this point in my career because I want to compete as much as I can. I think the most important thing for a competitor is to be confident. The only way that you are going to be confident is to win a lot and for me that means attending as many tournaments as I can.

Q: What else do you do to build confidence?

Moriarty: The most important thing about competing is confidence, and confidence comes from experience. You cannot win the big tournaments unless you are competing all the time because at the big ones there is even more pressure. You have to be able to go in thinking, "I can do this, no problem; I have done this a thousand times."

Most people do the best when they are at their own school competing among friends with no pressure and nothing to worry about. That is where they can do their craziest moves, take chances, and just play the game like they want to. But when they go to a competition, they usually compete at about 50 or 60 percent of their ability because they are nervous and intimidated. Now, if a guy goes to several tournaments in a row and starts winning, he will build momentum and confidence. Eventually he should be able to compete in a tournament at 80 to 95 percent of what he is able to do back in class. Once you can translate your whole in-class game to competition, your confidence will be very high.

CHAPTER 4

OPEN GUARD

The open guard is formed anytime that one fighter has his legs in the other fighter's way. There are many variations of the open guard, including the seated or butterfly guard, the inverted guard, the spider guard, the DelaRiva guard, the biceps splice guard, and many others.

In the last 15 years or so, the open guard has evolved from a purely defensive position to a dynamic and fully functional part of the offensive game. A fighter with a good open guard can sweep or submit his opponent with an endless variety of techniques.

The open guard is no joke, and the techniques, tactics, and strategies described below will provide you with a solid understanding of this part of the game. Two interviews on the topic of strategy follow at the close of this chapter. The first is with world-famous Alliance competitor and black-belt instructor Roberto "Spider" Traven. The second is with his wife, sports nutritionist Flavia Traven, who speaks on the extreme importance of nutrition in high-performance sports.

OPEN GUARD TOP WITH THE GI

There are many attacks that can be executed from the open guard top position, including ankle locks, knee bars, and knee crunching techniques. These techniques are important options to be sure, but the prime objective of the fighter who finds himself in the top position of the open guard is generally to pass the guard. According to Royce Gracie, "If you observe two athletes sparring, you will see that they spend a majority of their time either passing or defending the guard. Thus, a good Jiu-Jitsu game begins with a strong foundation in those skills."[1]

It is important to pass your opponent's guard as soon as possible because the fighter in the bottom position has a huge variety of attack options. One of the most reliable guard passing techniques is the over-the-thigh pass described below.

Figure 4-1. Hold your opponent's pants at the knees and push his left leg to the mat.

Figure 4-2. Control your opponent's right sleeve and left collar as you drive your right knee over his right thigh.

Figure 4-3. Hold under your opponent's left arm and put your weight on top to gain side control.

Core Technique: Over-the-Thigh Pass

To pass the guard and get to a superior position such as side-control or the mount, you must get past your opponent's legs. There are three ways that you can physically get past the legs: You can go under, around, or over them. There are dozens of techniques for each of these three paths.

Follow the steps in Figures 4-1 though 4-3 to execute the common and effective pass known as the over-the-thigh pass. You must keep low and close to your opponent as you execute this pass. It is important that you control your opponent's hips with your weight and keep his back pinned to the ground as you pass. If you do not, your opponent may be able to swim under your arm and climb to your back.

Tactical Option

The seated guard (also called the butterfly guard) is one of the most effective of the open guard positions. It affords many options to defend

Figure 4-4. While executing the over-the-seated-guard pass, you must gain control of your opponent's elbow.

Figure 4-5. Force your opponent onto his back so that you can break your hips to the side and pass his guard.

and to attack. It can be very challenging to pass the seated guard; one of the best ways is shown here.

Over-the-Seated-Guard Pass

When your opponent assumes a seated guard position, lean forward and swim your right arm under his left. At the same time, control your opponent's right elbow with your left hand. (Figure 4-4) Then drive your body forward. Use your right shoulder to force your opponent onto his back. (Figure 4-5) Then break your hips to your left and pass your opponent's guard.

You must be continuously aware of your opponent's hooks when he is in the seated guard. The hooks provide serious leverage. You will find yourself flying, rather than passing, if you aren't careful.

OPEN GUARD TOP WITHOUT THE GI

This game is quite different from the version with the gi. As the one trying to pass the guard, you have nothing to grab but flesh and bone and that's a challenge. Your advantage is that your opponent does not have any cloth to grab either. It is much harder for him to hold you in open guard without the cloth advantage.

Core Technique: Neck Turn Pass

When your opponent assumes a seated guard, you can pass by following the steps shown in Figures 4-6 through 4-8. Remember to watch out for the hooks as you execute this technique.

This pass is a variation of the over-the-leg-type pass. It differs somewhat because in this case you will be moving your opponent's body around rather than moving your body over his legs.

Figure 4-6. Wrap your right arm over your opponent's head and grab his chin.

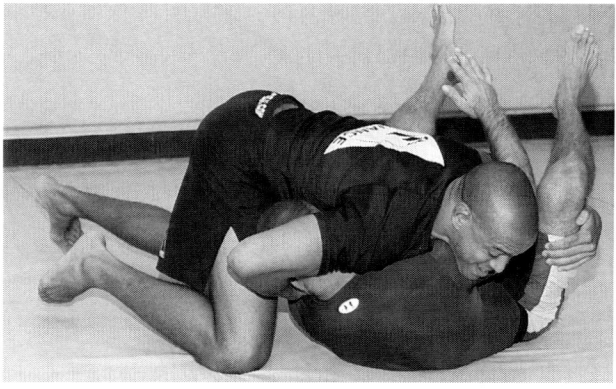

Figure 4-7. Scoop your left arm under your opponent's right leg and turn his body to the right.

Figure 4-8. Establish side control.

Figure 4-9. Executing a somersault pass.

Figure 4-10. After you land, you can assume side control.

Tactical Options
In the last few years, the seated guard has gained enormous popularity in jiu-jitsu competition. This is especially true in no-gi matches, where passing the seated guard has become a major challenge.

Somersault Pass
When your opponent assumes a seated guard, you should use your weight to press forward until he is flat on his back. Then reach around your opponent's thighs and hold his ankles. Once in this position, place your head on the floor to the right (Figure 4-9) and somersault over your opponent's legs. When you land, you will be clear of your opponent's legs and able to assume side control. (Figure 4-10)

No striking is allowed in sport no-gi matches, so you don't have to worry about getting punched as you make your way over and around your opponent's guard. You must be concerned, however, with your opponent's hooks. Maintain control of your opponent's legs all during the somersault to avoid them.

Figure 4-11. Executing the squeeze-both-knees pass.

Squeeze-Both-Knees Pass

This pass is most easily initiated against an opponent who is working from a seated guard position. Begin by sitting on your knees in a wide base. Advance on your opponent very quickly and squeeze his legs together between your thighs. Reach under both of your opponent's knees with your right arm. Clasp your right wrist with your left hand and squeeze your opponent's legs together very tightly. (Figure 4-11) Drop your weight on top of your opponent's legs and force them to your left. Place your head across your opponent's waist and pass his guard. Assume side control.

You must make certain that both of your opponent's feet are on the mat before you reach under to control his legs. Otherwise your opponent will use his feet to block your hips or hook your legs.

OPEN GUARD TOP FOR NHB

Remember: Your opponent can punch you, kick you, sweep you, or use any number of submission attacks and counterattacks against you from the guard position. Your goal, therefore, must be to pass his guard quickly and safely.

Figure 4-12. Advance on your opponent while he is on the ground in an open guard position.

Figure 4-13. Hook your opponent's left ankle with your left hand and move diagonally to your right.

Figure 4-14. Step forward, placing your left foot near your opponent's left hip.

Figure 4-15. Place your left knee on your opponent's belly and your left hand on his throat. Punch with your right.

Core Technique: Throw-the-Legs Pass

Use this technique when you find yourself in a situation in which you are standing and your opponent is on his back. Follow these steps in Figures 4-12 through 4-15 to execute the throw-the-legs pass.

This pass depends on timing and the placement of your foot as you step forward.

Tactical Options

The guard game changes a lot when striking is allowed. Few fighters, for example, like to use the seated guard as a primary position when strikes are allowed because they are vulnerable to punches and kicks. Most NHB fighters are extremely aggressive and like to go on top as soon as possible. The guard, while still dangerous, is primarily used as a defensive position in NHB matches.

Push-and-Pull Leg Pass

The push-and-pull leg pass is also best used when you are standing and your opponent is on his back. It is similar to the throw-the-legs pass described above except for the pumping of the legs. To make this pass work you must grab your opponent's ankles and push his legs forward, then immediately pull your opponent's legs toward you, causing him to slide forward a bit. (Figure 4-16) When your oppo-

Figure 4-16. Executing a push-and-pull leg pass.

Open Guard   71

Figure 4-17. An over-the-thigh pass.

nent's legs are stretched forward, push them to the right and step forward with your right leg. Place your right foot very near your opponent's hip and then drop your knee into his belly. Placing the foot close to the hip is an important step, as it can prevent your opponent from turning before you can lower your body to assume knee-in-the-belly or side-control.

Over-the-Thigh Pass

This technique also works best against an opponent who is working from a reclining open guard position. To execute, step forward and place your left foot between your opponent's legs and near his tailbone. Then drop your right knee to the mat and control your opponent's right and left legs with your hands. Follow up by driving your left knee over your opponent's left thigh. Be sure to reach under his right arm as you move forward. Sit onto your left hip and thrust your left leg forward. Continue to press your left leg forward and sink your weight onto your opponent to keep him firmly pinned as you finalize the pass.

OPEN GUARD BOTTOM WITH THE GI

You have several options when your opponent stands up. You can sit up with him and go for a single- or double-leg takedown for example. You can also stay on your back or side and use your arms and legs to execute a wide array of sweeps. One of the most reliable of these open guard sweeps against a standing opponent is the open reaping sweep.

Figure 4-18. Control your opponent's left arm and place both of your feet onto his hips.

Figure 4-19. Hold your opponent's right ankle with your left hand and swing your right leg against his left foot.

Figure 4-20. Continue to control your opponent's sleeve as he falls, then scramble to go on top.

Figure 4-21. Scramble to go on top and gain side control.

Core Technique: Open Reaping Sweep

This technique is performed when you are on your back or on your side and your opponent is standing. Follow the instructions in Figures 4-18 through 4-21 to execute a reaping sweep. First, control your opponent's left arm and place both of your feet onto his hips. Then hold your opponent's right ankle with your left hand and swing your right leg against his left foot. Continue to control your opponent's sleeve as he falls. Scramble to go on top and gain side control.

You must push with your left leg and pull with your right hand in order to make the sweep work. Follow your opponent as he falls and pass the guard as quickly as you can. It is a good idea to swing your body along an arc that is close to the floor as you move forward to assume top position. This will minimize the chance that your opponent will block your body as you rise up.

Tactical Option

As long as your legs are between you and your opponent, you are said to be in the open guard. This is true whether you are lying back, upside down, turned sideways, or sitting up. The seated guard works especially well against an opponent who is on his knees.

Seated Guard Hook Sweep

Sit upright with your legs extended between your opponent's knees. Then slide very close to your opponent and reach under your opponent's left arm with your right and hold onto his belt. Hold your opponent's left elbow with your left hand. Hook your right foot under your opponent's left leg and lean onto your left shoulder to execute the sweep.

This type of sweep is sometimes called an elevator because the sweeper uses his hooking foot to lift the other person into the air and over. Sitting sweeps are surprisingly effective, hard to defend, and relatively safe to employ.

OPEN GUARD
BOTTOM WITHOUT THE GI

The following core technique for no-gi, the outer reaping sweep, is performed from the open guard position when you are on your back. It works very well in both gi and no-gi competition.

Figure 4-22. Control your opponent in your open guard.

Figure 4-23. Adjust your position to the left and lower your left leg.

Figure 4-24. Assemble the X-guard and hold your opponent's left ankle.

Figure 4-25. Sweep your opponent.

Figure 4-26. Go on top.

Figure 4-27. Assume side control.

Core Technique: Outer Reaping Sweep

Execute the outer reaping sweep by following the procedures in Figures 4-22 through 4-27.

Start in an open guard position. Place your feet on your opponent's hips and control his arm. Control his right ankle and adjust your body to the left. Lower your left leg so that your knee can pass under your opponent's right thigh. Then place your feet in the X-guard position. Hold your opponent's left ankle with your right hand and sweep him onto his back. Follow him over and go on top. Assume side control and continue to attack.

This sweep is extremely reliable. If your opponent manages to evade it he will be vulnerable to a number of tactical options, including the inner reaping sweep, hip-thrusting sweep, and the over-the-head sweep.

Tactical Option

In gi and no-gi matches much of the guard game is played from the seated position. Many of today's top competitors consider the seated position to be the safest and most stable guard position. The seated guard hook sweep, described below, is one of the reliable standards from this position.

Figure 28. Start with your hooks inside your opponent's thighs.

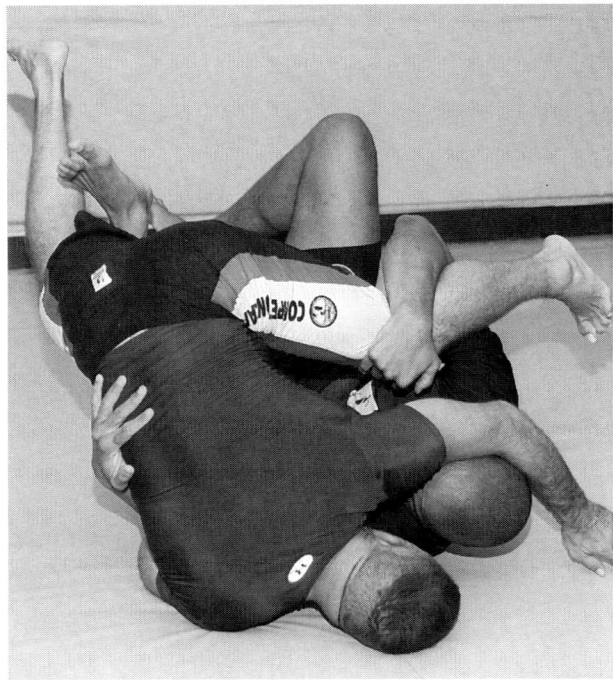

Figure 29. Scoop your hips under your opponent and sweep him over.

Figure 30. Assume side control.

Seated Guard Hook Sweep

The seated guard hook sweep is a bread-and-butter sweep. It is hard to stop and it opens the door for many tactical options. Begin by moving forward until your hooks are inside your opponent's thighs. Turn slightly to your right and reach under your opponent's right arm with your left. (Figure 4-28) Place your head against your opponent's chest and reach under his left leg. Scoop your hips under your opponent and sweep him over. (Figure 4-29) Follow your opponent over and assume side control. (Figure 4-30)

You must sweep immediately upon assuming proper positioning because your opponent will fight to place his arms under yours and defend your sweep. Follow your opponent instantly as he goes over with your sweep; otherwise, you will end up in a scramble for position.

OPEN GUARD BOTTOM FOR NHB

The open guard can be effective in NHB situations. It is important to move quickly and with explosive power to avoid your opponent's punches. In general, your goal when in the guard should be to reverse the situation and go on top.

Figure 4-31. Place your hands on your opponent's shoulder and neck.

Figure 4-32. Push your opponent away from you and assume a clinching seated guard position.

Figure 4-33. Lean to your right and sweep your opponent over to gain side control.

Open Guard 77

Core Technique: Clinch Elevator Sweep

Any sweep that uses a hook to lift an opponent up and over is a type of elevator sweep. The clinch elevator sweep is a useful variation that is easy to execute and difficult to defend.

Follow these steps to do a clinch elevator sweep from your seated guard: Place your hands on your opponent's shoulder and neck, then push him away from you and assume a clinching seated guard position. Lean to your right and sweep your opponent over to gain side control. (Figures 4-31 through 4-33)

If your opponent defends by placing his left hand on the ground, you can move into several tactical options as shown below.

Tactical Options

Two fundamental open guard sweeps are described below. Each of these tactical options relies on position and timing rather than brute strength.

Figure 4-34. Shift forward and clasp his left elbow with your left arm.

Elbow Clasp Sweep

The elbow clasp sweep is simple and effective. To make it work you need to do something that causes your opponent to place one of his hands on the mat. This can be accomplished by pulling him forward with your legs, or by offering your arm as bait. When your opponent places his left arm on the floor, uncross your ankles and reach over his elbow with your right hand. Place your right hand on the mat behind you and lift your hips to throw. (Figure 4-34) Follow your opponent over and assume mount control. (Figure 4-35)

Figure 4-35. Complete the elbow clasp sweep.

Open Guard Outer Reaping Sweep

The open guard outer reaping sweep is a solid basic technique. To begin, use your feet to keep your opponent from advancing. Hold your opponent's right ankle with your left hand and hook your right foot inside his left knee. Push into your opponent's hip with your left foot to sweep him over. (Figures 4-36 and 4-37)

This version of the outer reaping sweep is slightly different from that recommended for no-gi matches (see above). In the NHB version the fighter on bottom executes the sweep with his legs while using his right hand to defend punches.

STRATEGIES FOR THE OPEN GUARD

Following are strategies for confronting each of the four fighter types—aggressive, deceptive, defensive, and interceptive—from the open guard.

Figure 4-36. Use your feet to keep your opponent from advancing.

Fighting an Aggressive Opponent

Aggressive fighters who choose to fight from the open guard are rare but not unheard of. Most aggressive fighters like to go on top from the get-go, but a few will use the guard as a weapon.

When you run up against such a fighter, you can be certain that he will come after you with one aggressive sweeping technique or submission technique after another. The thing that you have going for you is that aggressive fighters tend to be redundant. They attack and attack relentlessly but not deceptively.

An interceptive strategy can work well for you against an aggressive guard fighter. Win against this individual by setting traps that take advantage of predictabil-

Figure 4-37. Push his hip with your left foot and sweep him over.

ity. Employ counterattack traps that feature ankle locks, knee bars, guillotine submission, and the like.

Fighting a Deceptive Opponent

The M.O. for the deceptive fighter is to fake one thing and then do another. Deceptive fighters are masters of distraction and timing. They are typically very fast and they know how to use their speed. You can win against a deceptive guard fighter by aggressively charging in on his guard. Force him to defend. Do not allow the deceptive fighter time to set the pace or establish the game.

Fighting a Defensive Opponent

Defensive guard fighters love to lock you up with their open guard. Their goal is to make you fight and fight to pass while taking few if any risks in the process. Just when you think you are finally going to get around the defensive fighter's guard, he will recompose the position and make you start over again. This is an extremely frustrating game.

To beat a defensive guard fighter you must find a way to force him to go on the offense. One way to achieve this is with an interceptive strategy.

You can do this by sitting back into your guard and pulling your opponent toward you. Offer openings until he takes the bait and makes a move to go on top. Then sweep or submit him from your guard.

Fighting an Interceptive Opponent

The open guard is the natural domain of the interceptive fighter. It is the perfect condition from which to set counterattacking traps. The open guard allows the fighter on the bottom to use both feet and both hands to control the situation while laying the trap. The typical strategy of an interceptive fighter in an open guard position is to establish a secure guard grip with one hand and one foot, then "open" the way for you to pass. That opening is invariably a trap and your best bet is not to enter.

You can win against an interceptive fighter who employs the open guard by making him switch games. You can cause the game to change by pulling back and bringing him into your open or closed guard. Or you can change things up by faking one thing and doing another. For example, you can fake like you are going to take the bait and attempt to pass, then move instantly to attack an extremity, i.e, ankle, wrist, knee, or arm.

ENDNOTE

1. Royce Gracie and Kid Peligro. *Ultimate Fighting Techniques, Volume 1: The Top Game.* Montpelier, VT: Invisible Cities Press. 2005, p. 15.

INTERVIEW: ROBERTO TRAVEN ON STRATEGY

The following interview contains the strategy used by Roberto "Spider" Traven of the Alliance Team. Traven is a Cavalcanti black belt and a veteran competitor with a prestigious record. He operates the Alliance Martial Arts Center in downtown Atlanta.

Highlights from his competitive career include Champion of the AFC Russia Ultimate Fighting (No Rules), Russia, 1997; Champion of the World BJJ Championship, Brazil, 1998; Champion of the open class in the Abu Dhabi Combat Club (grappling), Abu Dhabi, 1999; Champion of the Rings (No Rules) Japan, Japan, 2000; Vice champion of the super fight in the Abu Dhabi Combat Club (grappling), Abu Dhabi, 2000; Champion of the Master's World Cup super heavyweight (BJJ), Brazil, 2002; Champion of the Master's World Cup heavyweight (BJJ) Brazil, 2003; Champion of the Pan American Senior I, open division and super heavyweight division, 2006.

Question: How soon do you begin to prepare for a major jiu-jitsu competition?

Traven: Two months before the tournament.

Q: What do you do to prepare yourself?

Traven: Just train hard, and train more. Keep focused on the tournament. Start training harder as the tournament gets closer. Train a little harder every day. If you train hard you will be ready. This is so because everything you need to do to be ready is happening in the course of your hard training.

If you train your hardest, you will know that your opponent cannot be training more. He can train the same intensity but not more. So your mind is OK and your confidence will be high.

Q: How many hours a day should you train to get ready for a big tournament?

Figure 4-38. Roberto "Spider" Traven.

Traven: You should run two times a week and lift weights three times each week and train jiu-jitsu six times a week. You should split your daily training into two parts: Train in the morning and in the afternoon, or evening.

Q: You should take one day off each week?

Traven: Yes. One day.

Q: Do you train the same every day or change the intensity from day to day?

Traven: If you train hard for two days straight, like Monday and Tuesday hard, then Wednesday should be a little bit lighter. Thursday and Friday you can push again. Saturday take it easier and then rest all day Sunday.

Q: Do you vary the intensity of your training over the two-month period?

Traven: Go easy for the first two weeks, then start to push.

Q: Do you rest before the fight?

Traven: If you are going to fight on Sunday, you should take Friday and Saturday off.

Q: Do you alter your diet before a tournament?

Traven: I maintain a very healthy diet all the time. My wife helps me with this. She is a dietitian.

If you need to lose weight you should alter your diet with care. Don't lose weight too fast. For me it is always the same. Weight is not a problem and I always eat well.

Q: How did you prepare for some of your biggest fights?

Traven: In 1998, when I won the World Championship for the first time, my training to prepare included jiu-jitsu five days a week, running two times a week, lifting four days a week, and one day to rest. In that tournament I fought in the heavyweight division so I didn't care about my weight.

Q: They call you Spider because of your famous spider guard, right? What is your favorite way to fight? What is your game?

Traven: I prefer to play on top. But I like to fight on the ground, so I don't like to waste a lot of time standing up and trying to take the guy down. So I pull the guy to my guard and try to sweep.

Q: So you like to be on top?

Traven: Yes, it is much better to be on top.

Q: Are you a more aggressive fighter or a more cautious fighter?

Traven: More cautious.

Q: If you know who your opponent is going to be in [an NHB] match do you train differently depending on the guy's style?

Traven: If I am going to fight against a wrestler, I know that it will be really hard to take him down. So I will train more on the bottom with the intention of improving my game on the bottom.

I always train in boxing and wrestling. But if I know the guy is a really good wrestler, I

Figure 4-39. Roberto Traven after winning the ADCC Submission Wrestling World Championship in United Arab Emirates in 1999.

am going to focus on preparing my guard game.

If I know that the guy is not a good wrestler, but that he is a good striker, then I will focus on training my wrestling skills because I will try to take him down and play on top. This strategy helped me when I fought the second time in Japan. I knew in that tournament that my first two fights would be against two guys who were strikers. So I focused my training more on my clinching skills and on ways to take those guys down.

My goal in Japan was to close the distance. I am not a striker, so my plan was to clinch and take the fight to the ground.

Q: What is your favorite kind of submission?

Traven: I like chokes—arm triangles, rear naked chokes, and regular triangles.

Q: If you have a choice will you go to the side, the mount, or to the back?

Traven: Back.

Q: What if your opponent is not a wrestler or a striker but another jiu-jitsu guy? How would you approach that fight?

Traven: I would play the same game. I would push him to close the distance and take him down and play on top.

Q: What if you were up against a guy that is a lot stronger and a lot bigger than you, would you change your game or play it the same way?

Traven: I am always going to try to play on top, but if the guy puts me down, then I will change my game and play on bottom.

I try to have good technique for all aspects of the fight so if something happens in the middle of the fight I can change games right away. If you don't have good technique for all aspects of the fight, you can get locked into one way, and this no good.

Question: Is there ever a time when you tell one of your fighters to play on his back?

Traven: Yes, sometimes it is better to fight from the guard. Each fight is different. Each fighter is different and each opponent is different. Sometimes I will tell my fighter to pull the guy to his guard.

Q: What is your strategy for points during a jiu-jitsu match?

Traven: I always try to make a lot of points. If I have a chance to submit the guy I am going to try. But if the guy does not give me this chance, I will try to make a lot of points.

Q: Do you try to tap the guy first or get points first and then submit him?

Traven: I look for points first.

Q: Do you count your points or have someone counting for you at ringside?

Traven: I count my own points. But it helps to have a coach or partner telling you the time and the points.

Q: What do you do to prepare your guys for a tournament?

Traven: I put them into a lot of situations that are likely to happen in the tournament. I create situations, nothing really special; I just have the guys start in many different positions and work from there. For example, I will put one guy on the bottom and have the other guy try to pass his guard for 10 minutes, then switch.

Q: What is your advice for guys who are new to jiu-jitsu and want to become really good competitors?

Traven: Train hard. Train seriously with a good coach in a good school. If you have a good coach and train in a good school, you have all that you need to become a really good fighter.

Q: If a student of yours wants to become a serious competitor, how many tournaments should he go to each year?

Traven: As many as possible.

Q: Is it good to compete in gi and no-gi?

Traven: Yes. Today everybody does both.

Q: Do you think one is better?

Traven: I prefer gi.

Q: Why?

Traven: Because I think the game is more technical with the gi.

Some guys have a really good talent and highly technical skill for fighting without the gi, like Marcello Garcia and Roger Gracie, but most of the guys who fight no gi don't have a lot of technical skill. You can just take off the gi and defend yourself. I think the game with the gi is more technical.

Q: Is the gi game more difficult?

Traven: It is more difficult for the guy that doesn't have much technique. You need to know more to fight well with the gi.

Q: What do you do to encourage your guys to compete?

Traven: I tell my guys to go and do their

best. I tell them that it doesn't matter if they win or lose. I tell them that they will get something out of it if they go. They will learn something.

Q: What do you do after a jiu-jitsu tournament?

Traven: Take a rest. One week of no training.

Q: What about after an NHB match?

Traven: It depends on how much you are hurt.

Q: Anything else you would like to add?

Traven: Just stay focused and train hard. When you train hard, you will feel good. You will feel confident. By fight time you should be thinking, "I have trained as hard as I could. I am ready. This guy cannot have trained more that me. Maybe he trained the same but he cannot possibly have trained more. Whatever happens, I am ready."

INTERVIEW: FLAVIA TRAVEN ON NUTRITION

Nutritionist Flavia Traven, wife of Roberto Traven, advises her husband and many other top jiu-jitsu competitors in nutritional strategy. She says proper nutrition is an essential and often overlooked element in fighter strategy.

Question: Nutrition is a big part of strategy. What are some of the key things that you recommend?

Flavia Traven: The majority of fighters try to lose weight one week before the competition. I try to convince them not to do this. One year when Traven went to the Abu Dabi, there was a Russian guy who tried to lose 20 pounds in two days. He stayed in a sauna for the better part of two days. People die doing this sort of thing. My job is to convince fighters not to do this. Start losing weight at least two months before the competition.

You can lose weight healthy at a rate of up to 9 pounds per month. When you are training, you burn a lot of energy—eat a small amount. People often eat their whole amount for the day at nighttime, [but] this is when you should eat less. Divide your calories through the day.

You can eat at night. You should divide your calories—30 percent in the morning, 30 percent at lunch, and 20 percent in the afternoon, then 10 percent at night.

If you eat more than you burn, you are going to gain. If you are lifting weight, you will gain muscle. If you want to gain muscle, you must lift weights.

Q: Is the nutrition strategy for jiu-jitsu competitors and for other athletes just the same?

Flavia Traven: Absolutely not. Jiu-jitsu, [NHB], wrestling, and boxing athletes all have similar nutritional needs, but athletes from other sports have very different nutritional needs. For that reason I am currently writing a book that specifically addresses the unique nutritional needs of the martial sports.

Q: What should you eat when you are training to increase performance in jiu-jitsu and maintain your weight?

Flavia Traven: Eat lightly before training or you will be uncomfortable at training. Eat some carbohydrates [such as] cereal or fruit. Different people have different tolerances. You have to train yourself. Remember, your stomach is like a muscle. You have to train your stomach. You have to try different things to see what works for you.

Q: What about after training?

Flavia Traven: After training you must eat protein and carbohydrates. This is what we call the recovery phase. Within one hour after the training is the best time to eat.

Many athletes think they only need protein, but you need both protein and carbohydrates. To absorb the protein you need carbohydrates in your system.

Q: No fat, right?

Flavia Traven: I do not recommend a high intake of fat, especially saturated fat. You need essential fat, [such as] vegetable oils. You need fat but in the right ratio. I recommend a balance of 6 percent carbohydrates, 20 percent fat, and 20 percent protein.

Q: Should you stay away from fried foods?

Flavia Traven: Yes.

Q: Do you recommend supplements?

Flavia Traven: Sometimes. Especially when you don't have time to eat right. The problem is that people think supplements are the key factor, but they are not. Supplements are food. For example, you can get the same protein from a lot of common foods that you can get from a protein shake. It is the same.

The good thing about supplements is that they are easy to prepare. And you have a high concentration in just one cup. Sometimes I recommend this because it is easy.

Q: Do you recommend any of the designer supplements for jiu-jitsu athletes?

Flavia Traven: I do not. If you are getting a good diet, you don't need supplements.

Q: What about taking a lot of vitamins?

Flavia Traven: If you take more vitamins than your body needs, your body will not be able to absorb them. You will just be wasting your money.

Q: How much water should you drink?

Flavia Traven: It depends on how many calories you are eating. In general I recommend at least two liters of water per day.

It is a good idea to check your weight before you train and after you train to see how much water weight you are losing. Then try to replace the same amount of water by weight that you lost during the training session.

For example, if you weighed 190 pounds before the cardio and 187 pounds afterward, try to replace three pounds of water over the next several hours.

CHAPTER 5

HALF GUARD

The half guard occurs any time a fighter has one of his legs between his opponent's legs. In general, the fighter who is on top will seek to get out of the half guard and assume side control or mounted control. In general, the fighter on the bottom will attempt to sweep the fighter on top and gain a superior position. Both fighters, however, are in continual danger of a variety of submission attacks when in a half-guard state. Because both fighters have attack options, some practitioners consider the half guard to be a neutral state providing equal opportunities to both fighters.

This chapter includes techniques and tactical options for fighting in the half guard. It concludes with an interview on the topic of strategy by Alliance black-belt competitor and instructor Bull Shaw.

HALF GUARD TOP WITH THE GI

The technique described above and the tactical option shown below (knee leverage half-guard pass) are guard passing maneuvers. Remember that it is also possible to submit an opponent from the half guard top position.

Figure 5-1. Reach over your opponent's right shoulder with your right hand and move your left foot inward until your shin is perpendicular to the mat.

86 Brazilian Jiu-Jitsu Fighting Strategies

Figure 5-2. Grab your opponent's belt and drive your right elbow under his right arm.

Figure 5-3. Control your opponent's right knee with your left hand and place your right knee onto his hip to get leverage to pull free of the half guard.

Core Technique: Knee-in-Hip Half-Guard Pass

It is very difficult to escape from a skilled grappler's half guard. The fighter on top has gravity on his side, but the positions are almost equal. To pass you must gain enough leverage to extract your leg while maintaining your balance to avoid being swept. The knee-in-hip half-guard passing technique, described in Figures 5-1 through 5-3, will allow you to do just that.

You must keep your opponent's shoulders pinned when executing this pass. Otherwise your opponent may be able to turn toward you and reverse your position.

Figure 5-4. Pin your opponent's back flat to the floor.

HALF GUARD TOP WITHOUT THE GI

Passing the half guard is a bit like walking a tightrope. Even the slightest imperfection in your position will leave you open to a sweep. You must maintain your balance, and you must keep your opponent's hips and/or shoulders pinned as is illustrated in the cross over half-guard pass described below.

Figure 5-5. Press your opponent's right knee with your left hand and move your left foot inward.

Half Guard   87

Figure 5-6. Put your shoulder into your opponent's neck and drive your left knee over his thigh.

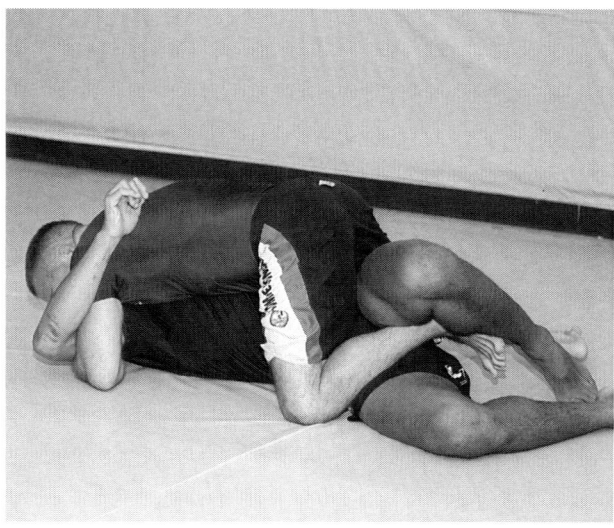

Figure 5-7. Stabilize your position.

Figure 5-8. Use your right foot to break your left foot free.

Core Technique: Cross Over Half-Guard Pass

The cross over half-guard pass is so named because the grappler on top will pass his shin over his opponent's. Perform it by following the steps in Figures 5-4 through 5-8.

When your opponent realizes that you are going to pass, he will likely attempt an explosive escape maneuver. Be prepared for such an attempt just at the moment in which you assume mount control.

Tactical Option

The tactical option that follows differs only slightly from the gi version (knee-in-hip half-guard pass) described above. In the no-gi version shown below, proper hand placement must be used in place of gi gripping positions.

Knee Leverage Half-Guard Pass

To execute this tactical option, begin by holding around your opponent's right shoulder. Press your weight onto his chest. Then place your right knee into your opponent's lap. (Figure 5-9) Use the leverage from your right leg to pull your left leg free and pass the half guard.

Figure 5-9. Knee leverage half-guard pass.

Figure 5-10. Stabilize your position to avoid a reversal sweep.

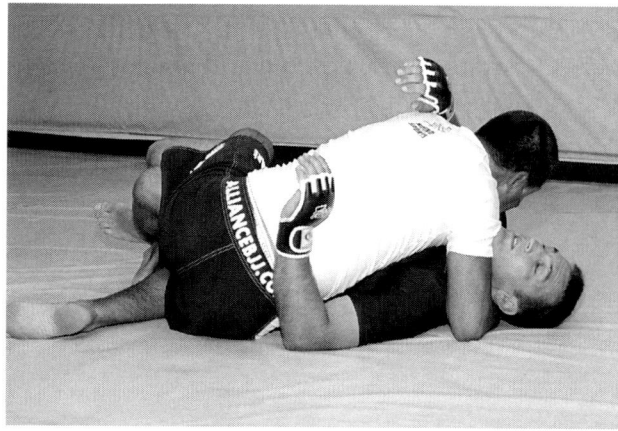

Figure 5-11. Reach under your opponent's neck with your right and under his left arm with your left arm as you drop your hips to the floor and bring your left leg inward.

Figure 5-12. Drive your left knee over your opponent's right thigh to pass the half guard and assume the mount.

HALF GUARD TOP FOR NHB

The most important thing for the fighter on top to do is to pin his opponent's shoulders to the mat. The most important thing for the fighter on the bottom to do is to turn toward the fighter on top and stay off his back.

Core Technique: Over-the-Thigh Pass

In the over-the-thigh pass technique, you must stay very tight with your opponent. Keep your weight on your opponent's neck at all times as you execute the steps in Figures 5-10 through 5-12.

Tactical Option

The half guard condition is not an equal opportunity for the fighter on top and the fighter on bottom in no-rules situations. The fighter on top has a clear advantage because he can generate leverage for effective strikes, such as the elbow attack shown below. The fighter on bottom cannot get the space needed to throw effective strikes.

Half Guard

Figure 5-13. Attack with the elbow from the half guard.

Figure 5-14. Move your hips to your left, grab your opponent's belt with your left hand, and grab his left wrist with your right hand.

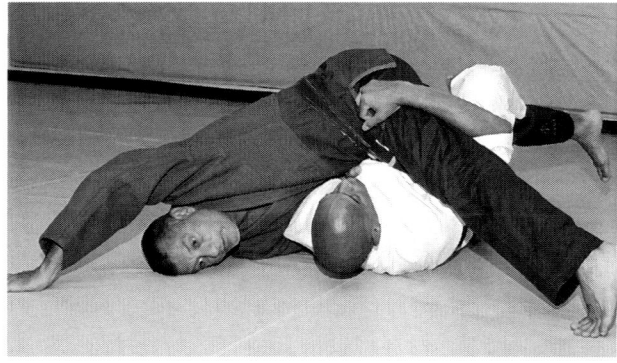

Figure 5-15. Move your hips to your right to position them under your opponent's hips and scoop your right arm under his left thigh.

Figure 5-16. Throw your opponent over and assume side control.

Attack with the Elbow from the Half Guard

To execute this tactical option you must first stabilize your position to avoid a reversal. Then swim your left arm under your opponent's right arm and hold it tightly against your body. Follow by striking your opponent with your right elbow. (Figure 5-13) When your opponent lifts his arms to defend against your elbow strikes, you should be able to slip your left leg free and pass the guard.

HALF GUARD BOTTOM WITH THE GI

The half guard can be divided into two primary varieties: closed half guard and open half guard. The closed half guard is a condition in which the fighter on the bottom has one of his legs threaded between the other's legs. The open half guard is usually described as a condition in which the fighter on the bottom and has one leg threaded between his opponent's legs and the other knee pressed into the opponent's abdomen. The core and tactical techniques that follow start from the closed half-guard position.

Core Technique: Sweep Over

If your opponent reaches under your arm and grabs your lapel, you can easily sweep him over from the half guard position by following the steps in Figures 5-14 through 5-16.

With this, and most half-guard bottom techniques, it is very important to prevent your opponent from reaching under your neck. The placement of the arm under the neck is sometimes called "cross facing." If you allow your opponent to cross face you, he can easily flatten your back to the mat. Once there, your escape options will be very limited.

Tactical Option

The tactical option described below is just one of many available to the fighter on the bottom in a half guard situation. Take care, when executing this or any technique from the half guard bottom position, to duck your head downward to avoid the cross face and to avoid being choked.

Figure 5-17. Grab your opponent's left ankle with your right hand.

Figure 5-18. Reach over his leg with your left hand and grab his ankle.

Figure 5-19. Sweep him over and assume side control.

Figure 5-20. Reach over your opponent's back with your left arm.

Figure 5-21. Reach under his left leg and hold his ankle with your right hand.

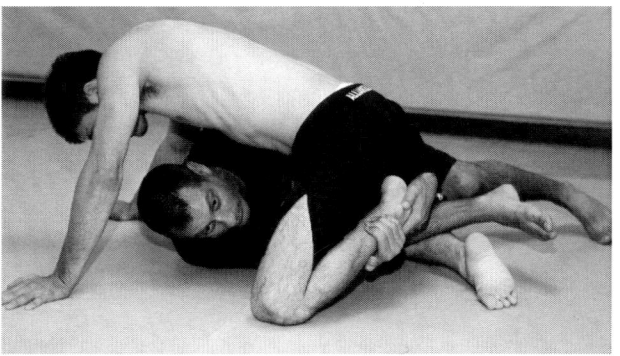

Figure 5-22. Reach over his thigh and hold his andkle with your left hand.

Figure 5-23. Hold his left knee with your right hand.

Hold the Ankle and Sweep

Execute this tactical option by first moving your hips away from your opponent and swimming your arm under his arm. Then reach under your opponent's left ankle with your right hand and hold. (Figure 5-17) Rock a little to get position, then reach over your opponent's leg with your left arm and grab his ankle. (Figure 5-18) Base your right hand on the mat, and sweep your opponent over to gain side control. (Figure 5-19)

HALF GUARD BOTTOM WITHOUT THE GI

In order to do the hold-knee-and-sweep technique described below, you must move from the closed half-guard to the open half-guard position. Do this by placing one knee in your opponent's abdomen while keeping your other leg threaded between his legs.

Figure 5-24. Sweep him over and go on top.

Core Technique: Hold Knee and Sweep

Execute the hold knee and sweep technique by following the steps in Figures 5-20 through 5-24.

To make this sweep work you must plant your left foot on the floor and push off. It is also important to hold your opponent very tightly as you perform the sweep.

Tactical Option

When you are in the half-guard bottom position, you have several basic options. You can sweep your opponent to the right or to the left. You can elevate your opponent and establish the full guard. You can move your opponent away and capture an open guard position. You can attempt a submission from the half guard, or you can go through the "back door." Any technique, including the one described below, in which you climb down and go under your opponent's legs, is a "backdoor" maneuver.

Half Guard Sweep

Execute this half guard sweep tactical option by reaching under your opponent's right arm with your left and driving your head downward toward his left knee. Scoop your right arm under your opponent's left leg and clasp your hands together. (Figure 5-25) Move your hips to the right and lift your opponent's leg upward. This action will cause your opponent to fall backward and free you from the half guard. (Figure 5-26)

The half guard escape is also a commonly used approach for establishing the X guard. Remember, the X guard is an open-guard position in which you hold one of your opponent's legs with one arm while trapping and controlling his other leg by placing one foot behind the knee and the other at the top of the thigh. In the X-guard position your legs will be crossed.

Figure 5-25. Executing the half guard sweep.

Figure 5-26. When your opponent falls, it will free you from the half guard.

Figure 5-27. Scoot your hips away and reach over your opponent's back.

Figure 5-28. Pull yourself upward and clinch your opponent by reaching under one arm and around his neck.

HALF GUARD BOTTOM FOR NHB

Any time you find yourself in a half guard bottom position in a no-holds-barred match, you should be thinking of escaping and doing it as soon as possible. One of your best options will be to move to your opponent's back as shown in the following example.

Core Technique: Escape and Take the Back

Follow the steps in Figures 5-27 through 5-29 to escape from the half guard bottom position and assume control of your opponent's back.

In a half guard situation, the fighter on top has a major advantage when striking is allowed. The fighter on bottom must concern himself with defending strikes while simultaneously trying to reverse positions.

Figure 5-29. Place your left foot around your opponent's left thigh to sink the "hook" and establish full back control.

Tactical Options

In order to prevent you from going to his back, your opponent must react quickly. This may provide you with an opportunity to reverse positions by executing either of the tactical options shown below.

Figure 5-30. Executing the ankle pin sweep.

Figure 5-31. Assuming side control.

Ankle Pin Sweep

This tactical option requires that you tuck your head downward near your opponent's knee. Then swim your left arm under your opponent's right arm and move your hips to your left to establish a stable position and make space. At this point, hook your right arm under your opponent's left thigh and pull him forward. (Figure 5-30) Move your hips to the right as you sweep your opponent to your left. Maintain control of your opponent's left arm and right leg, drive your weight on top, and assume side control. (Figure 5-31)

Half Guard Sweep

You must not let your opponent hook his arm under your neck when in the half guard position. If this happens, your opponent will be able to pin your back flat onto the floor and greatly restrict your defensive options. Prevent your opponent from doing this by controlling his left arm with your right and moving your hips to the left. Then hook your right arm under your opponent's left leg and move your hips to the right. (Figure 5-32) Follow your opponent over as you sweep him. Assume side control immediately. (Figure 5-33)

Figure 5-32. Reach under your opponent's thigh with your right arm.

Figure 5-33. Sweep him over and go on top.

STRATEGIES FOR THE HALF GUARD

Following are four different strategies, one strategy for confronting each of the four fighter types—aggressive, deceptive, defensive, and interceptive—in the half guard.

Fighting an Aggressive Opponent

When you are on the bottom in half guard, you must prevent your opponent from putting his arm under your neck. This position is called the "cross face." If your opponent gets you in a cross-face position, he will be able to put your back flat on the floor and eliminate most of your attack and escape options. No matter what type of fighter you are up against, you must avoid the cross face.

If your opponent is highly aggressive, you should take special care to protect your neck and arms. An aggressive opponent will try to submit you from the half guard, so your first reaction should be to turn your hips toward him and duck your head. When you duck your head down near your opponent's thighs, you gain leverage and reduce the risk of being submitted. From here you can work your attacks and or sweeps.

It is wise to proceed aggressively and make every effort to get out from under the half guard when facing a truly aggressive opponent. This is true in gi, no-gi, and especially in NHB matches. Stay on your side, duck your head down, and employ any one of the sweeping techniques described in this book.

Fighting a Deceptive Opponent

An aggressive escape by sweeping strategy works well when facing a deceptive opponent from the bottom half of the half-guard condition. Do not linger or stall in the half guard because this will give the deceptive fighter time to set you up for an attack or a crafty guard-passing technique. Turn the tables by turning your opponent over and onto his back as soon as you can.

Fighting a Defensive Opponent

If you find yourself on the bottom, in half guard, when fighting a defensive opponent, you have a real opportunity to gain a submission. Many defensive fighters are weakest when they are on top in a relatively offensive position. You can use this to your advantage by attacking them with a deceptive strategy. For example, you can fake a sweep, then go for an arm bar. Make him stay on top. Execute your half-guard bottom submission techniques to win against the defensive opponent.

Fighting an Interceptive Opponent

Interception works best from the bottom. A truly interceptive fighter will likely be at his weakest when on top in the half guard. Take advantage of this by aggressively pursuing submissions and sweeps. Do not allow him to pass your half guard or to back out of it.

INTERVIEW:
BULL SHAW ON STRATEGY

In the following interview, Bull Shaw discusses his strategy. Shaw is an Alliance black belt and a veteran sport jiu-jitsu and NHB competitor. He owns and operates the Alliance Martial Arts academy in Marietta, Georgia.

Shaw won many competitions including World Masters Championship Gold Medalist, Brazil, 2001; World Masters Championship Gold Medalists Absolute Division, Brazil, 2001; Pan American Masters Division Gold Medalists, 2002; Pan American Masters Division Absolute Division, 2002; NAGA (North American Grappling Association) Gi Expert Division Champion 2004. Shaw's NHB record is 5 wins and 1 loss.

Figure 5-34. Bull Shaw.

Question: Why did you take up Brazilian jiu-jitsu?

Shaw: When I first started, I was 28 and I weighed almost 400 pounds. I was looking for a sport to do. I was unhappy; I was looking for something different. I knew I was not going to go out and run sprints or lift weights for the rest of my life. Then I discovered jiu-jitsu. I knew right away that this was something that I could see myself doing lifelong. That was the main focus for me to find something physical to do that I could stay with for the rest of my life.

Q: Your sparring partners always say, "Bull is really big, but he is also really technical." It seems that it would be natural for a big person to win with strength. Would you describe yourself as being a technical fighter?

Shaw: As far as being a big guy and using technique it just applies more leverage. I think if you come into jiu-jitsu with the mentality that you are going to muscle somebody, it actually limits you. It limits how far you are going to go.

A lot of big guys rely too much on their strength. They spend a lot of time lifting weights to get even stronger and bigger. Then they go out and they fight with too much muscle and waste a lot of energy. Relying too much on strength and size puts a ceiling on their game and their ability to use technique. What happens is they can beat the white belts, they can beat the blue belts, but when they go against the upper level blue belts and purple belts who have really slick stuff, they have trouble.

Q: Is there ever a time to emphasize strength over technique?

Shaw: In the old days, no-rules matches didn't have rounds and technique was more important than strength. But a guy can't do a 20-minute fight with no rounds all-out on pure muscle. He would be blasted. Now the rules have changed and we have rounds. Rounds are far friendlier to the muscle head and to the stand-up guy.

Q: But you have never been a strength fighter?

Shaw: That's right. It was easy for me to be technical from the start because I had been in sports where you had to be technical. Remember, I weighed 400 pounds at the time I started training. I would blow myself out really quickly when I tried to use power. It hit me very early on that I needed to be able to control the situation, to control the other guy with posture and things like that.

Q: How do you "control the situation"?

Shaw: Well, when you roll with a guy like Leozinho [Leonardo Alcantara "Leozinho" Vieira, one of Cavalcanti's black belts], no matter how long you can go, he can go farther. He can go faster. Think about it like this, almost everybody is Leozinho to me. Everybody is more flexible. Everybody is faster. A guy who weighs 200 pounds and trains the same amount of time that I do is going to be in better cardio shape than I can ever be. Think about it—at my size going from point A to point B costs me more energy than it does him. I just learned to get to a certain point and rest and to control the situation

Q: Then a big part of your strategy is conserving energy?

Shaw: More controlling than conserving. If the guy wants to go crazy, I try to make it so that he can't without getting into a worse situation.

Q: Can you give an example of how you set that up?

Shaw: I stay very tight. Some of the most dangerous people are guys who are so limber that they can turn all the way in either direction and you can't get to their back. So I just drop my weight on them. I put my knee in their side and control their ability to move. You have to take the guy down a path of your choosing.

The very best guys at any sport can basically do everything, but there is usually one thing they are better at than anybody else. Like, I do the Kimura and a couple of other things; you could jump on me in the middle of the night and grab me and I would wake up with you in the Kimura. Most people worry about learning lots of new techniques as fast as they can. You can learn 50 moves a day and that is not going to make you win anything.

Your technique has to be something that you just do automatically without thinking, like putting your blinker on and turning right in your car.

Q: What is your strategy for defense?

Shaw: Students often ask me how to defend against some guy's super-secret move or whatever. I don't think that way. For me, if you do the things you are supposed to do—the things people don't talk a lot about like posture, keeping your balance, and proper placement of your arms—then defense will mostly take care of itself.

A lot of guys are too impatient to work on the fundamentals. I can think of several people who went from one school to another school to learn flashy and new "secret" moves. They don't win a single tournament more now than they used to. In fact, it goes the other way. All these flashy moves that you don't really know work well might work on a guy who is at a lower level, but that's about it. I can beat a guy who is better than me if I control him and take him out of his element.

Q: You make it sound easy.

Shaw: You have to force him down a path that he is not good at. That is the only trick. You do this with posture and where you put your hands and most importantly where you put your hips. That is what I tell my students. I am a very boring teacher because you can take my class then go over to someone else who shows a dozen moves a day when I show one. But you are going to be better than the guy with a dozen moves because I teach the fundamentals—like where you put your hands on the collar, how to control the other guy's hips, little things like that. If you try to throw a guy and your hand is slightly out of place, you won't have any leverage; put it in the right spot and it is a different game. Little things make the difference.

Students ask me what I do in this or that situation. I often tell them I don't know—because of my posture and hand placement I never get in that situation.

Q: So posture is a big part of the equation?

Shaw: Good posture affects all of your moves. I really fight to keep my posture. I think a lot of purple belts have poor hand placement, poor posture, and poor base. A lot of guys have trouble with this so when they learn a new move they are starting from zero. You can learn 50 moves but if your base sucks, what have you got? If you learn a move and get good at it, then it makes other similar moves better because you don't have to learn all the parts of the move.

Take a guy whose whole game is to pull you into the guard and then lead you to this favorite sweep. He has swept a thousand people a thousand times with that sweep, people with different body types. After a while he realizes that half the people react in a certain way when he attempts the sweep and half react in another way. Then he starts to do the next thing that sets him up for the finish. All this experience this guy has is worthless against you if you have good posture, the right posture, and if you shut him down with your hips. Good posture is often all that you need to defend against some of the very best guys out there. Most guys have to set you up before they attempt a sweep or other attack. Just sit up and solidify your posture so he can't pull you, can't get your neck, or your arm.

The guy who is up against a guy with good posture feels like he is being attacked even if he is the attacker. This is because everything he tries doesn't work against the stable posture. If you maintain solid posture, eventually he will be forced to try stuff that he is not as good at.

Q: What about when you are attacking?

Shaw: When I attack, I make it work the first time. I don't want to attempt it two or three times. I am very particular. I attack in measures. I try to be perfect about it and get it right the very first time. I don't jump into one thing then go back and jump in again, so for me it is a very measured thing.

When I attack I stay very low. When I pass the guard, my hips touch the floor. Controlling the legs and hips, that is how I pass. I keep control the whole time and I never raise my hips. I make continuous contact.

Q: Do you ever change your game to deal with a particular opponent?

Shaw: Usually you don't know the guys that you are going to go up against. There has only been one time when I really changed my game plan. This guy I fought at the Pan American—his throws were so good compared to mine that I just wanted to stay out of that. I did some things that you can't do in judo; I held on to his belt the whole time so he could not throw me.

But generally I might know that this is the way a guy will start and he has a good triangle or something it just means I am not going to risk my arms as much to deny him that.

Q: Would you play a different game with a guy who was particularly good at the guard?

Shaw: The only thing I might change, if he has a really good guard and I know that he is going to try to pull me into it, is to deny him the opportunity to pull me in. I might back away, or pass at that time and then sit on his hips. But this is really the same thing that I always do, just deny the guy what he likes.

Just keep your posture, and for something specific you can make a change. Once you get him on the ground and you pass the guard then it is always the same thing. It is a procedure.

Q: Is that the bottom line for your strategy, deny the guy what he likes?

Shaw: Partly. Let's say you have a great open guard and you are up against another guy with a great open guard. If he pulls you into his guard first, then he denies you one of your best tools.

Q: When did you start using the half guard?

Shaw: I injured my knee and passing the guard was difficult. I wanted to try something new. When I started using the half guard, not many people in the U.S. had really figured it out yet. I won a lot because of it. Now it's several years later and everybody does it. I use it in an unorthodox way but I am still effective with it.

I discovered the half guard because I wasn't flexible enough to do the X guard. It was popular, at that time, to start in the half guard and then go to the X guard. I tried this and found that I just didn't have the flexibility to do it. So I figured out a way to be effective from the half guard without going to the X guard. It took me a couple of months of losing to everybody at the school to work it out. I was determined and for three or four months I would do that to people over and over until I got it down.

Q: Do you usually play from the bottom regardless of how big your opponent is?

Shaw: No. You are better off being on top, especially with bigger guys. In some cases it is easier for a smaller guy to squirm out from under me than it is for a big guy. I don't mount small guys; they are almost escaping the second I mount. The big guy is easier for me to mount; he is easier for me to work with in certain positions.

Q: Do you use the half guard against someone as big as or bigger than you?

Shaw: Yes, I do. I am not great at passing the guard so I usually get in the half guard and sweep to pass to side control.

Q: You don't think that you are strong at passing?

Shaw: When I first started, I was better at passing the guard than working my own guard. This is the way it is for bigger guys. Most smaller guys are better at being on their backs than they are at being on top because a smaller guy gets put on his back all the time. A guy who starts out in the sport who weighs 250 or 300 pounds and is strong is going to be able to knock anybody on their back, I don't care who it is, especially when you start on your knees. So he is always starting in that position. It is hard for a strong guy to break that habit and learn to work from his back. I really started learning to do the guard and the half guard when I hurt my ankle. I couldn't push off. So I just watched guys and learned the guard, then I went to the half guard. I knew had to be able to do it. Finally I came up with something different.

Q: When did you start trusting the half guard enough to make it a main part of your strategy?

Shaw: After I'd been working the half guard for a while, I went to the Masters. It was my intention to stay with my old strategy of staying on top. One time a guy got me down for some points, he was ahead and I just swept him from the half guard. I won my division and then I went to the Absolute. I was tired but I kept winning one match after another. This went on until I got to the point where I was so tired I didn't want to stand up. So, in the next match I just ran up and pulled the guy to the half guard. It caught him completely off guard. I worked him like a $2 hooker for the next two minutes and tapped him out. Everybody was shocked that a big guy, in the Absolute division, pulled a smaller guy into the half guard. At this point I was exhausted and I didn't want to compete anymore, but I kept going. In another match a guy swept me as we went over in mid-air. I jumped into the half guard and swept him back and got my points. That was the day that I really got faith in my half guard. The Absolute was a huge division. I think I went eight or nine matches that day.

Finally I got it to a point where almost no one could defend against my half guard. That was what I was doing at the end of my peak competition time.

To me, the half guard is not a passive thing. When I go, I attack the guy's legs and stay so tight in the half guard that he can't cross face me or anything.

Q: Is there a type of fighter that you would not use your half guard on?

Shaw: It works better on some guys than

others. For example it is very difficult to put a guy who is a bulldog and just leans into you all the time into the half guard.

Q: Do you have a strategy for managing your points during a match?

Shaw: Yes, after several tournaments I learned how to manipulate the points a little. I think that is why they are thinking about changing the rules now to keep people from doing that too much. There were times when I would take the guy down and be up on points and then never risk anything from that point. I would move him around some to show aggression but not commit as much as I should have.

In general it is best to be the first one on top. A lot of times, if you stay on your feet for a long time, trying to take the guy down, the guy will finally pull you into his guard. If he does this with a minute to go, from that point all you have to do is not get swept or tapped for one minute because the guy on top, if it is zero to zero points and advantages, is going to win. This is a simple strategy that is good especially for a guy that is more of a beginner.

Q: What advice do you give your guys before they go to a tournament?

Shaw: It is different for every guy. I tell beginners not to pull the guy in their guard. I might tell a student who is a purple belt and weighs 122 pounds to pull his opponent into his guard if that is the best part of his game. I might tell an upper level blue belt who weighs 250 pounds to work on top and warn him that if he pulls his opponent into the guard, I will make you run sprints when you come back to the school! So it is different for different guys.

The thing that I tell everybody is to be relaxed, to focus, and to take their time. What happens is that guys feel very rushed during a match, especially when they are standing. They think, "I have to take this guy right now." I tell them, yes, you have to try to take him down, but you don't have to do it right now, this second, because the guy does not have any more points than you.

Q: So in some cases you advise your guys to go on bottom if that is where they play best. Why not always try to stay on top and only go to the bottom if you have to?

Shaw: You just never play to a guy's strengths. For example, the first time I fought Robbie Ferguson I was a blue belt and didn't know anything about judo. Robbie has strong judo skills. He grabbed me and threw me over his head without even touching my collar. You might need to pull a guy to the guard if you go against a guy like that who has stand-up skills that are so good that you can't do anything to short-circuit him.

Q: What is your prediction for the sport of Brazilian jiu-jitsu in the United States?

Shaw: The art is growing a lot, but it is not institutionalized like other sports. It is not likely to be accepted in schools where it would quickly become institutionalized. The legal risks are much greater these days than they were in the past. Do you think that football, if it were invented tomorrow, could get into a school system in the U.S? I can hear the school board and the parents saying, "So, you are going to give these guys armor and they are going to crash into each other? My 10-year-old?" Getting football into a school system now would be very tough. This is what jiu-jitsu is up against.

This may soon change due to a little-known group of guys from the Army. I think we are going to see a lot of former U.S. military people entering into the sport very soon. Right now the U.S. military is paying jiu-jitsu instructors to train what they call Army Combatives. In Army Combatives they teach a version of martial arts based on jiu-jitsu, Muay Thai Boxing, and stick fighting. The Army's approach focuses on how to fight a guy that does not know jiu-jitsu. This is very different from sport jiu-jitsu. For example, I have worked in the sheriff's department, police departments, and as security in bars, and generally if the guy does not know how to fight but he is aggressive or strong, he is going to

Figure 5-35. Bull Shaw (right) and Cavalcanti.

put you in a headlock. Eighty-five percent of the time an untrained guy will go to a headlock and start swinging. So in Army Combatives they show the guys how to get out of the headlock. In sport jiu-jitsu everybody knows not to put a guy in a headlock because if he gets out he goes to your back. So what they really teach in Army Combatives is how to fight beginners over and over again. So, those guys in the U.S. Army are getting a taste for jiu-jitsu, but those guys don't have enough stable training time to advance like they should because they are all over the place. But when they return to the civilian world and train with advanced guys, they will shoot right up.

Q: Are you doing some work with the Army at this time?

Shaw: Yes.

Q: Is the Army Combatives/jiu-jitsu program growing?

Shaw: Absolutely. Here in Georgia, at Fort Benning for example, they have many instructors in place. They have some of the biggest mat space in the world. There are hundreds of Zebra mats. It is like an airplane hanger. They are running groups of instructors through on a daily basis. The army is putting money behind it because in modern confrontations they have a lot of police actions, check points, and situations where they are snatching bad guys; jiu-jitsu training gives them an option rather than just shooting someone in the head every time.

There are approximately 10,000 people in the army that have been trained by Army Combatives at this time. There are four certification levels in Army Combatives. There is a big push to have everyone in the entire U.S. Army trained in level one and two combatives. That means 1,052,000 people eventually that will have contact with combatives instruction. At present, Army Combatives train 423 instructors a year. Those instructors can train between 50 and 70 level-one students a week. About 30,000 will be trained next year.

This program will continue to grow exponentially. It is not unreasonable to assume that within five years everyone in the army will have had contact with jiu-jitsu through Army Combatives. The army is rarely a permanent career. I don't know how many people exit the military yearly—50,000, 100,000—but when these former soldiers go looking for a sport for their kids or for themselves to be involved with, it will probably be jiu-jitsu.

CHAPTER 6

SIDE CONTROL

The side control condition is created when one fighter places his body over and on top of another fighter's body. Side control, also called cross-body control, is an extremely stable position for immobilization. It is also a good position for submissions.

The fighter on top is in a massively superior position. The fighter on bottom must be concerned with three things: survival, escape, and preventing the fighter on top from assuming a position of even greater control, such as the north-to-south, knee-in-the-belly, or mount.

This chapter contains Brazilian jiu-jitsu techniques and tactical options for gi, no-gi, and NHB fighting from the side control top and side control bottom positions. The final section of this chapter contains an interview on the topic of strategy by Alliance black belt Felipe Neto.

SIDE CONTROL TOP WITH THE GI

The side-control top position occurs when your opponent is on his back and you are on top and roughly perpendicular to his body. The side-control position is extremely stable. In this section, you will learn hard-core submission that can be done from side control beginning with the shirttail choke.

Figure 6-1. Assume side control against your opponent on his right side and feed his shirttail to your right hand.

Figure 6-2. Switch grips and press your weight forward.

Figure 6-3. Grab your opponent's lapel with your left hand.

Figure 6-4. Lower your weight and execute the shirttail choke.

Core Technique: Shirttail Choke

Execute the shirttail choke by following the steps in Figures 6-1 through 6-4.

The shirttail choke described above is just one of many "shirttail" chokes. Remember, the gi is a weapon. In the hands of a skilled practitioner, the gi provides a massive array of options for choking, binding, and submitting an opponent.

Tactical Options

Many jiu-jitsu players see side control as a stepping-stone to the mount. Some fail to realize that a wide range of attack options are available from side control. Two more examples follow.

Under-Collar Choke

The under-collar choke, also known as the "paper cutter," is one of the most powerful hand chokes in jiu-jitsu. It is also one of the most stable because it locks up your opponent's arms and does not require you to give up your side-control advantage. Execute the under-collar choke by following these steps: Assume side control against your opponent on his left side. Reach under your opponent's left arm with your right. Trap your opponent's arm

Figure 6-5. Under collar choke.

Kimura

Assume side control on your opponent's left side. Reach over your opponent's right shoulder with your right arm. Reach around your opponent's right arm and hold your left collar. Move to the north-south position. Place your left knee on your opponent's left biceps. Squeeze your knees together. Hold your opponent's right wrist with your left hand. Hold your left wrist with your right hand to establish the Kimura grip. (Figure 6-6) Jerk your opponent's hand free. Move your opponent's arm behind his back to execute the Kimura submission.

on your thighs as you grab his collar with your right hand. Grab your opponent's left collar with your left hand (thumb down). Press your left elbow to the floor to choke. (Figure 6-5)

It is essential that you keep your opponent's left arm trapped at all times during this submission. If your opponent frees his left arm, your leverage will be greatly reduced.

It may be necessary for you to move your body in a north-to-south position in order to get the under-collar hold. It may also be necessary for you to break your hips before trapping your opponent's arm. With this submission, as with all submissions, your opponent's reaction to your attack will dictate many of the details.

Figure 6-6. Executing the Kimura.

Figure 6-7. Assume side control and place your right arm over your opponent's torso and trap his left arm.

Figure 6-8. Put your weight onto your opponent's trapped arm.

Figure 6-9. Place your left hand on your right biceps and place your right hand on your opponent's head. Squeeze your arms toward yourself to execute the submission.

SIDE CONTROL TOP WITHOUT THE GI

There is less friction in no-gi competition than there is in gi competition. Less friction means more speed and more opportunity to escape. It is essential, therefore, to minimize space and maintain pressure at all times when attempting no-gi techniques.

Core Technique: Arm Triangle

The arm triangle is a submission in which you use your arms to create the exact same pressure that you would use in a standard triangle that is done with the legs. Follow Figures 6-7 through 6-9 to complete an inside arm triangle from a side-control position.

This submission requires extremely close contact. You cannot allow your opponent to remove his arm so you must keep the pressure on at all times. Once in place, and properly locked, this choke is very powerful.

Tactical Options

The arm triangle can be obtained from a wide variety of positions, including the closed guard. From side control, it is possible to catch your opponent in an arm triangle from the outside as described above, or from the inside as shown in Figure 6-10.

Side Control 107

Figure 6-10. The inside-arm triangle.

Inside-Arm Triangle

Execute the inside-arm triangle by forcing your opponent's left arm across his neck. Then reach under your opponent's neck and clasp your arms together. Apply your body weight against your opponent's arms and squeeze to submit him.

Arm Bar

You can capture an arm bar submission from side control by isolating your opponent's inside arm and placing your shin against his armpit. Step over your opponent's head, then sit back to execute the arm bar. (Figure 6-11)

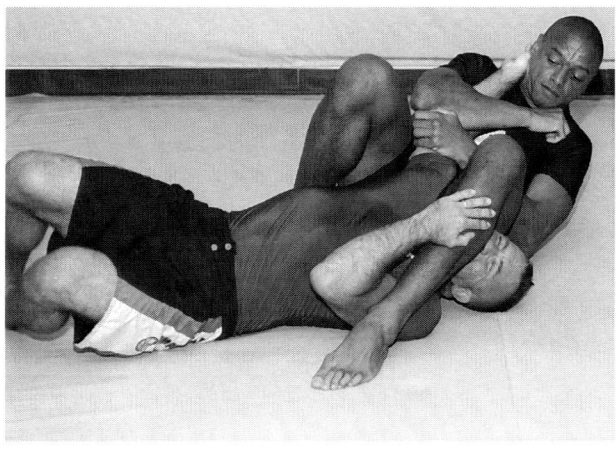

Figure 6-11. The arm bar.

SIDE CONTROL TOP FOR NHB

You can strike your opponent from a side controlling position. The most common types of strikes are elbow and knee strikes. It is common for the fighter on top to throw a few knee or elbow strikes to shake his opponent's defenses and go for a choke or arm attack.

Figure 6-12. Assume side control.

Figure 6-13. Reach over your opponent's left shoulder with your right arm.

Figure 6-14. Secure the Kimura grip by holding your opponent's right wrist with your left and your left wrist with your right. Step over your opponent's head with your right foot and pull your opponent's arm to your left, away from his body.

Figure 6-15. Keep your opponent's arm trapped against your chest as you turn to your right to execute the Kimura submission.

Core Technique: Kimura

The Kimura is a standard side-control technique. Follow Figures 6-12 through 6-15 to execute.

Remember to use your body, not just your arms, to move your opponent's arm into submission position. Keep your chest pressed to your opponent's arm the entire time. This will increase your balance and greatly amplify your strength.

Tactical Options

When your opponent defends the Kimura, he may create an opening for you to attack with a cross-body key lock. Take advantage of the situation by quickly adjusting your grip as described in Figure 6-16.

Cross-Body Key Lock

Assume side control with your arms clasped around your opponent's neck and under his left arm. Attempt a Kimura grip and when your opponent defends, move fast to capture a key-lock grip (also known as the Americana). Do this by placing your right hand on your opponent's wrist and your left hand on your right wrist. Swing your left leg over your opponent's head. Lift his arm as you press down with your leg to execute the key-lock submission. (Figure 6-16)

Figure 6-16. The classic key-lock submission.

Figure 6-17. Assume side control.

Figure 6-18. Move your hips away from your opponent and push against his hips with both hands.

Step-Over Arm Bar

Assume side control with your arms clasped around your opponent's neck and under his left arm. (Figure 6-17) Pull your opponent toward you. Maintain control of your opponent's left arm as you move to your left. Maintain control of your opponent's arm and place your left foot near his back. Swing your left leg over your opponent's chest and fall backward and at a diagonal to execute an arm bar.

SIDE CONTROL BOTTOM WITH THE GI

The side control position is very stable and therefore difficult to escape from. Most opportunities for escape occur when the attacker allows some space in preparation for an attack or in preparation for moving to the mount or to north-to-south control. If an opponent does not allow any space, by virtue of his skill or perhaps just to stall the game, it will be necessary for you to create your own escape-space as shown in the technique descriptions that follow.

Figure 6-19. Turn to your knees and control your opponent's legs.

Figure 6-21. Gain side control.

Figure 6-20. Press your head against your opponent's body and pull on his legs to execute a double-leg takedown.

Core Technique: Turn to Knees for Double-Leg Takedown

In the description shown below, your opponent is on your right side and has you in side control. Follow the steps shown in Figures 6-18 through 6-21 to escape and regain the advantage by executing a double-leg takedown.

You must protect against arm bar attack during the bridging phase of this escape. When you spin onto your stomach and drive forward to grab your opponent's thighs, you must be fast or he will move to your back. When you place your head against your opponent's side, take care to avoid the guillotine.

Tactical Options

If you are unable to turn to your knees and get the double- or single-leg takedown, you can attempt to escape to the guard. These two techniques, turning to the knees and escaping to the guard, follow each other naturally. If you miss one, take advantage of the moment to go for the other.

Sit to the Guard

Place your right palm against your opponent's left hip. Place your left hand across your opponent's neck. Bridge

Figure 6-22. If your opponent sprawls, sit to the guard.

Figure 6-23. The shovel escape.

Figure 6-24. Use your leverage to go to your opponent's back.

upward with your hips and push against your opponent at the apex of your bridge. Turn your hips toward your opponent and shoot your right knee under his hips. Move your hips counterclockwise to bring them under your opponent. Adjust your legs to assume the closed guard. (Figure 6-22)

If you are not able to free your right leg, you can assume a seated guard or other version of the open guard rather than the closed guard. It is important that you avoid letting your opponent pin your right leg during this process or you will quickly end up back under side control.

Shovel Escape

The shovel escape works, but be warned that you must risk an arm bar to pull it off. It goes like this: When you are locked down in side control, scoop your arms under your opponent. (Figure 6-23) At the very instant your arms extend, lift your hips and spin your body 180 degrees. Use this momentum and leverage to go to your opponent's back. (Figure 6-24)

Figure 6-25. Lift your hips and push with your arms to create space.

Figure 6-26. Turn to your knees and hold your opponent's thighs.

Figure 6-27. Put your right leg to the side and use your head to push your opponent over.

Figure 6-28. Put your weight onto your opponent's midsection.

SIDE CONTROL BOTTOM WITHOUT THE GI

Many jiu-jitsu competitors claim that it is easier to escape from side control in no-gi matches than it is in gi matches. They claim that the fabric of the gi makes it harder to get free and gives their opponents more places to hold and to impede their escape maneuvers. Whether it is easier or not is a matter for debate, but there can be no doubt that the game speeds up when the gis come off.

Figure 6-29. Assume side control.

Core Technique:
Escape to Single-Leg Takedown

Perform the escape to single-leg takedown escape from the side mount by following the steps in Figures 6-25 through 6-30.

In order for this technique to work you must swim your arm under your opponent's arm before he can swim under your arm and pin you down. You must then turn your hips before your opponent presses your back flat on the floor. If you wait until your opponent has you flattened out, it will be much harder to escape.

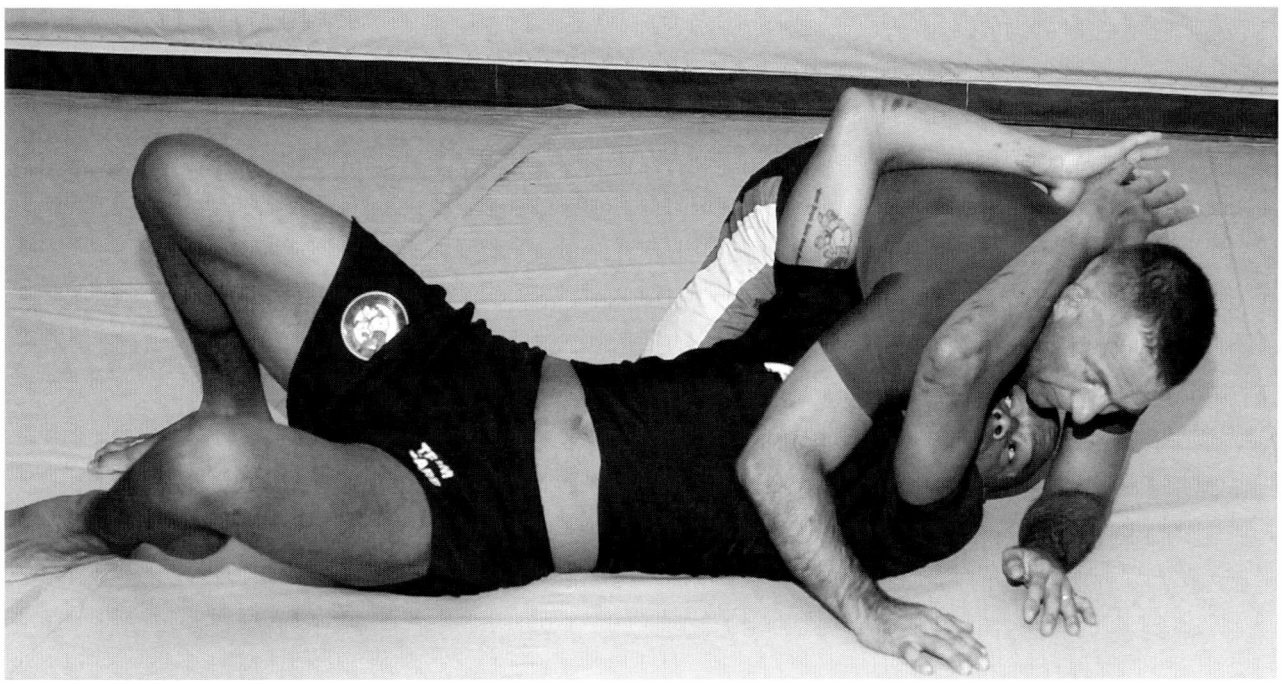

Figure 6-30. Shovel escape.

Figure 6-31. Turn to your left and control his neck with your right arm.

Tactical Option

The shovel escape described below is essentially the same as the gi version discussed above. In the no-gi version, however, there is a slightly smaller risk of getting caught in an arm bar as you make your way free. This is so because you will be able to move more quickly without the gi.

Shovel Escape

To escape from side control using the shovel technique you must first place one arm under your opponent's neck and one arm under his body. (Figure 6-30) Then lift your hips and twist toward your opponent's head. (Figure 6-31) Continue to twist until you are on your knees and free from side control.

Figure 6-32. Keep your elbows in and place your hands against your opponent's throat and chest.

Figure 6-33. Lift your hips and push your opponent away and to your left.

Figure 6-34. Swim your right arm under your opponent's left arm.

Figure 6-35. Bring your left leg under your right leg.

SIDE CONTROL BOTTOM FOR NHB

If your opponent gets you in side-control position in an NHB match, you are in big trouble. From this position your opponent can submit you or strike you with serious leverage. You must defend such attacks, and above all, you must not allow your opponent to mount you. If mounted, you will be at the mercy of your opponent's fists. You urgent goal, therefore, must be to escape and to do it quickly.

Side Control 115

Figure 6-36. Turn to your knees, place your head against your opponent's stomach, and hold his left leg.

Figure 6-37. Take your opponent over.

Rollout Escape

Swim your left arm under your opponent's torso and your right arm under his neck. Lift your hips and use your arms to elevate your opponent and create space. Twist your body and reach over your opponent's back with your left arm and around his left arm with your right. (Figure 6-39) Bring your left leg under your right so that your belly is facing the floor. Clinch your opponent and press your body forward to place your weight on top of his back.

Figure 6-38. Pass your opponent's guard to assume side control.

Core Technique: Turn to Knees Reversal

To execute the turn to knees reversal, follow the steps shown in Figures 6-32 through 6-38.

Tactical Options

The two tactical options shown below will work, but only if the conditions are right. You have two choices: You can wait for your opponent to leave an opening, or you can move in a way that creates an opening.

Figure 6-39. The rollout escape.

Figure 6-40. Executing the escape to take the back.

Figure 6-41. Finish by going to your knees and taking your opponent's back.

Escape to Take the Back

Swim your left arm under your opponent's torso. Place your right arm under your opponent's neck. Lift your hips and elevate your opponent. (Figure 6-40) Turn to your right and push yourself out from under your opponent. Go to your knees and take your opponent's back. (Figure 6-41)

STRATEGIES FOR SIDE CONTROL

Following are strategies for confronting each of the four fighter types—aggressive, deceptive, defensive, and interceptive—in the side-control condition. Keep in mind that these are examples, not absolutes. There is no one best strategy. Use these examples as a baseline for customizing your own approach.

Fighting an Aggressive Opponent

If you are fighting an aggressive opponent and you manage to get him under side control, a good strategy would be to slow the game down and establish complete control. Work methodically for submission or for a superior position. Take your time and stay very tight. Shift your position as needed to keep your opponent pinned. Be ready for bold, aggressive jerks and pushes. Aggressive fighters hate to be pinned.

Should you find yourself under side control from an aggressive opponent, you should be watchful for submission attacks from every possible angle. Block your opponent's hips with your arm and block him from mounting with your knee. Do not let him get the north-to-south, knee-in-the-belly, or the mount position.

Once on top, an aggressive fighter will become even more aggressive. You must escape and do it soon—but don't waste your energy on lost causes. Make your escape attempts at moments in which you have a real chance of getting free. Some of your best opportunities will appear when your opponent repositions to attack.

Fighting a Deceptive Opponent

When you have a deceptive opponent on the bottom, chances are good that he will try to fake you into leaving an opening. Maintain control and be on guard for quick escape attempts and for movements designed to throw you off balance and leave a space through which he can maneuver. Watch also for those few submission techniques that can be executed from the bottom.

When under side control by a deceptive fighter, you must constantly watch for tricky attacks. Double and triple attacks are the specialty of the deceptive fighter. He might, for example, set you up for a paper-cutter choke but let you defend it with your outside arm. The moment that you reach over to defend, he will lock you down and put you in a painful arm triangle. Thus, you must move aggressively to escape from the side control of a deceptive fighter. Turn toward him and push to create space. Work hard and fast to execute one of the escape techniques taught in this book.

Fighting a Defensive Opponent

Getting a truly defensive fighter under side control is like locking Houdini in a cell. If you look away for one second, he is going to escape. Defensive fighters are all about survival. They tend to be extremely difficult to submit and really hard to hold down. Stay tight and work methodically to submit the defensive fighter.

In those rare times when you may find yourself under side control from a defensive fighter, you can expect him to move with extreme caution. Being on top provides the defensive fighter with another opportunity to stall and make you waste your energy. You can escape by offering an opening in your defense that requires space to exploit, then moving quickly to take advantage of the space offered. The more defensive your opponent, the larger the gambit move must be in order to bait him into action.

Fighting an Interceptive Opponent

When on top of an interceptive fighter, you must be ever watchful for submission attempts from the bottom. Interceptive fighters tend to leave openings that require their opponents to position themselves in such a way that space will be created. Then, watch out for a counter-attack from the bottom or a perfectly timed escape attempt.

When an interceptive fighter has you under side control, you should expect to be offered opportunities to "escape." These chances to escape are likely to be submission traps. Your strategy should be to proceed aggressively to make your own space and escape from an angle that you create rather than one that he allows.

INTERVIEW: FELIPE NETO ON STRATEGY

The following interview contains the strategy used by Alliance black-belt instructor Felipe Neto, a veteran competitor and winner of many, many jiu-jitsu matches in local Rio tournaments.

His record also includes Rio de Janeiro

Figure 6-42. Felipe Neto (center) with trophy.

State Championship, first place; Los Angeles Tournament for American Federation of Brazilian Jiu-Jitsu Champion, first place; Calhoun Submission no rules, open division, Champion, Florida State Championships, first place; and Pan American Jiu-Jitsu tournament, second place.

Question: How old were you when you started training?

Neto: I was 16.

Q: How old were you when you got your black belt from Jacare?

Neto: I was 27.

Q: Are you still competing now?

Neto: Last year I fought in the Brazilian Championship in the open division. I didn't win but I did pretty well. I am 33 years old now and I am not competing much. I am focusing on teaching now. I am a jiu-jitsu professor and a physical education professor. I teach in a very nice club.

Q: What should you do to prepare for a major tournament?

Neto: I think you have to have at least two months to prepare. The first four weeks you train jiu-jitsu one day and cross train on the next day. So three times a week you cross train and work your cardio and lift weights that are proper for the activity of jiu-jitsu.

After the four weeks you should quit the cardio and stop lifting weights and just train jiu-jitsu. Then train your jiu-jitsu a little harder each day as you count the last weeks down.

Q: How much rest do you allow each week?

Neto: You have to rest at least one day, maybe two. As you get older you require more rest, more recovery time.

Q: Do you keep training hard right up to the day of the tournament?

Neto: I quit everything and just rest two to three days before the tournament.

Q: Do you recommend losing weight to get into a lower weight class?

Neto: I don't recommend this if you have low body fat. If you have some body fat to lose, then I recommending losing three to five pounds, not too much. There is no energy in fat in your body. It just sits there. But if you are already lean and strong, it is best to train hard and stay in your weight class. If a lean guy loses weight, he is going to get weak.

Q: Let's say you go to a tournament—you might have to fight several times and you might not know all of the guys. Do you try to watch and analyze the guys that you will face or do you just show up?

Neto: I watch them. I pay attention to what they are doing. If I see that a guy is aggressive, I will build a strategy to fight that guy. If I see that one of the guys in my category likes to stall a lot and hardly ever attack, I will be more aggressive and make the guy fight back.

To win in a competition you have to pay attention to everything, not only when the guy is fighting, but after the fight when he runs off the mat. Notice how he acts. Pay attention to his body language. See if he makes eye contact. Notice whether he is afraid or not. I am always aware of those things. I pay attention to what the guy is doing and I build my strategy on top of that.

Q: Can you describe your style?

Neto: I like to pass the guard and be on top. I am very strong in side mount control. I try to be on top because when I am on the side mount the guy can hardly move. I like to fight on top because it works well for me and because I believe it is the best approach for scoring in a tournament.

Figure 6-43. Felipe Neto (left).

Q: What does it take to be a winner?

Neto: Seventy percent of winning is in your mind. Sure, you have to train hard, but from my experience in competition—and I have been doing this since I was a kid—a good fighter is the one that can really get focused all the time. He concentrates and maintains a positive state of mind. I think this is the key.

The mental game is a big aspect of all sports. For example, golf players imagine the ball going inside the hole. I think this works for every sport. I think to be good in jiu-jitsu competition you need to do a lot of this; you need to imagine good things happening.

Q: Do you do this during the competition?

Neto: Yes, during the fight you have to imagine what you want to happen and what you want to do, to make happen. Some guys get so nervous that they can only think bad things. If you think that you are not going to make it, then you will not do well. You have to think positively and imagine yourself winning. Imagine the referee lifting your arm. That is what I do before the fight, and that is a big part of my strategy.

Q: Do you also do this visualization in weeks before the fight?

Neto: Yes, I do this in the weeks before, and I do it during the day of the fight. Most of the time things happen the way that you visualize because your mind is so powerful. Of course, there are times when it doesn't happen the way you visualize, but usually, when you think positively and imagine things going the way that you want, it will happen like that.

Q: Would you describe this as meditation?

Neto: It's not really meditation. It is just that you have to believe in the power of your mind. It is not anything mystical or anything. It is something that works for me. It is part of my strategy to win the match. I haven't talked about this to many people before, just a few of my students. I think it is a very important thing to put in the book.

Q: How would you approach an opponent who is extremely flexible and very fast?

Neto: This is a hard guy to fight. To fight him you have to be in good condition. Go on top and smash his legs. Pass the guard.

Q: Do you change your game if you go up against a fighter who has the same style as you?

Neto: When I see a guy fight, I can tell a lot about his game. Maybe he has one or two sweeps that are very good. I know how to counter those sweeps, so if he pulls guard, I am going to be ready to counter with this or that technique.

You can do this analysis on your own, but it is a good thing to get your instructor involved. Ask him to help you build your plan for your opponents. Ask him to watch the fights with you and share his ideas on what you should and should not do to fight this guy or another guy.

When I fought last year, my friend Fernando Gurgel helped me. Together we watched my opponents and he helped me devise my strategy. He saw one thing that I didn't see, an important little detail that I didn't notice about the way that one of my opponents worked his guard. It is a good thing to have somebody to pay attention with you and help you build a strategy. Two heads think better than one.

Q: Do you have a strategy for managing points during a match?

Neto: I have my style—to get side mount control, to be on top, to pass the guard. Once I pass the guard and get on the side, I always fight to finalize the guy. My goal, my objective is to make the guy tap; submit. I always try for this.

Nowadays the guys just want to fight to score points or advantages. I think I have an old type of fight game. I fight to win by submission. Of course, if I see the guy is very aggressive and I am up one point when I finally get side mount control, I am not going to give the guy a chance to recompose his guard again. In this case I wouldn't take a big risk to submit him because most of all I want to win the match.

Every case is different. That is why it is hard to tell you that this is what I do because you are dealing with a fight, with movement of the body. A lot of things are involved. It is hard to tell you exactly what I would do. For every match you have to see what the guy is doing. You have to read his body language before the fight, imagine yourself winning, but you never know until you are in the fight.

Things can happen and you have to adapt your fighting game to what is going on in the real situation.

Q: What is your recommendation for new guys who want to become great jiu-jitsu competitors?

Neto: To be a good fighter you have to practice constantly and cross train your body with specific things to build muscle and flexibility and to avoid injury. If you want to be a top competitor or a professional fighter, you have to have a healthy life. You must build good habits. Eat right and avoid drinking and partying hard. I don't say never party, but you want to be moderate. Proper sleep, proper food, good practice—it all comes together. If you eat wrong, you can't train right. If you don't sleep right, you won't be able to practice right. If you are young, OK, you can get away with bad habits for a little while, but over time you are not going to succeed. Your life must be in balance. You need to maintain a good relationship with your family, your girlfriend, your jiu-jitsu professor, your school, and your fellow students. Remember, as you train more, your responsibility to others will increase. You need to be a good example for the new guys. This is my strategy for life, not only for being a good fighter.

Q: What kind of weight training do you recommend for jiu-jitsu competitors?

Neto: Jiu-jitsu requires explosive power. The lifting program should be tailored to build muscle and strength but also to build explosive power. There are three different kinds of resistance training that I teach that lead up to explosive-power weight training.

Q: Did you study judo?

Neto: Yes, when I was very young.

Q: Would you recommend that jiu-jitsu competitors train in judo too?

Neto: I recommend training some judo because when you fight, you start on your feet so you can have an advantage and get two points for the takedown. Fabio Gurgel taught me that if you want to put judo in your fight game that is fine, but you have to have in your mind that you are a jiu-jitsu practitioner, not a judo practitioner. You cannot be good at both.

Add some of the judo techniques to your fight game. That is what I recommend. Select one to three judo techniques that work well for your body type and add them to your jiu-jitsu game. I don't think it is worth it to learn the whole range of judo techniques.

Q: Is their anything that you would like to add?

Neto: Train right, eat right, live right, and sleep right. Be good with yourself and with the people around you. Avoid injuries. The rest is inside your mind. Think positive, get focused. Believe that you will win. Even if the guy might be better than you, you have to believe that you can make it, that you can do it. Concentrate. Visualize good things happening during the competition. Be positive, play smart.

You have to have a balance in your life, your mind, your soul, your brain, your body—everything has to be together. If you do everything right but have your mind messed up in your life, this is going to interfere in your fight. Be a good person, do things for people—it comes back to you during the fight, during your work, whatever you do.

Finally, I just want to say that Jacare is a very important person in my life. I am very grateful to him for everything that he taught me. I learned a lot of things from him about being a good person and doing things right.

CHAPTER 7

NORTH-TO-SOUTH CONTROL

The north-to-south control position describes a condition in which one fighter is on top of the other in an inverted state. In other words, the fighters have their faces at each other's bellies. The fighter on the bottom will hardly be able to breathe. It is a truly miserable position to be caught in, but it is a really great position to catch someone in.

The north-to-south position is hard to escape from. It affords the fighter on top a variety of attack options. Even if the fighter on top does nothing, the fighter on bottom must expend a great deal of energy just to keep breathing.

This chapter explores techniques and tactical options for fighting in and defending against the north-to-south condition.

The last part of the chapter contains an interview on the topic of strategy with Alliance black belt Fabio Gurgel.

NORTH-TO-SOUTH CONTROL TOP WITH THE GI

The most common attack from the north-to-south position is the Kimura submission. The technique described below is a variation. Rather than attack the shoulder, with this technique you will attack your opponent's wrist.

Figure 7-1. Stabilize your opponent in the north-to-south position.

Figure 7-2. Place your right shin across your opponent's right arm, then wrap your opponent's shirttail over his arm to trap.

Figure 7-3. Execute the Kimura position wristlock submission.

Core Technique: Kimura Position Wristlock

Follow the steps in Figures 7-1 through 7-3 to execute the Kimura wristlock from the north-to-south control position.

To make this work you must keep your opponent stable. Remember to squeeze your knees together and keep your chest close to your opponent's arms at all times. The wristlock is most often captured by surprise. Cause your opponent to think that you are going for a regular Kimura or arm bar to create an opportunity to go for his wrist.

Tactical Option

You can use the north-to-south position to set up a number of submissions, like the arm bar shown below. You can also use the north-to-south as a way to navigate into a better or different side-controlling position. It is also possible to use the north-to-south position as a platform from which to take the back.

Arm Bar

Like the Kimura, the arm bar can be captured from a variety of positions. You can easily catch an arm bar from the north-to-south control position by using the same basic setup done with the Kimura and the Kimura wristlock described above. Circle your left arm around your opponent's right arm and grab your own collar. Bring your knees up and turn your opponent onto his right side. Straddle your opponent's upper torso and sit on his head. Grasp your opponent's left wrist with your right hand. Grasp your own right wrist with your left hand. Pull your opponent's left arm up and away from his body. Hold the Kimura grip as you swing your left leg over your opponent's body. Sit back and execute an arm bar. (Figure 7-4)

You can also execute the arm bar with your left knee against your opponent's ribs rather than over his torso. Both methods are effective.

Figure 7-4. The arm bar.

Figure 7-5. Capture the Kimura grip from the north-to-south position.

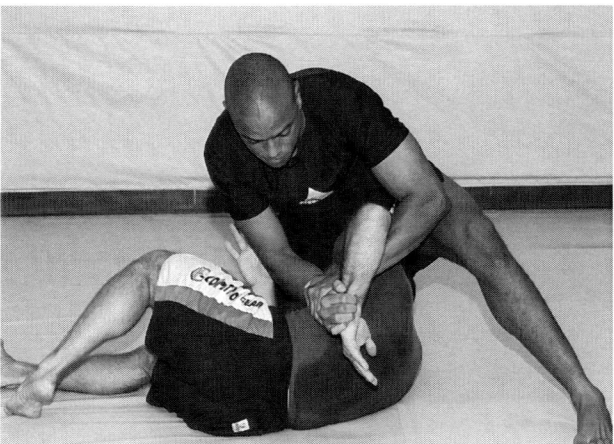

Figure 7-7. Pull your opponent's left arm up and away from his body and execute the Kimura submission.

NORTH-TO-SOUTH CONTROL TOP WITHOUT THE GI

North-to-south control works the same with or without the gi. While it is true that there are a few more options for attack when the gi is worn, the big difference is in the speed of the game. No-gi is faster.

Core Technique: Kimura

You can capture the Kimura from the north-to-south control position by using the procedures shown in Figures 7-5 through 7-7.

Tactical Option

The fighter on bottom should always try to

Figure 7-6. Bring your knees up and turn your opponent onto his right side.

keep the fighter on top from gaining north-to-south control. Once in position, the fighter on top will prove difficult to displace and will have a variety of submissions at his disposal.

Inverted Crank

To pull off an inverted crank submission you must first stabilize your position in north-to-south control. Then reach under your opponent's neck with your left and right arms. Hold your own arms at the elbows. Drop your hips and squeeze to submit. (Figure 7-8)

Figure 7-8. The inverted crank.

Figure 7-9. Maintain pressure and move from side control to north-to-south control.

Figure 7-10. Place your right shin on your opponent's right arm and capture a Kimura grip on his left arm.

Figure 7-11. Jerk your opponent's arm to the right.

Figure 7-12. Fold your opponent's arm to the left, over his back, to execute the Kimura submission.

NORTH-TO-SOUTH CONTROL TOP FOR NHB

When you are on top and in north-to-south control position, you have your opponent at a dangerous disadvantage. You can attack your opponent with reliable submission standards like the Kimura attack described below.

Core Technique: Kimura

Perform the Kimura in NHB situations by following the steps in Figures 7-9 through 7-12. (This scenario assumes that you have your opponent under north-to-south control.)

Tactical Options

If you miss the Kimura attack described above, you can always substitute other techniques such as an arm bar attack, a wrist attack, or a leg choke attack. These three attacks work from the Kimura position so they are natural follow-ups to a missed Kimura. If all of these options fail, you can lower your weight and flatten your opponent onto the mat then attack him with an inverted crank/choke.

Strike with the Knee

From the north-to-south position you can generate tremendous power with your knees. Follow the steps in Figures 7-14 and 7-15 to attack with your knees from the north-to-south control position.

Use caution not to give up too much space when you strike. Expect your opponent to scramble hard to escape when you launch knee strikes at his head. Don't attempt knee strikes unless your position is solid.

Figure 7-14. Assume north-to-south control at a slight diagonal.

Figure 7-13. Inverted crank/choke.

Inverted Crank/Choke

The inverted crank/choke is a mean and nasty submission. Perform it by assuming north-to-south control with your body at a slight diagonal to your opponent's. Reach over your opponent's neck with your right arm and under it with your left. Clasp your right elbow with your left hand. Drive your hips down and pull up with your arms to execute the inverted crank/choke submission. (Figure 7-13)

Figure 7-15. Strike your opponent's head with your right knee.

Figure 7-16. Place your palms on your opponent's hips.

NORTH-TO-SOUTH CONTROL BOTTOM WITH THE GI

The north-to-south control position is very stable for the person on top. Escape options are limited. The best option is to prevent your opponent from moving into north-to-south control by blocking his hips. If your opponent manages to get you into this condition, you may be able to escape by turning to your knees as described below.

Core Technique: Turn to Your Knees to Escape

Follow the procedures in Figures 7-16 through 7-18 to escape from north-to-south control by turning to your knees.

It is important to stay relaxed when under north-to-south control. Avoid panic and control your breathing. As Dr. Patrick Harvey explains, "When guys get under stress, they start gasping for air and forget to exhale. Make yourself breathe out. Don't worry about breathing in. Your body will naturally breathe in."

Tactical Option

If you are unable to turn to your knees to escape, you can hold tight and defend and wait for your opponent to move back to side control, or you can attempt to sweep him. As is evident in the tactical option that follows,

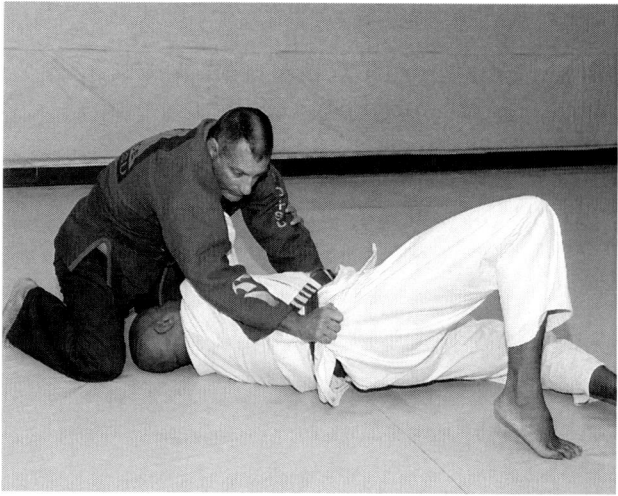

Figure 7-17. Push upward against your opponent's hips and turn to your left.

Figure 7-18. Go to your knees and grab your opponent's left leg for a single-leg takedown.

you will need a good deal of flexibility in order to sweep your opponent from this disadvantaged position.

Use Both Knees to Sweep

Keep your elbows at your sides and wait for an opportunity to grab both of your opponent's wrists. Immediately after grabbing both

North-to-South Control

NORTH-TO-SOUTH CONTROL BOTTOM WITHOUT THE GI

Escaping from the north-to-south position is difficult. Make no mistake about it. The most commonly used escape techniques are described below. "The best strategy is to avoid getting caught in bad positions like the north-south in the first place," says Bull Shaw.

Figure 7-19. Use both knees to sweep.

Figure 7-20. Escaping from north-to-south control.

Figure 7-21 Place your hands on your opponent's hips.

Figure 7-22. Lift your hips and push with your arms to gain space to turn.

of your opponent's wrists, place both of your knees inside of his armpits. (Figure 7-19) Extend your legs to sweep your opponent away and escape from north-to-south control. (Figure 7-20) Follow your opponent as he falls away and assume side control or mounted control as quickly as you can.

130   Brazilian Jiu-Jitsu Fighting Strategies

Figure 7-23. Turn to your knees and grab your opponent's legs for a double-leg takedown.

Figure 7-24. Take your opponent down and assume side control.

Core Technique: Escape to Your Knees

Follow the steps in Figures 7-21 through 7-24 to escape from the north-to-south in a no-gi situation.

Tactical Option

The secret to escaping from the north-to-south position or any position of disadvantage is timing. Power can help, but timing and leverage are far more important than power.

Escape to the Guard

You may be able to escape from the north-to-south position by pushing upward on your opponent's chest and quickly lifting your knees. (Figure 7-25) Immediately hook your right leg over your opponent's neck to gain leverage. Use your leg to spin your body out from under your opponent. (Figure 7-26) Then establish your open guard to regain control of the action.

Figure 7-25. Push your opponent upward and lift your knees.

Figure 7-26. Hook your right leg over your opponent's neck and spin around to your guard.

Figure 7-27. Keep your elbow bent and place your forearms on your opponent's chest.

Figure 7-28. Bridge your hips and push your opponent to gain space.

Figure 7-29. Hold your opponent's elbows and place your knees in his armpits.

Figure 7-30. Rock forward.

NORTH-TO-SOUTH CONTROL BOTTOM FOR NHB

The fighter on bottom should do all in his power to prevent the fighter on top from going north-to-south. If the fighter on top assumes this inverted control position, there is little to stop him from throwing powerful knee strikes. In addition, the fighter on top has a significant number of submission options available to him.

Figure 7-31. Throw your opponent.

Figure 7-32. Maintain your grip on your opponent's arms and assume side control as he lands.

Core Technique: Knee Leverage Escape

Execute the knee leverage escape in a no-rules situation by following the procedures shown in Figures 7-27 through 7-32.

Tactical Options

The fighter who is on top in a north-south control position must pin your shoulders and head to the mat in order to hold you down, which makes it difficult for him to simultaneously immobilize your hips. If your hips are free, you can move your legs. If you can move your legs, you may be able to mount an escape like the one described here.

Figure 7-33. Swing your legs to create space.

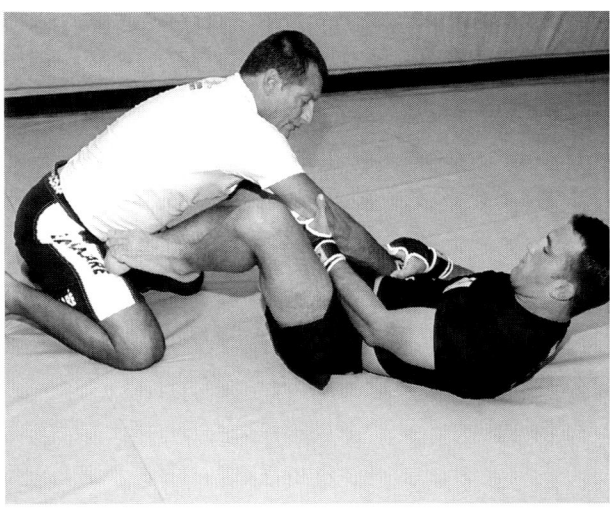

Figure 7-34. Place him in your open guard.

Swing Legs and Go to the Guard

You may be able to create the space that you need to escape from a north-to-south control position by swinging both of your legs from side to side. (Figure 7-33) You may need to swing your legs many times at fast speed in order to create an opening. If an opening appears, you must immediately spin toward the opening and push against your opponent's hips with your arms as you go. If the space is large enough, turn your legs toward your opponent and place him in your open guard. (Figure 7-34)

Turn to Single-Leg Takedown

A second tactical option for escaping from the north-to-south control position in a no-rules situation is to turn to your knees and take your opponent down with a single leg. Do this by using your arms to push on your opponent's hips in order to create a small space. When a space appears, immediately turn so that your stomach faces the floor. Then drive forward and grab one of your opponent's legs. (Figure 7-35) Keep driving forward and take your opponent over. Keep going until you have side control.

STRATEGIES FOR THE NORTH-TO-SOUTH CONTROL

Following are strategies for confronting each of the four fighter types—aggressive, deceptive, defensive, and interceptive—from the north-to-south control condition. Remember that your strategy will need to change somewhat with each opponent that you face.

Fighting an Aggressive Opponent

The north-to-south position is a great position to use to control an aggressive fighter. Use the superior leverage and control that this position affords to slow down the pace of the fight and force your opponent to waste energy. Go

Figure 7-35. Drive forward and grab your opponent's leg.

slowly and set up your attacks methodically. Expect your aggressive opponent to try drastic escape attempts. Be prepared to adjust your position to maintain control.

When under north-to-south control from an aggressive opponent, you must keep your head calm and your arms in. Expect to be attacked constantly. Watch for every sort of attack but be especially careful to defend Kimura attacks and inverted choke/crank techniques. Save your energy and watch for openings through which to escape. When you create an opening or one is offered, burst through it boldly and aggressively. Be ready for a violent scramble when you get free.

Fighting a Deceptive Opponent

When you have a deceptive opponent in the north-to-south position you can be sure he has an escape plan in mind. Watch out for the setup. Do not allow him to fake you out and escape. Keep the pressure on by attacking quickly. Force your opponent to defend against your game.

When under north-to-south control of a deceptive fighter, you should expect the unexpected. Watch for and defend against odd-angle submission attacks. Fight hard and aggressively to escape. Your aggressive attempts to escape will pull your deceptive fighter off his game. Your opponent will have to react to you, and this will give you the advantage you need to escape.

Fighting a Defensive Opponent

An interceptive strategy can work well against a defensive opponent when you have him pinned under north-to-south control. Create an opening and allow your opponent to enter. Plan a submission attack to take advantage of the specific movements that he will have to make in order to escape through the provided opening. With this strategy you will risk letting the defensive fighter escape should you miss the submission trap. Losing a defensive fighter from a superior position is, however, a far lower risk to you than losing a more aggressive opponent.

If a defensive fighter gets you under north-to-south control, you can expect him to stay there for as long as possible. Holding someone down from the north-to-south is an extremely low-risk job, especially if you are up on points. You cannot allow your opponent to stall you out in this condition. Escape quickly by aggressively creating space and then executing techniques taught in this book.

Fighting an Interceptive Opponent

An interceptive opponent is always hard to submit. This is so because his pattern is to continually create openings for you to attack him that are actually ploys to create space from which he can escape. You must control the pace by attacking in patterns that force him to play to your rhythm. You can use an aggressive approach or a deceptive approach, but you must make him dance to your tune.

When under north-to-south control from an interceptive opponent, you need to be afraid, very afraid. Remember, the interceptive personality is the most analytical of the four styles. Every motion from an interceptive fighter is intended to cause a reaction that works to his advantage. Generally speaking, these are "opportunities" that look like escape routes but in fact lead to submission traps. Do not take the bait. Make him play your game. Move aggressively to create the space that you need to escape on your own terms.

INTERVIEW: FABIO GURGEL ON STRATEGY

The following interview contains the strategy used by Alliance black-belt instructor, UFC Contender, NHB fighter, and Brazilian jiu-jitsu competition champion Fabio Gurgel.

Figure 7-36. Fabio Gurgel (left) with Jacare Cavalcanti.

Gurgel's impressive jiu-jitsu competition record includes countless wins and championships in blue, purple, brown, and many black-belt competitions. As a black belt he won his division at the World Championship in 1996, 1997, 2000, and 2001. Gurgel also won his division and the open division at the World Masters Championship 2002 and 2005.

Question: How old were you when you started training in jiu-jitsu?
Fabio Gurgel: 13 years.
Q: When did you get your black belt?
Gurgel: I got my black belt from Jacare in 1989. I was 19 years old.
Q: That was really fast.
Gurgel: Yes. Actually, my generation was the first generation to train twice per day in the professional way. In the previous generation it sometimes took 20 years to get a black belt because a lot of guys trained just twice a week.

Q: When did you open your first school?
Gurgel: I started teaching at a club in Rio de Janeiro when I was a brown belt, 18 years old.
Q: You have had an amazing personal competition career.
Gurgel: I started to compete in blue belt at 15 years of age. At that time, Jacare was Rickson Gracie's student, so we would go to Rickson's school to compete against his students to earn a spot to compete at the tournament. Later Jacare started his own team, Team Jacare.

My first tournament was the Rio de Janeiro tournament, and I got second place. Then I started to compete in every tournament in my division and the open division. I was champion in blue belt, purple belt, brown belt. And, then [in 1989] I got my black belt and that is when my career really started. Black belt is the real thing. Starting in 1989, I competed in black belt at many events. I won the first World Championship in 1996 and I won in 1997, I lost in the final in 1998, I lost in the semifinal in 1999, I won in 2000, and 2001. After that I began competing in the World Masters Division, over 30 years old. I won the World Championship in Masters in 2002 in my division and in the open division. I had a rib injury and did not compete in 2003 and 2004. Then I won again this last year in 2005 in my division and the open division.

Q: So you are still competing?
Gurgel: Yes, but just once a year. Just to shake the body out.
Q: You had one UFC fight and some other no-holds-barred fights, right?
Gurgel: My first no-holds-barred was in 1991 when I fought a match between jiu-jitsu and Lutra Libre.
Q: How did you do in that fight?
Gurgel: I won by knockout from the mount position. It was a really good fight. It

was very important for jiu-jitsu. Today, of course, the guys are professional fighters; they fight for the money. At that time we were fighting to defend the position, the jiu-jitsu flag. It was quite different from nowadays.

Q: How did you prepare for the UFC?

Gurgel: I went to the U.S. to train with Rickson for two months before the fight. I did three training sessions every day. I trained a lot of boxing in the morning, and then I trained with Rickson for two hours in the afternoon. At night I did conditioning. It was a really tough time. I was really well prepared for that fight, but things didn't go as I expected and I lost by decision.

Q: In terms of conditioning, is it a lot different to prepare for a no-holds-barred match than it is to prepare for a jiu-jitsu tournament?

Gurgel: It is about the same as far as conditioning goes. Of course, when you have the gi, you use the grip a lot more. For no-rules you train boxing and train without the gi, but basically it is the same.

Q: What do you do that is different from your normal training when you get ready for a big jiu-jitsu tournament?

Gurgel: Nothing is different, really, because you need to prepare yourself all during the year. You must train beginning in January to get into good shape for July. You need to compete in small tournaments along the way to prepare yourself for the bigger competitions. It is not special training for some competition—I don't believe that. You just train, always. Of course the month before the tournament you need to rest, you need to pay attention, and to get ready.

Q: So you rest for one month before a major competition?

Gurgel: Sometimes when you train too hard for a competition you get injuries. You have to take a lot of care to avoid injuries. So beginning about one month before the competition you must pay a lot of attention to what you are doing to avoid injury.

A lot of people push themselves very hard before the competition. It is better to push hard three months before so that in the last month you can rest more and pay attention to technique. In the last month you should try to change some things that you don't do well.

Q: You were one of the founders of the Alliance Team. How did this team get started?

Gurgel: My students were beginning to compete against Jacare's students. The same thing happened with Roberto Traven and some of Jacare's other black belts who had their own academies. Jacare had the idea to form the Alliance and we started working together.

Q: Why was the Alliance Team so successful?

Gurgel: We were the first to have all our academies competing together. We went to many tournaments over the years and did very well. The highlight was in 1998 when we won the World Championship. Then we did it again in 1999. This was the best time for the Alliance.

Q: What is your strategy for preparing your team so that you win as many events as possible and win the team competition?

Gurgel: In my academy most of the guys want to compete. In the World Championship, for example, everybody wants to go. So you have to give the training to everybody.

In my academy, for example, we have Marcello Garcia; he is the biggest star in the Alliance nowadays, but the training session is not just for him—it is for everybody, for all the students. You have to build the whole group.

Q: Speaking of Marcello Garcia, he is one of the most successful competitors in the world and you are his teacher and his coach. To what do you attribute his success? Is it from your coaching, natural ability, a combination? Why is Marcello so great?

Gurgel: It is a combination. When I was a champion, it was not just from natural qualities but from Jacare coaching me and teaching me, telling me what is right and what is wrong. This is the same thing that I try to do with Marcello. I try to put the things in a really simple way. It is not a big deal. The preparation he does for a tournament is exactly what he does every day. I give him exactly the same attention that I give to all my students. But Marcello is really good. He has a natural quality. He is very dedicated. He is really, really professional. That is why he is one of the best competitors nowadays.

Q: Strategy is about planning, about trying to figure things out in advance. Do you have a different strategy for fighting guys who have different talents?

Gurgel: When you go to a jiu-jitsu tournament, you must fight against at least five different guys. They are going to have different qualities. So you have to build your strategy to compete with different guys.

Q: What is your primary strategy?

Gurgel: I try to put my game on everybody, so I try to do something ahead of them. That is what jiu-jitsu is all about. When you are one step ahead, you are winning. If you let the guy do something to you first, then you must defend; then the guy is going to do the next step, and you have to defend again, and you must wait for him to make a mistake. I prefer to stay ahead all the time. That is my main strategy for fighting.

Q: So your main strategy is to stay one step ahead of your opponent all the time no matter what type of fighter he happens to be?

Gurgel: Yes. Even if the guy is bigger than me or smaller, or faster, or stronger, it doesn't matter. Of course, if the guy is heavier than I am, I am going to try to stay on top. But sometimes you can't stay one step ahead. Sometimes the guy puts you down and you must do something different to reverse the situation. But I try not to think too much about positions and situations. I try to let the thing go.

Q: Let the thing go?

Gurgel: Yes. If you think, "I am going to do this and then this," but the thing doesn't work, you are going to be paralyzed. You should go with an open mind where you remember that anything can happen. The most important thing is to stay one step ahead.

Q: So you don't plan to do certain moves, you just plan to stay ahead and keep a very open mind as you go through the fight?

Gurgel: Yes. Of course, when you go to fight, you have to have your preferred techniques. For example, if I am trying to put the guy down, I will think about techniques for doing that. But if I can't do the movement that comes to mind, that is no problem at all. I will change immediately. I might pull the guy into the guard or something else. The problem is when you go with one shot and the shot doesn't work, you are done.

Q: What is your strategy for managing points in a jiu-jitsu match?

Gurgel: I am a competitor and I know the rules very well. I pay attention to advantages and to points. I know if I am winning or losing the fight. If I am losing, I know that I need to add some speed or try to do something different. If I am winning the fight, I know that I can go slowly. You must understand the rules to play the game.

Q: Some people say that a big part of winning is in the mind. Do you agree? Do you teach your students to play a mind game?

Gurgel: Yes, I believe that. If you go to a tournament and trust yourself, your conditioning, your training you have a lot of chances to be successful. If you go to the tournament with some doubts about your ability, it is going to be hard for you to win. To get this confidence is very important. That is why I put my fighters to compete in every tournament.

Sometimes a fighter is not in good shape, but it is important for him to go just to learn how it is to fight without being in good condition. To be a complete fighter you must learn how to deal with different situations. I fought many times when I was not in good shape and sometimes I won. Sometimes I lost the fight. But I always learned something very important. That is why it is so important to compete every time.

Q: What are some of the changes that you have seen in jiu-jitsu in the last several years?

Gurgel: It is not about changes in the art really, but a lot is happening all the time. Every day when I go to my academy I learn something new. That is the movement of the art.

If you mean change in competition, the people in the old times didn't think about points or advantage; they wanted to submit their opponents. It is very romantic to remember those times, but is impossible now to win tournaments with this thinking. That is maybe the biggest change that I have seen, that people now think more about the points, more about advantages, more about how to play in the rules. The art itself, the jiu-jitsu, is still basically the same.

Q: What are your plans for the future?

Gurgel: My main academy in San Palo is doing very well and I have 13 satellite academies in San Palo. I have satellite schools outside of Brazil in Germany, Greece, and Venezuela. Soon I am going to have even more academies abroad. My goal is to continue this. I will continue my efforts to get more and more people to learn the real jiu-jitsu, the philosophy of jiu-jitsu, and how jiu-jitsu can be good for your life. This is my most important goal.

Q: Jiu-jitsu is your full-time job right?

Gurgel: Yes. I start at 7 AM and go until 9 PM.

Q: Since it is your job, are you able to train as much as you would like?

Gurgel: Of course, it is different now. Now my goal is not competing anymore. Now I compete in only one tournament a year, the Masters World tournament. I do this just to have fun, because I like it. But competing is not a profession for me anymore. It is no longer my job to compete and fight. Now I try to do my best for my students and teach all my classes the best way that I can. I train for myself because I like to stay in good shape but it is not about competing anymore, so I don't need too much time to train. For me, one hour per day is enough.

Q: Is there anything else that you would like to say?

Gurgel: Stay one step ahead. Jiu-jitsu is like a chess game—it really is. If you know what your opponent is going to do, it is much easier to get the position, to get the chance to submit.

CHAPTER 8

KNEE-IN-THE-BELLY

The knee-in-the-belly position is widely used in Brazilian jiu-jitsu. The position is formed when one fighter places his knee across the hips, belly, or chest of another fighter. The effect of the knee in the belly is to pin the opponent to the mat while freeing up the hands of the person on top. This position causes almost all the weight of the fighter on top to drive straight down into the belly or chest of the fighter on the bottom. Needless to say, it is not much fun being the person on bottom.

This chapter contains techniques and tactical options for using the knee-in-the-belly for attack and for defending against it. The last part of this chapter features an interview on the topic of strategy with Alliance black-belt instructor Abdul Mutakabbir.

KNEE-IN-THE-BELLY TOP WITH THE GI

The most common way to get to the knee-in-the-belly position is from a side control position. You can slide your knee into place with very little risk any time that your opponent leaves an opening. In no-gi matches, placing the knee in your opponent's belly and establishing the position for a few seconds will result in points earned. From this position, many submissions are possible, including the shirttail choke described here.

Figure 8-1. Assume knee-in-the-belly control.

Figure 8-2. Reach under your opponent's right shoulder for control as you free your right shirttail.

Figure 8-3. Feed your right shirttail over your opponent's neck and place it in your left palm.

Figure 8-4. Place your shirttail into your right palm.

Figure 8-5. Place your left hand across your opponent's neck and choke him.

Core Technique: Shirttail Choke

To perform a shirttail choke, follow the steps in Figures 8-1 through 8-5.

When you place your knee in your opponent's belly, you will be focusing the majority of your body weight onto him across a small area. This action alone will make it very hard for your opponent to breathe.

Tactical Options

It is not uncommon for the competitor on the bottom to panic and risk his arms. Be prepared to take advantage if this happens and strike quickly with an arm bar submission like the one described here.

Figure 8-6. Arm bar.

Arm Bar

Place your right knee onto your opponent's belly. Keep your left foot flat and your left leg fairly straight. Stabilize your position and wait for your opponent to push against your knee. If your opponent pushes with his right arm, go for an inside, or near-arm arm bar. (Figure 8-6) If your opponent pushes with his left hand, go for an outside, or far-arm arm bar. Do this by scooping your opponent's left arm at the elbow with your right hand. As soon as you scoop the arm, step over your opponent's head, place your shin onto his side, and sit back to execute the arm bar.

Cross Choke with Shirttail

Assume a knee-in-the-belly position. Once in place, loosen your opponent's right shirttail. Feed his shirttail to your right hand. Hold your opponent's collar with your left hand and execute the choke. (Figure 8-7) Step over your opponent's head to add leverage as needed. (Figure 8-8)

KNEE-IN-THE-BELLY TOP WITHOUT THE GI

Placing your knee in your opponent's belly allows you to have the "high ground." You gain freedom of movement for your hands while maintaining maximum pressure on your opponent's body. This frees you up to attack your opponent's legs, neck, and arms.

Figure 8-7. Cross choke with shirttail.

Figure 8-9. Place your knee in your opponent's belly.

Figure 8-8. Cross choke with shirttail.

Figure 8-10. Gain control of your opponent's right arm.

Figure 8-11. Plant your left foot on the ground over your opponent's neck.

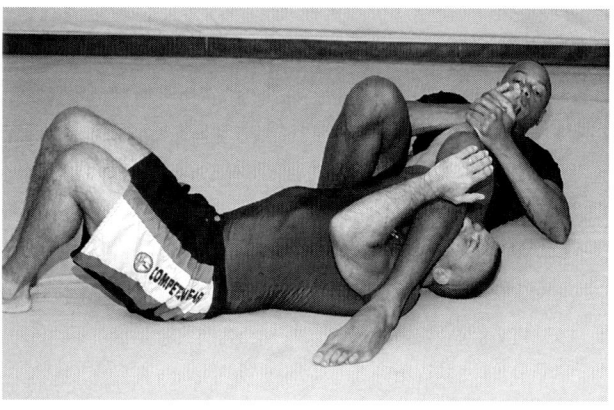

Figure 8-12. Execute the arm bar.

Core Technique: Near Arm Bar

When you assume a right knee on the belly control position, your opponent's right arm is the "near" arm. If he gives you an opening, you can execute the near-arm bar from the right knee on the belly-control position using the procedures in Figures 8-9 through 8-12.

Squeeze your knees together as you do the arm bar. Be sure to stay tight against your opponent as you sit back to execute the arm bar. He will likely turn to escape if you allow even a small amount of space between your bodies.

Tactical Options

Your opponent may expose his neck in order to mount and escape from your knee-in-the-belly control. Keep the pressure on and wait for your opponent to lower his arms and push on your knee. Should this happen, respond quickly with one of the tactical options described below.

Baseball Choke

Assume the knee-in-the-belly on top position. Reach under your opponent's neck with your left hand. Place your right arm over your opponent's neck. Clasp your hands. (Figure 8-13) Drop your knee off your opponent's belly to execute the baseball choke.

Figure 8-13. Baseball choke.

Knee-in-the-Belly 143

Figure 8-14. Arm-bar trap.

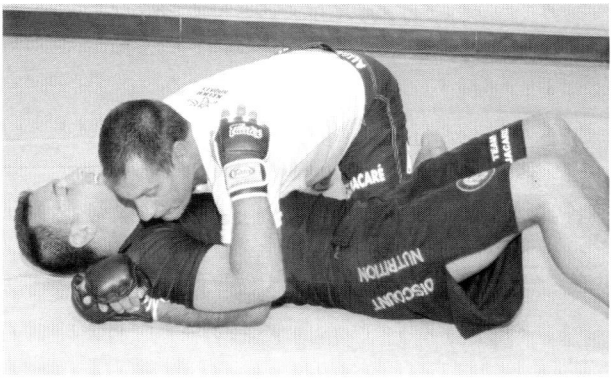

Figure 8-15. Hold around your opponent's neck and arm in a tight clinch.

Arm-Bar Trap

Place your knee solidly into your opponent's belly. Put your weight forward and trap your opponent's left arm across your thigh. Hold your opponent's left leg for control. Swing your left leg over your opponent's neck and sit back to execute the arm bar trap. (Figure 8-14)

KNEE-IN-THE-BELLY TOP FOR NHB

You can use the knee-in-the-belly position in no-holds-barred fighting, but you must protect your groin. Your opponent might make a desperate attempt to grab or strike you in this area, so be careful.

Figure 8-16. Place your hands on your opponent's neck as you bring your knee into place on his belly.

Core Technique: Punch

You can throw punches and elbow strikes at your opponent from the knee-in-the-belly position by following the steps in Figures 8-15 through 8-17.

You can generate considerable power from the knee-in-the-belly position, but you can get a lot more power and control if you mount. Most NHB fighters use the knee-in-the-belly as a transition to the mount if they use it at all.

Figure 8-17. Maintain your hold on your opponent's neck with your left hand as you punch and throw elbow strikes with your right.

Tactical Option

The ability to punch generates a range of responses that will open doors to a number of submissions including chokes, knee bars, and arm bars like the one described below.

Opposite Side Arm Bar

This tactical option for the knee-in-the-belly position requires that you control your opponent's outside arm. In this case you will slip your left knee into his belly and cup his right arm inside your left. (Figure 8-18) Then step around and fall back to capture the arm bar. (Figure 8-19)

KNEE-IN-THE-BELLY BOTTOM WITH THE GI

If your opponent gets you under side control, he will likely go for a knee-in-the-belly position. Remember, your opponent will earn points just for placing his knee in your belly. This position is a particularly uncomfortable one to be under. You will also be at risk for a wide variety of submissions if your opponent gets you into this position. Your primary goal, therefore, is to prevent your opponent from getting you under knee-in-the-belly control. Failing that, you can attempt to escape by reaching under his shin as described below.

Core Technique: Reach Under Shin to Escape

If your opponent gets past your defenses and places his knee in your belly, you must remain calm. It is difficult not to panic from the pressure, but you must stay cool. Control your

Figure 8-18. Slip your knee into his belly and cup his arm.

Figure 8-19. Capturing the arm bar.

Figure 8-20. Keep your elbows in when your opponent assumes knee-in-the-belly control.

Knee-in-the-Belly   145

Figure 8-21. Reach under your opponent's left leg with your left arm and grab his belt. Push on his chest with your right hand.

Figure 8-22. Roll your opponent over and gain side control.

breathing. When you see an opportunity, you can escape by following the steps shown in Figures 8-20 through 8-22.

While there are other techniques for escaping the knee-in-the-belly position, the best course is to prevent it. Keep your opponent from getting this position by blocking his knee with your elbow and your knee. Turn toward your opponent and push on his hips. You can also use your knee to rake your opponent's knee away if he comes close to sinking the knee-in-the-belly position. There is no tactical option for this technique because the objective is to avoid getting put in this position in the first place.

KNEE-IN-THE-BELLY BOTTOM WITHOUT THE GI

Your opponent will earn points for placing his knee in your belly so do all that you can to avoid this situation. If it happens, avoid the temptation of exposing your arms by flailing or pushing wildly against your opponent's legs. Use caution and escape to your knees as shown below.

Core Technique: Escape to Knees

Follow the steps in Figures 8-23 through 8-25 to escape from knee-in-the-belly control.

Remember not to panic. Wait for an opening before attempting this or any knee-in-the-

Figure 8-23. Place your hands on your opponent's hip and knee and push your hips away from him.

Figure 8-24. Turn to your knees and grab your opponent's right leg for a single-leg takedown.

Figure 8-25. Take your opponent down and assume north-to-south control.

belly escape and your chances of getting free will be much greater.

Tactical Option

It is possible, although quite difficult, to submit an opponent that has you under knee-in-the-belly control. One example, the knee-bar counterattack, is described next.

Knee-Bar Counterattack

When your opponent has you under knee-in-the-belly control, turn toward him and push. Target your push against your opponent's knee and hips. Then immediately swing your left leg over your opponent's head and capture the leg lock. (Figure 8-26)

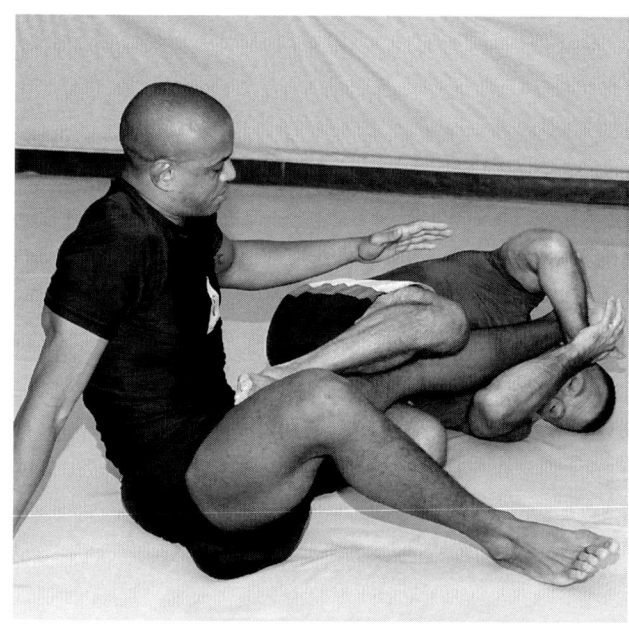

Figure 8-26. Executing the knee-bar counterattack.

Figure 8-27. Defend the punch by controlling your opponent's arms.

Figure 8-28. Push your opponent's right leg downward with your right leg and trap it between your thighs.

Figure 8-29. Move your hips to the right and move your body out from under your opponent's. Reach over your opponent's back as you slide out.

Figure 8-30. Climb onto and take your opponent's back.

KNEE-IN-THE-BELLY BOTTOM FOR NHB

In an NHB match you have an additional worry if your opponent puts you under knee-in-the-belly control—he can hit you.

Figure 8-31. Push against your opponent's knees as you move your hips to the side.

Figure 8-32. Swing your legs forward and trap him in your open guard.

Core Technique: Under-Ankle Push Escape

Before you can execute this or any knee-in-the-belly defense in an NHB fight, you must defend against punches. Follow the steps in Figures 8-27 through 8-30 to execute an under-ankle push escape while defending against strikes.

Tactical Option

Most of the knee-in-the-belly escape techniques require you to use your arms. You must keep in mind that your opponent knows this. Your opponent's strategy for putting you under knee-in-the-belly control is to cause you so much discomfort that you will expose your arms. When you are ready to attempt an escape, you should move quickly to minimize the exposure of your arms to attack.

Hip Escape

Place both of your hands on your opponent's knee. Push against your opponent's knee and simultaneously move your hips to your left. (Figure 8-31) Swing your legs forward and contain your opponent within your open guard. (Figure 8-32)

STRATEGIES FOR KNEE-IN-THE-BELLY CONTROL

Following are strategies for confronting each of the four fighter types—aggressive, deceptive, defensive, and interceptive—in the knee-in-the-belly control condition. As you know, no single strategy is best. Each fighter must devise his own strategy. Build your strategies to play on your strengths and take advantage of your opponent's weaknesses.

Fighting an Aggressive Opponent

When fighting an aggressive opponent, you should expect a major struggle the moment that you place your knee in his belly. Maintain a solid position to avoid being overturned within the first seconds. Use your grips, or hand placements, to add control. A deceptive strategy works well against this type of fighter in this condition. Use the knee-in-the-belly control position to set up fakes followed by quick attack combinations.

When an aggressive fighter has you under knee-in-the-belly control, you should expect attacks to your neck, arms, and legs. Defend these attacks and work to free yourself using the escape techniques taught in this chapter. Do not allow the aggressive fighter to mount.

Fighting a Deceptive Opponent

Deceptive fighters love the knee-in-the-belly position because it affords the maximum number of attack options. Once your opponent gets his knee in your belly, attack options for choking, arm bars, leg bars, and ankle locks are instantly available to him. Your best option is to keep your arms tight and work aggressively to create space and escape.

A deceptive opponent will likely try to escape the knee in the belly in a way that results in an advantage. This type of fighter is likely to fake one type of escape and go for another. He may attempt a submission from the bottom. Attack quickly and aggressively to keep him off plan. Make your opponent play your way.

Fighting a Defensive Opponent

A deceptive strategy works well against a defensive fighter under knee-in-the-belly control. Defensive fighters are notoriously calm when on the bottom. You can use the knee-in-the-belly to shake your defensive opponent loose. Attack him with a series of double and triple submission attempts. Force your opponent to open up. Switch from neck to arm to leg attacks to mix things up.

Don't expect a defensive fighter to stay in the knee-in-the-belly position on top for very long. This position is typically less secure than the side mount or the mount. Expect your defensive opponent to attempt a mount or fall back to the side mount. Plan your escape to take advantage of space created when he makes this move.

Fighting an Interceptive Opponent

One approach that works well with an interceptive opponent is to be defensive with him at first, and then switch to interceptive mode.

An interceptive fighter will always be planning ways to reverse a bad situation in a way that brings him advantage. He might, for example, allow an opening for you to mount while planning a swift escape from that position. You must press the fight aggressively and force the interceptive fighter off his game. Mount when and if you want to. Attack constantly to keep him confused and on the run.

An interceptive fighter will likely bait you into thinking that you can escape from under his knee-in-the-belly control position. When you make your escape attempt, he will attempt a submission. To avoid this trap, you must take the initiative. Act aggressively to create an escape opening. Break your opponent's balance and escape in a direction that he does not expect.

INTERVIEW: ABDUL MUTAKABBIR ON STRATEGY

The following interview contains the strategy used by Alliance black-belt instructor Abdul Mutakabbir, who began his study of Brazilian jiu-jitsu under Professor Cavalcanti when he was in his late forties. Mutakabbir is a lifelong martial artist with a stellar record. Highlights of his accomplishments in competition include: Tri-Area Semipro Grand Champion, 1985; Harlem Goju Champion, 1984 and 1985; New York Golden Cup Champion 1985; and Ying Yee Peter Urban Cup Invitational Karate Grand Champion from 1977 to 1988. Mutakabbir was undefeated for 10 consecutive years as a Triple Crown competitor in the Martial Arts/Karate Circuit.

Figure 8-33. Abdul Mutakabbir with some of his trophies.

Abdul Mutakabbir is the founder and director of the SWAM Academy of Modern Martial Arts. He is also the owner of Hail/Swam Security Services and is responsible for protecting many of the world's high-profile actors, actresses, musicians, and diplomats. Mutakabbir's unique perspective on strategy follows.

Question: How old were you when you started training in martial arts?

Mutakabbir: For the first three years I taught myself. Then I started to study formally at 13.

Q: Where did you grow up?

Mutakabbir: New York City. Harlem.

Q: What style did you start with?

Mutakabbir: I studied karate first, then kung-fu and Japanese jiu-jitsu. I studied kung-fu for over 20 years. Currently, I hold nine black belts. My newest black belt is in Brazilian jiu-jitsu. I am working on a 10th black belt in Aikido.

Q: With so many black belts, why did you decide to study Brazilian jiu-jitsu?

Mutakabbir: I consider myself to be an archaeologist of the martial arts. I love the martial arts and I like to probe deep into its circles of mystery. Brazilian jiu-jitsu held a mystique for me. It was very different from the other styles that I knew, so it was a challenge. I started training in Brazilian jiu-jitsu at the age of 44, ten years ago.

At that time I was extremely comfortable with the stand-up world and the weaponry world. I wanted to improve my ground game.

Q: Worlds?

Mutakabbir: I like to call them the three worlds of combat: weaponry, combat, and the ground. I met a gentleman who knew some jiu-jitsu. I thought that he studied the same jiu-jitsu that I studied. We began to spar one day and I took him to the ground. I let him back up. He said, no, let's finish on the ground. He put me in arm bars, leg locks, triangles, I said, "Man, what is that?" So I became aware of Brazilian jiu-jitsu and was very enthusiastic about learning it. I worked out with this gentleman for some time, maybe six months. Then one day I saw an ad for Brazilian jiu-jitsu in Atlanta. I started training with Professor Jacare and have been learning from him ever since.

Q: What is your general recommendation for approaching a violent confrontation?

Mutakabbir: I tell my students that there are three different ways, or concepts, for training. One is to train for reality, two is to train for sport, and three is to train for hobby. These are the three mentalities that people can approach the martial arts with. Most people today are confused; they think sport is reality. It is not. On the street there are no rules. On the street there is survival and that's it.

I always teach my students that violence is strictly forbidden except in the instance of legitimate self-defense. I teach them that they must have the intelligence to be able to handle any type of derogatory remark that is made against them. I teach them that once an attacker puts his hands on them in a violent manner, they have a God-given right to defend themselves.

My philosophy is that I always come in peace but I am always prepared to take you to pieces. I train like a warrior and I pay attention like a soldier. That is the philosophy of the SWAM. That is what the SWAM acronym means—Spiritual Warriors Against Madness. That means mental madness and people that behave like beasts in human form. We live in a very volatile society. Everybody is not nice and civilized like we are.

When we leave our homes and go out on the streets, sometimes it can come down to do or die. I have a family that I love very much and I want to go back home to them so I have to be prepared. Coming up in New York City, in a very hostile area, I always trained my art in the most real way possible. That is why my system is called Getto Ryu jiu-jitsu—that means whatever works. It is a street fighting art. Reality fighting.

Q: Reality fighting?

Mutakabbir: When I say reality fighting, it means anything can happen. There is no such thing as going to an arm bar or an ankle lock. You are not going to be going through all those types of changes in a street situation. God forbid, if I get into a situation on the street, I am going to do whatever I can do to prevail. I will do what works that is as simple, as effective, and as inconspicuous as possible.

Q: Inconspicuous?

Mutakabbir: Understand that it doesn't matter who starts a fight—if the authorities come to the scene, you will both be incarcerated. I am a security consultant for many diplomats from different countries, high-profile movie stars, and individuals from the music world. I teach my people that you have to be inconspicuous, that you have to deal with a threat situation as discreetly as possible. Whether by yourself or in the service of a client, you do not want an audience. You have to make things as effective and as invisible as possible.

Q: How should you prepare for a tournament?

Mutakabbir: It is like this: Before you have a physical technique, you must have a mental and spiritual technique; you need a psych game. If you think that you are going to lose, you have already lost. Before you walk into the competition you must be psyched up. Your spirit must be on a very high level. Your confidence must be at a high level. You must condition yourself psychologically as well as physically. The mental and spiritual part of the game is more than half of the fight.

Q: Do you need a lot of techniques to be a champion?

Mutakabbir: You can win with just a few basic moves if you perfect them and condition yourself mentally and physically. You can defeat a person who has a thousand techniques who is not in condition and does not have confidence in himself.

Too much technique can become confusing. It can blind you. Look at Professor Cavalcanti, for example. His game is focused on applying the basics. He doesn't do a lot of flamboyant stuff. Look at Roberto Traven—he fights the same way.

Q: So your approach is to keep it simple and use what works?

Mutakabbir: My game is to relax the body and calm the mind. This allows me to see things before they happen. There is a difference in relaxation and calmness. Calmness belongs to the mind. Relaxation is of the body. I always pray before I begin a match with anyone in the school. I pray that I don't get hurt and that I don't hurt others. I put my mind in a state of fun. These are my brethren. I am not trying to kill them; they are not trying to kill me.

My whole approach is nonconfrontational. This is the reality that I am looking for in the martial arts to keep me sane in an insane world. That is why I try to be the first one that greets everyone that I see at the school. My thing is to be more humble than those around me. I am like an uncle in the school. I have an obligation to set an example. It is my duty to do that. We are a family.

Q: When you were competing, did you hold this peaceful concept or did you approach it differently?

Mutakabbir: I used the same approach in competition. I always approach things spiritually first. I got that from Mohammad Ali—he inspired me. I was always careful not to hurt the people that I was competing against. I gave a lot of mercy in my matches. I didn't go overboard to hurt anybody.

Q: There is a difference in a martial artist and a fighter, isn't there?

Mutakabbir: Yes, there is. Martial art is an art that is conducted with the humane part of our mind. A fighter unleashes his individual energy from an animalist state of mind. All of us have the animal in us. We all have this beastlike quality. We have to govern it with our humane part. That is what makes us different from the beasts that walk the field. We have to make sure that we are always upright, not so much physically walking upright but mentally, we have to think upright. We have to be civilized.

Q: You are not talking about good and evil, you are talking about civilized versus uncivilized, right?

Mutakabbir: That is right.

Q: In a street confrontation, should you give way to the animal? Is this a time to unleash the beast within?

Mutakabbir: A street confrontation is totally different. Now we are talking about life or death. In this type of situation it may be necessary to let the beast off the chain completely. I am talking about a situation where someone is breaking into your house or about to do violence to your family, your friend, or to you.

Q: Then you have a personal code for releasing different levels of energy based on the situation?

Mutakabbir: Yes, based on the situation. That is the warriors' code, the way of the samurai. In the old days, the samurai—the real samurai, not the rogues—were some of the most peaceful people that there were. But once a samurai's sword was out of its scabbard, it meant the beast was released. When that sword was drawn, it was about life and death.

Q: The warrior poet?

Mutakabbir: That is right, and that is what I aspire to be. In my religion, the scholar is greater than the boxer. I want the scholar part of me to be much more brilliant than the warrior part of me. If you ask me what I want to be known for most, the sword or the pen, I will say the pen.

Q: OK, back to the sports world; when you go to a tournament and see that you are up against different types of fighters, some stronger, some faster, and so forth, do you approach each one differently?

Mutakabbir: Yes. You have to be like a chameleon; you have to adapt to the environment, to the person's energy. If, for example, you have an opponent who stays stationary all the time, then you have to move. You can't stand there with him or you are going to be in his game. If you are up against a person who moves around all the time, don't dance around him or you will be in his rhythm, his game. You have to break your opponent's game by doing something contrary to what he is used to. The different art forms that I have studied help me with this because they all have different patterns. I've learned that you can't be too structured and too rigid in one particular way.

It is just like communicating your message verbally; you can't think in just one way, or you become so narrow minded, so rigid, that your way is the only way and that is it. There are many roads, many different ways to approach an opponent, just as there are many different methods as far as talking to different people.

Q: Would you say that people fall into general groups? Commonalities of style?

Mutakabbir: Yes, absolutely. Jacare always teaches us not to be one-dimensional. This is his philosophy. Learn to fight on top and on the bottom because you are going to be up against someone who plays in your game or is going to try to take you out of your game. If you are not used to that other type of game, and it is foreign to you, then you are going to be in trouble. You won't know how to respond.

Q: How should you prepare for a tournament?

Mutakabbir: Let's say you are my tournament training partner. If I am working with you, I don't need to work the best parts of my game, I need to work the weakest parts of my game. I don't care if you tap me and you don't care if I tap you because you are my training partner. We are not competing against each other; we are trying to learn. We should try to perfect our weaknesses in training so there won't be any in the tournament.

Q: What advice do you have for young guys that want to learn BJJ and are looking for a good instructor?

Mutakabbir: Integrity. Look for an honorable person who has the spiritual qualities that are necessary for a leader. I don't care how good a person's technique is, that is the least important thing. You are giving part of your life to this person. This teacher is going to become a leader in your life.

Q: What should you watch out for?

Mutakabbir: Watch out for people that aggrandize themselves. Watch out for instructors who brag on their titles and abilities. Look out for teachers that hold themselves above everybody else and have to be addressed by flamboyant titles such as "grandmaster." At the first sign of this you know you are looking at a manipulator. A manipulative person is going to try to make you subservient to him. His whole thing is to take over your life. There are a lot of people like that in the martial arts.

You see, the bushido, the way of the warrior, is almost gone in the martial arts world. It has been replaced by the dollar bill. Brazilian jiu-jitsu is one of the last arts that is still teaching the warrior spirit. Look at the great warriors that are coming from Jacare like Fabio Gurgel and Roberto Traven. You see the humbleness in those guys. You don't see that much in a lot of the other arts.

Another thing to watch out for is people who have been teaching longer than they trained. You have instructors out there that were a student for three years and have been teaching for 20 years. This is bad.

Q: You are working on your 10th black belt. You have 40 black belts under you, but you are modeling being a perpetual learner, aren't you?

Mutakabbir: I am one who is seeking knowledge from cradle to grave. I am always training and learning. I do my kung-fu, my karate, my stand-up jiu-jitsu, my aikido, stick training, all of it. I am getting ready to start training in another art. I train seven hours a day.

Q: What are some of the highlights of your career?

Mutakabbir: My family is a martial arts family. My wife has been training for 26 years. All my sons have been training all of their lives. We make part of our living by teaching. The other part is the security consulting business. I do security work for big motion picture films. My company provided security for most of the major motion pictures that have been made in New York City in the last 10 to 12 years, including *Malcolm X, Godzilla, Men in Black* 1 and 2, *Stuart Little* 1 and 2, *Spider-Man* 1 and 2, *Carlito's Way, Red Heat*—it goes on and on. We have provided security services to many major stars, including actors Sean Connery, Harrison Ford, Robert DeNiro, Al Pacino, Denzel Washington, Wesley Snipes, Whoopi Goldberg, Brad Pitt, Meryl Streep, Ving Rhames, Robert Redford, Dustin Hoffman, and musician Teddy Riley.

Q: You do the security work yourself?

Mutakabbir: Yes. My crew and I do the work. For example, one of my clients right now is Adam Sandler. One of my black belts is with him every day.

Q: Anything else that you would like to say?

Mutakabbir: I trained with many different teachers in my life, 17 masters including Jacare Cavalcanti. I respect Jacare as a martial arts master and even more so as a human being. He is a concerned person. He is a good father figure for the young guys. He is an elder brother for the older students that are there. He is a great family person and an excellent teacher. You can see the result in the people he has trained. He is a great person and I am just happy to be one of his students and to be his friend.

Figure 8-34. Mutakabbir (left) and an associate protecting Meryl Streep.

Figure 8-35. Mutakabbir and an associate protecting actor Ving Rhames (center).

Chapter 9

Mount

The mount is defined as any position in which one fighter has both of his legs on either side of an opponent's torso. There are many variations on the mount, including the forward-facing low mount, the forward-facing high mount, the cross mount, and the "S" mount.

The mount is one of the most dominant positions in jiu-jitsu. In gi and no-gi matches, the mount position offers maximum control. Many attack options are available from the mount, and escape is always difficult. In NHB matches the mount is even more devastating because punches are so difficult to defend from this position.

This chapter contains techniques and tactical options for fighting in and against the mount. At the end of this chapter veteran Alliance jiu-jitsu competitor and NHB champion Ryan Ellison shares his strategy for victory on the mat and in the ring.

MOUNT TOP WITH THE GI

When you first assume a mounted control position, your opponent will likely try to escape before you solidify your position. For this reason, it is wise to begin in a low-mount position in which you keep your knees over your opponent's hips. Press your weight down onto your opponent's hips, lean forward, and extend your arms to establish balance and control.

Figure 9-1. Place your right foot under your opponent's left shoulder.

Figure 9-2. Capture your opponent's right arm; place your body weight over his hips.

Figure 9-3. Hold your opponent's right leg with your right arm as you sit back at a diagonal and execute the arm bar.

Core Technique: Arm Bar

Once stable in a low-mount position, move your knees forward. Drive them under your opponent's elbows. Execute an arm bar by following the steps in Figures 9-1 through 9-3.

Holding your opponent's leg as you execute the arm bar helps to keep him immobilized. This gives you added control and minimizes the chances that your opponent can escape.

Tactical Options

While the high-mounted position opens up the largest number of submission options, there are a number of attacks that can be done from the low-mounted position. One example is the sleeve choke described below.

Sleeve Choke

Stabilize your mounted position by lowering your weight onto your opponent's hips. Place your chest down and put your arms over your opponent's head. Reach under your opponent's neck with your right hand. Place your right palm into your left sleeve. Put your left hand over your opponent's neck and choke him out. (Figure 9-4)

The advantage of attacking from a low-mounted position is stability. It is very hard to overturn an opponent who has you locked down in a low mount.

Figure 9-4. Sleeve choke.

Figure 9-5. Knife-hand choke.

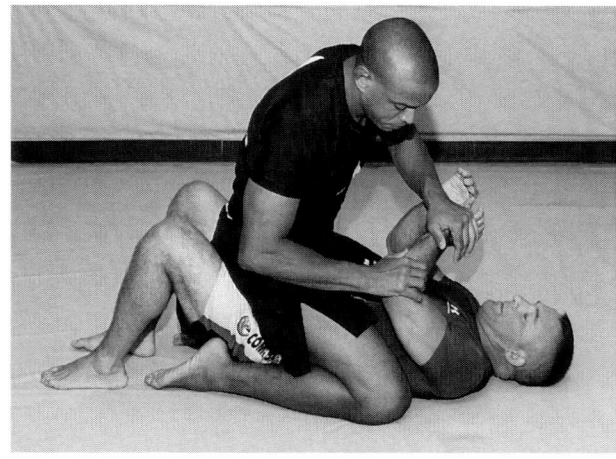

Figure 9-6. Control your opponent's left arm.

Figure 9-7. Press your opponent's left arm to the mat and assume a key-lock grip with your left hand holding his wrist.

Figure 9-8. Lift your opponent's elbow to execute the key-lock submission.

Knife-Hand Choke

From a high-mounted position, force your opponent to turn to his right side. You can force your opponent to turn by attacking his arm, or by wedging your knees under his shoulder and back. Once your opponent turns, place your left foot in his hip. Reach under your opponent's neck and grab his collar with your right hand. Put your left arm under his left arm and across his neck. Then execute the knife-hand-choke submission. (Figure 9-5)

MOUNT TOP WITHOUT THE GI

In order to hold an opponent under mount control, you must relax and flow with your opponent. Keep your center of gravity low and stick to your opponent much in the same way that you would ride a horse. When ready you can attempt any number of submissions such as the key-lock submission described below.

Core Technique: Key Lock

Applied correctly, the key lock (also called the Americana and the paint brush) puts serious joint-cracking pressure on the shoulder. The key lock is simple to execute and really difficult to defend. In the example shown in Figures 9-6 through 9-8, the key lock is described as if one were starting in a high-rid-

Figure 9-9. Frontal crank.

ing, straight-body mounted position and fighting with an opponent who has his arms bent and is prepared to defend a choke.

It is important to keep your weight down as you execute the key lock. Remember to pull your opponent's elbow downward as you lift up or you will not have sufficient leverage for a break.

Tactical Options

It is very important to keep your legs tight against your opponent when in the mount position. Your opponent will be watching for any gap in your position from which to gain leverage for an escape.

Frontal Crank

Stay in a low-mount position. Wrap your right arm around your opponent's neck. Place your right palm in your left elbow. Place your left hand on your opponent's head and execute the frontal crank. (Figure 9-9)

A crank, by definition, is an attack to the neck or other joint in which twisting or bending pressure is applied. A cranking submission may or may not have a choking element. Neck cranks are legal in most no-gi matches but usually are not allowed in gi matches.

Arm Bar

Assume a high-mount position by driving your knees forward and under your opponent's elbows. Isolate your opponent's right arm by attempting a key lock. When your opponent defends the key lock, capture his arm. Then step over your opponent's neck with your left leg. Sit back and execute the arm bar. (Figure 9-10)

Figure 9-10. Execute the arm bar.

MOUNT TOP FOR NHB

Most NHB fights are called by the official within seconds of one fighter mounting the other. It is extremely difficulty to defend punches and elbow strikes from underneath mount control. The "ground and pound" technique described here is therefore known as one of the truly terminal attacks of NHB fighting.

Core Technique: Ground and Pound

Ground and pound attacks are often done from a high-riding, straight-body mounted control position. Follow these procedures to execute this devastating attack.

Clear your opponent's arms out of the way and rain punches into his face. (Figure 9-11) You can use elbow strikes, forearm strikes, and a variety of punches, and that's about all there is to the ground and pound from the mount technique. Take care not to seriously injure or kill your opponent as this attack has the potential of doing enormous damage. You are responsible.

Tactical Options

Your opponent must expose his arms in order to defend against your punches. This act of defending will expose your opponent to a number of arm-submission attack options, including the arm bar and the key lock.

Arm Bar

Under the rare circumstances in which punches don't do the trick, you can isolate one arm and execute an arm bar. (Figure 9-12) This option is commonly taken in gi and no-gi matches but is seldom used by NHB fighters because going for the arm bar means giving up the supremely dominant mount position.

Figure 9-12. Arm bar.

Figure 9-11. Ground and pound.

Figure 9-13. Key lock.

Figure 9-14. Hold your opponent's left arm and place your right foot outside of his left ankle.

Figure 9-15. Lift your hips and roll to your right.

Figure 9-16. Land in your opponent's closed guard.

Key Lock

If your opponent is adept at deflecting punches and does not offer an arm bar opportunity, you can attack him with a key lock. (Figure 9-13) Be sure to keep your hips down and your center of gravity low as you execute this submission; otherwise, your opponent may be able to sweep you over.

MOUNT BOTTOM WITH THE GI

Being under the mount is tough in gi and no-gi matches, but the mount is not the show-stopper that it is in NHB fights. In fact, some jiu-jitsu grapplers would rather defend against the mount than defend against side control or back control. Keep your cool and you can escape from the mount by using the techniques described here.

Figure 9-17. Place both hands on your opponent's left knee and push yourself away..

Figure 9-18. Escape to the full guard.

Core Technique: Trap-and-Roll Escape

Execute the trap-and-roll escape (also called the umpa) by following the steps in Figures 9-14 though 9-16.

Your odds of escaping with the trap-and-roll technique are much greater if you catch your opponent off guard or off balance. You can set him up by faking a move in one direction, then going for it in the other. You can also wait until you see an opening and go for the escape in a swift, surprising motion.

Tactical Options

If your opponent is stronger or heavier than you, it will be more difficult for you to escape with a trap-and-roll technique. You can use leverage from your hips and elbows to wedge out space to escape as described next.

Elbow Escape

Keep your arms folded against your chest. Turn to your right and wedge your right elbow against your opponent's left knee. Shrimp backward a bit, then place both hands on your opponent's left knee and push yourself away. (Figure 9-17) Turn your hips to your left and establish a half-guard position. Repeat the motion to free your leg and escape to the full guard. (Figure 9-18)

Figure 9-19. Press upward on your opponent to gain space.

Figure 9-20. Swing your left leg over your opponent's thigh as you push him away.

Figure 9-21. Trap your opponent's ankle and extend your body to execute the submission.

Figure 9-21a. An alternate view.

MOUNT BOTTOM WITHOUT THE GI

Escapes from under mount control are limited. You can roll your opponent over, use your elbows to pry yourself free, or you can wiggle out the back door. You can also undertake an escape that terminates in a submission as in the example described here.

Core Technique:
Escape to Ankle-Lock Counterattack

Follow the steps in Figures 9-19 through 9-21 to escape from under mount control and engage an ankle-lock counterattack.

Tactical Options

Escapes from under mount control in a no-gi match vary only in that you have no fabric to grab. Substitute hooking and clasping positions for gi grips as explained in the tactical option that follows.

Figure 9-22. Elbow escape.

Figure 9-23. Defend with your arms to avoid getting punched.

Elbow Escape to the Full Guard

Use your elbows to press against your opponent's right knee. Turn your hips to the right and pull your left leg over your opponent's right. (Figure 9-22) Push downward on your opponent's hips and pull your right leg free. Put your opponent into your full guard.

MOUNT BOTTOM FOR NHB

If you find yourself under mount control in an NHB match, you must first control your opponent's arms to avoid being punched. You must also resist the temptation to escape the punches by turning to your stomach. If you turn, you will give up your back and likely become victim to the rear naked choke.

Figure 9-24. Lift your hips and push with your arms to escape the mount.

Figure 9-25. Wrap your right arm around your opponent's left ankle.

Figure 9-26. Trap your opponent's left leg between your legs and execute the heel hook.

Core Technique: Escape to Heel Hook

Escape from under mounted control by following the steps in Figures 9-23 and 9-24. Submit your opponent with a heel hook as described in Figures 9-25 and 9-26.

Tactical Option

You can escape from mount control in an NHB fight if you keep your head. Your best two options are the trap-and-roll technique and the elbow leverage escape described next.

Elbow Leverage Escape

Protect yourself from punches by controlling your opponent's arms. Turn your hips to the side and use your elbow to pry against your opponent's knee. (Figure 9-27) Shift your hips to the other side and recompose the open guard.

Figure 9-27. Elbow leverage escape.

STRATEGIES FOR THE MOUNT

Following are strategies for confronting each of the four fighter types—aggressive, deceptive, defensive, and interceptive—in the mount condition. Use these examples as a baseline from which to formulate your own strategy. Remember to emphasize your strengths and minimize your weaknesses when devising your fight game strategy.

Fighting an Aggressive Opponent

Start low and keep your hips down when you are mounted on top of an aggressive fighter. Work your way to a high-mount position with care. Expect bold escape attempts. Do not let him get control of your arms. Set up your attacks methodically. Take your time and keep your position solid.

When under the mount of an aggressive fighter, you can expect to be assaulted with vigor. Do everything you can to protect yourself but move quickly to escape. Use deceptive actions to create space and get away. Take advantage of any openings and bolt to freedom using the techniques described in this chapter.

Fighting a Deceptive Opponent

When you have a deceptive opponent under mount control, you can prevail with an aggressive strategy. Attack relentlessly and do not allow your opponent to mount an escape attempt.

When you find yourself under the mount of a deceptive fighter, one of your best strategic approaches is to use a deceptive style in return—fight fire with fire. Set up your escape quickly and deceptively. Make your move on your terms.

Fighting a Defensive Opponent

When you mount a defensive opponent, expect him to be extremely difficult to submit. Use an interceptive strategy to "invite" him to attempt an escape and provide an opening for attack in the process.

A truly defensive fighter is unlikely to be comfortable in the mount position. Defensive fighters are most comfortable on their backs. If you roll a defensive fighter over, you will land in his closed guard. This is "home" for the defensive fighter so you don't want to go there if you can avoid it. Instead of rolling him over, use your elbows to wedge your way into the half guard. Then sweep your opponent over and go on top.

Fighting an Interceptive Opponent

An interceptive fighter under mount control is likely to make a controlled effort at escape. Don't expect him to panic. Odds are the interceptive fighter will wait for you to make a move and try to escape via any opportunity that you provide. A deceptive strategy can work well in this case. Make your opponent think that you are going for one thing then change up and go for another. Keep him on the run until you sink a submission.

An interceptive fighter will likely offer you chances to escape then turn the tables on you when you try. Act aggressively to break free. Do not let him set up. Create your own space and use the techniques in this chapter to escape.

INTERVIEW:
RYAN ELLISON ON STRATEGY

Ryan Ellison is a veteran jiu-jitsu competitor and champion NHB fighter. Ellison's gi and no-gi jiu-jitsu competition record includes first place GA State Grappling Championship, 2002; first place NAGA Pro Am of Grappling (Florida), 2005; third place Budweiser Jiu-Jitsu World Cup, 2004; first place Budweiser Jiu-Jitsu World Cup, 2004; first place GA State Grappling Championship, 2004. His NHB record is six wins and no losses.

Figure 9-28. Alliance NHB fighter Ryan Ellison (top) applying a submission attack.

The interview that follows contains the strategy that Ryan Ellison uses to prepare for gi, no-gi, and NHB fights.

Question: How far in advance of an NHB fight should you begin to prepare?

Ellison: Six weeks, assuming you already have a good foundation and your cardiovascular is pretty good, your endurance is pretty good, your strength pretty good, and you are not injured. With six weeks to work with, you can develop a training cycle that is not too short and not too long.

You will train for six weeks specifically to perform at your very best on the day of the fight. You want to time your training cycle to peak on the day of the competition. You don't want to have your best day in the gym.

The fight is never won on fight night. It is won six weeks before. If you have two guys equal in strength, technique, and talent, it is the guy that did what he was supposed to do before the fight that I will put my money on.

Q: What does it really mean to "overtrain?"

Ellison: Overtraining and undertraining are the same, because you will be out of shape either way. If you prepare yourself correctly and time the performance cycle just right, you will enter the ring at a point where you have the ability to carry the fight beyond your normal capacity.

That is why you need a full six weeks if you can get it. For example, if you tried to prepare for a fight in three weeks, you would have to jam in so much training in that short time that you nearly kill yourself, and by fight night you wouldn't have the ability to do anything. You would be weak. You would be overtrained.

Figure 9-29. Ryan Ellison (center).

Q: How do you regulate your training over the six weeks to be at your best on fight night?

Ellison: I schedule everything and put it in

writing. It is important to have a written schedule because it is hard to keep up with it otherwise. You have to train on Monday in a precise way so you can come back and train well on Tuesday, same on Wednesday, Thursday, and Friday, and you have to plan days for rest. If you don't write things down and you just have your training plan in your mind, you can easily blow an entire day or week.

Q: What does your training week look like?

Ellison: I train twice a day, five days a week. I don't train both sessions as hard as I can. If I did that, by Wednesday I will be worthless and by Friday I will be overtrained. If I've overtrained by Friday, I won't have enough recovery time to be ready to return on Monday.

I might, for example, train Muay Thai hard in the morning and jiu-jitsu lighter in the evening. Then the next day, alternate and train Muay Thai lighter and jiu-jitsu very hard. My goal is to avoid neglecting any skill area and to avoid overemphasizing any skill area.

Q: Do you tweak your schedule as you go along and try to make it better?

Ellison: Your training schedule is built on a combination of two things: Your availability to train and the availability of the people that are training you. Sometimes there are communication issues, scheduling conflicts, you get sick or hurt, and you have to adapt.

Q: How do you know that you are at your peak, that you are ready for the fight?

Ellison: You feel it when you are ready. You just know that you are ready. Your body becomes so conditioned that you can fight no matter what happens to you. One time I was in an MMA match and got kicked in the head and almost knocked out, but my body was so conditioned that I continued to fight and won the match. I have no recollection of the fight. Of course I watched the video, but I don't remember any of it. It was the fact that I had trained so hard for that fight that enabled my body to continue when I was practically knocked out. That is why I say the fight is never won on fight night—it is won by who trained harder and who prepared himself better. It is like anything else in life. If you are in school and you don't go to class for six weeks, then you show up on the last day to take the final, you are going to fail. But if you were there every day and did the homework and studied hard, you will pass the final.

Q: What is the secret of your training program?

Ellison: It is not a secret. It is a matter of dedication. Training for six weeks for a no-holds fight is tough for many reasons. Partly because you take yourself out of your element and train in ways that are intentionally uncomfortable for you. You have to train in all kinds of situations where you are at a disadvantage. To do this you must accept the fact that you are going to have a tough training day every day and that you are going to get spanked a lot. It is very humbling to be a fighter. You have to put your ego aside.

Q: So your training for NHB should be scheduled to the minute?

Ellison: It does not have to be so detailed. Basically I am going to work BJJ, Muay Thai, or wrestling. I work Monday through Friday and take Saturday and Sunday off.

Q: You don't train at all on the weekend?

Ellison: No, because I will have gone two and one-half hours in the morning and two and one-half hours at night for five days in a row. So by the time I wake up on Saturday, I hurt. I am tired.

Q: Rest is part of the plan?

Ellison: I fully believe rest is one of the most neglected parts of training. I know guys that train and train and then they get to the fight and they feel week and drained. Then they complain, "I trained so hard, why did I feel so weak? Why did I lose?" I say it is good to train hard but your body has to rest. Over training is just as bad as under training.

Q: Lots of trainers and top athletes from different sports recommend training in six-week cycles. Is there something magical about the six weeks?

Ellison: I think six weeks is about the right amount of time for your body to adapt for the rigors of the ring. A lot of sports doctors write about anatomical adaptation. It is all about adapting your body to the physical constraints of the event. You have to prepare yourself physically and mentally. It takes your body at least three weeks just to get used to the extra workload. You can't wake up in the morning and go and run a 26-mile marathon if you haven't been training. You just can't do it. It takes time for your body to adapt.

Q: Can you describe what you experience over the six-week cycle?

Ellison: The first two weeks you are really sore and you will feel pretty low. During the third week you start to get stronger and feel better. At this point you can start to add to your workload. At six weeks you will be at or near your peak and you will also be close to the other side of the hill, the drop-off point.

Q: Is there always a drop after six weeks?

Ellison: You are traveling up this incline, your workload is constantly escalating, for some people it may be four weeks, maybe six weeks, maybe eight, but there always is a peak and a fall. The trick is to peak on the day of the fight.

Q: Why do you have to have a fall-off? Why can't you just keep going up in performance?

Ellison: You can push beyond, but when you push beyond your limits, you run a risk of burning your mind. With this intense training like this you are constantly working off of your adrenal glands. You can burn these adrenal glands. I have done this, trained and trained and not allowed myself to rest. I got to the point where I didn't get excited about anything. I become like a drone.

When you overtrain to this extent it feels kind of like you are watching life through a window. Nothing really matters. You don't find joy. You don't get excited anymore because your mind just can't process anything else. Your muscles start to ache. If you don't take care of your body, your body will break.

Q: What do you do in the days just after a fight?

Ellison: When you commit to a six-week training cycle for a no-holds-barred fight, you limit yourself on what you can do. You have to put your personal life on hold for six weeks. Think about it: You are training six hours a day, so you are not going out at night. By the weekend you are beat up and recovering. When 9:00 PM rolls around on Saturday night you are already asleep, not from choice but from utter fatigue. After the fight I like to take a week or two off just to rest. I reflect on the fight. I think about ways to fix things that didn't go well. I just basically rest and enjoy life for a while.

Q: Do you train at all during this week or two of recovery time?

Ellison: I walk and jog a little during recovery, but I do nothing that will push my body. Remember you just put yourself through six weeks of torture. Your body needs to heal. When you have recovered you can start to cycle up again.

Q: How does one six-week performance cycle fit with the next?

Ellison: We are talking about a curve that is going to go up and down over time. We can look at this curve as performance. If we train properly, the curve will rise; but after the six weeks or so when you hit your peak, if you keep pushing your performance will take a plunge. Push beyond a certain point and your performance will get lower even if you work harder.

Q: What happens to your performance over the course of several cycles?

Ellison: The six-week cycles are not taken in equal parts. It is not six weeks on and six weeks off. You go six weeks on and one or two weeks off. So when you return to a new six-week cycle after resting, you will have only lost 10 or 15 percent, not 100 percent of what you did at your peak. You will start back from a higher base point so the new six-week cycle will be a little easier to endure. With each cycle you can train a little harder and get to an even higher performance peak. Of course, if you were to take a long break, say a few months, you would lose ground.

Q: So your base is elevated over time and your performance peaks get higher and higher?

Ellison: Yes.

Q: If you know who your opponent will be in an NHB match, what do you do to get ready for him?

Ellison: You try to learn as much about your opponent as you can. Sometimes you will know a lot, sometimes a little, and sometimes you won't know anything about him at all. Even in the best case your information will be limited. It is not like you can go and train with the guy beforehand. You try to estimate what he will be like based on what you know.

I start with physical characteristics: Is he tall or short, heavy or light? Does he have a long reach, short reach, and so on. I do what I can to find out what his skills are. I try to determine if he likes to punch, likes to wrestle, likes to be on top, on bottom, is tricky or not, and so on. Then I try to find training partners with similar body type, style, and skill characteristics.

Q: What is your strategy for managing ring space?

Ellison: I don't want to charge and I don't want to be charged. I want to get into the center of the ring and show that I am not going to give any of my space. I have my boundaries of where I am going to go and not going to go. I want to play my game in the fight.

Q: You said you want to play your game. What are some of the common "games" that fighters have?

Ellison: Everyone has a game. Your game is doing the things that you do well and staying away from positions that you know can hurt you.

Q: Let's say you were in a jiu-jitsu match and you don't know who your opponent will be. You get on the mat and you realize that you are up against a guy that is very aggressive, and bigger and a lot stronger than you are. You see that he is pressing hard to play a top game. How would you approach this opponent?

Ellison: I like to always apply pressure. No matter if I am on defense or offense and no matter how aggressive my opponent.

Q: Are the aggressive guys the most dangerous?

Ellison: The most dangerous guys are the ones that are cautious and watch you and capitalize on your mistakes. For me, the easy ones are the aggressive guys that keep charging at me the same way.

When I have an opponent that keeps charging at me like a bull trying to take me down, then I know what he is after. Once I know what he is after, it is not hard for me to defend. I have a lot of confidence in my cardio so I will let the guy will wear himself down. After he tries for seven to ten attacks and starts to slow down, I will take him down.

I have faced bunches of guys that only do one thing, that are limited to one thing. It is easy to defend something that you know is coming. It is impossible to defend something that you don't see coming. That is why the cautious fighters are more dangerous. In MMA it is always the punch that you don't see that can knock you out—the ones you see, you can handle. It is the same in jiu-jitsu: You can defend the arm bar that you see coming, but you can't defend the choke that you don't see coming.

Q: So when you are up against an aggressive opponent, you try to wear him down first, you never go head-to-head with him?

Ellison: Yes, but there are times when you have to go head-to-head like two charging rams. For instance, when the score is zero to zero with one minute left. In this case, whoever gets the takedown, or is perceived to try to go for the takedown the most, could win. In this situation you have no choice. You have to try as hard and as fast as you can to make a point or an advantage.

Q: You adapt your game to the circumstances of the match?

Ellison: There are variables that are going to change the way you will react and your opponent will react. The story can change in the middle of the match because you could be down or up by points. Take single elimination jiu-jitsu, for example. In most matches it is free play for the first few minutes but after the halfway marker hits, the guy who is up on points is going to slow down, save energy, and wait and see what his opponent does. The guy who is winning knows he is going to have another fight, so he might switch from being very aggressive to very defensive. The guy who is behind has nothing to lose so he will take risks and go all out. So the way that you fight changes depending on the score of the match that you are in and the kind of elimination.

Q: How does a fighter's game develop?

Ellison: Every fighter has a game, and I think the game develops from the moment you first start training in jiu-jitsu. For example, you have guys who are stronger and they quickly develop a top game. The guys who are weaker or not as coordinated get pushed down so they tend to develop the bottom game more. This is a thing that stays with people.

As you get better and move up in belt progression, it is important to expand your skills. If you are a top player, you should learn to work the defensive game. If you have a defensive game, you need to learn to attack more. You can't just be defensive when you are losing by two points. You have to change your game with the direction of how the match is going.

Q: What if you are up against an opponent who is very defensive and cautious?

Ellison: You have to force a defensive fighter to change his game. It is hard to do anything to someone that is not going to attempt any offense at all, because he never opens up. But it is also hard for him to score points. If he won't open up, you don't have to worry about him trying to pass your guard, and you don't have to worry about him trying to submit you. If he is the kind of guy who is defensive until you make a mistake and counterattacks then, you have to be much more cautious. You can't just go wide open.

Q: OK, how do you force a defensive fighter to change his game?

Ellison: Let's say he is really defensive. What you can do is force that guy to move by putting him under a lot of pressure. You can draw him out by getting ahead by two points or by an advantage. At this point he has to work out of the backstretch: It is not like he can just sit and wait for you to move.

Q: How do you diagnose an opponent when you are in the ring?

Ellison: It is not like they are trying to hide anything from me. They are either really good or not; they like to play to their guard or they don't. Most guys that you face will give you a sign of what they are good at. They might jump to the guard, try to throw you; they tip their hand. You can't allow yourself to get so caught up in your opponent's game and forget what you are trying to do.

I train a lot of wrestling, Muay Thai, and judo. I know by looking at someone whether or not he is good at stand-up. I can tell a lot by the way he stands, the way he walks, the way he goes to grab me. I can tell if he is a good boxer by the way he holds his hands and walks around the ring. I know that if he crosses his feet or is shaky on his feet that he is weak at stand-up.

You have to probe your opponent. I have faced a lot of guys with really good guards and I have tried to pass one way three or four times without success and then tried the same pass on opposite side and it was easy. It is not about just running through people, everyone gives you some way you can beat them; you just have to find it.

Q: What is your game?

My game is to pressure my opponent at all times. My game is to put my opponent in uncomfortable positions by using my body weight or using the right leverage that takes his leverage away. I like to apply pressure on my opponent until he is stuck in a spot that is uncomfortable. I press him into a corner where he can't do anything without making a mistake.

I apply pressure all the time, always, no matter what, whether it is defensive pressure or offensive pressure. Pressure is a word that I use to describe a lot of things, like how much weight I am putting on my opponent, how well I am defending, how well I am attacking, and in what way I am forcing my opponent to move. Once he moves he is committed and then I take advantage.

Q: Would you say that the majority of your opponents try to play their normal game all the time no matter what or that they vary their game based on what happens?

Ellison: In the beginning they will try to play their game. A lot of guys will change because the points change. They will try to tip the scales to their advantage.

Q: Do you ever try to do things specifically to take advantage of a particular guy's game?

Ellison: I fought a really tough guy at a BJJ match in Florida. I watched his matches and saw that he was a phenomenal wrestler. He took everyone down like it was free. But I saw that when he took people down he left his head

Figure 9-30. Ryan Ellison in NHB competition.

out a little. So I planned to let him take me down and go for the guillotine as a counterattack. It worked. I caught him in a guillotine the first time, but we rolled out of bounds and he got out. He was so confident that he tried to take me down again, and I caught him in the guillotine again and won the match that way.

I try to go after the places where my opponent is weakest. When I am up against a guy that I know will try to jump to his closed guard right away, I sometimes jump to my guard first. If I am facing a guy with a great open guard, I don't walk over and give him my sleeves and collar so he can play the best open guard game he can. I make him reach for it. I force him to make mistakes. I make him come out of his element.

Chapter 10

Back

The back control position can be described as any condition in which one fighter is riding on the other fighter's back. The attacking fighter can be on top, underneath, or to the side of his opponent. The back can also be attacked if an opponent is standing or on the floor balled up in a turtle position.

Back control is greatly enhanced by placing of the hooks by the attacking fighter. "The hooks" refers to the placement of the feet on the inside of the opponent's thighs. The hooking feet of the attacker must be high on the opponent's thighs, near his groin.

This chapter contains techniques and tactical options for fighting from back control and for escaping from back control. The last part of this chapter contains an interview on strategy with Alliance black belt Fernando Gurgel.

BACK TOP WITH THE GI

The turtle position is a defensive position. It is formed when the defending fighter has his knees and elbows on the floor. Fighters use the turtle to try to prevent their opponent from sinking the hooks and gaining total back control. It is not always necessary, however, to sink the hooks to submit an opponent from the back. This can be seen in the description of the clock choke shown below.

Figure 10-1. Put your weight on your opponent's shoulders and hold his right collar with your right hand.

173

Figure 10-2. Control your opponent's left wrist and walk forward to execute the clock choke.

Core Technique: Clock Choke

If your opponent goes to a turtle position, submit him with a clock choke. Follow the steps in Figures 10-1 and 10-2 to execute.

To make the clock choke work you must keep your weight on your opponent's shoulder at all times. Don't lean too far over or your opponent will sweep you over.

Tactical Options

If you are not able to capture a clock choke against an opponent who is in the turtle position, you can use your positional advantage to sink your hooks. When you have both hooks in place, proceed with a rear naked choke as shown below.

Rear Naked Choke

Assume control of your opponent's back. Place your feet over your opponent's thighs without crossing them. Reach under your opponent's neck with your right arm. Place your left hand behind your opponent's head and execute the choke. (Figure 10-3)

Figure 10-3. Rear naked choke.

BACK TOP WITHOUT THE GI

The version of the rear naked choke described below varies from the gi version described above because of the setup. In this version the position is attained by a unique manipulation of the opponent's arms.

Core Technique: Rear Naked Choke

The rear naked choke is perhaps the most common back choke and certainly one of the most powerful of all choking submissions. To execute the rear naked choke against an opponent, follow the steps in Figures 10-4 through 10-7.

The rear naked choke, like all chokes, can kill your opponent if you hold it for too long. You are *absolutely responsible* for your attacker's life and you must learn when to let go. Most street fighters have had no training, so don't expect your attacker to tap when he's about to pass out! You have to know when to quit.

Figure 10-4. Place your ankles on top of your opponent's thighs and control his arms.

Figure 10-5. Bring your right arm across your opponent's neck.

Figure 10-6. Place your right hand on your left biceps.

Figure 10-7. Place your left hand behind your opponent's head and squeeze to execute the choke.

One former sheriff's deputy and jiu-jitsu practitioner who was interviewed for this book used a rear naked choke in a scuffle with a suspect. Even though he is no longer in law enforcement, he asked that his quote shown below be anonymous.

I was moonlighting at a nightclub. It was closing time and this guy jumped on some other guy in the parking lot. I stepped in and pulled him off and he started fighting with me. He was punching and screaming. He was fighting wild, like a crazy man. Somehow we ended up on the ground. I got on the guy's back and got my hooks in. He kept on trying to bite me so finally I put him in a rear naked choke. I put the squeeze on him. I had the choke really good and I choked him hard. He stopped struggling. Somewhere in my mind I was thinking, "He's going to give; he's going to tap." Then I realized that this guy didn't know to tap. I let my grip loose a little bit. He was out! I got up and started shaking him. He came to OK, but this really made me think. You have to understand what's going on when you are on the street like that. You have to know when to stop. I was in a fog. I could have killed that guy!

Many police agencies, by the way, have banned the rear naked choke, calling it too dangerous. This former law enforcement officer's experience is a lesson to all jiu-jitsu fighters. If you use chokes to defend yourself, you will be responsible for what happens to your attacker.

Tactical Options

Back control is an amazingly versatile position. You can attack your opponent in dozens of ways. The most common attacks are chokes, so going for a knee-bar or an arm bar provides the advantage of surprise.

Arm Bar

Sink your hooks and assume back control. Capture an arm bar from the back control by first pushing your opponent's head to your right (Figure 10-8), releasing your right hook, and moving your hips to your right. Slide your right leg out from under your opponent's body. Then swing your right leg over your opponent's neck to capture the arm bar. (Figure 10-9)

Figure 10-8. Push aside your opponent's head.

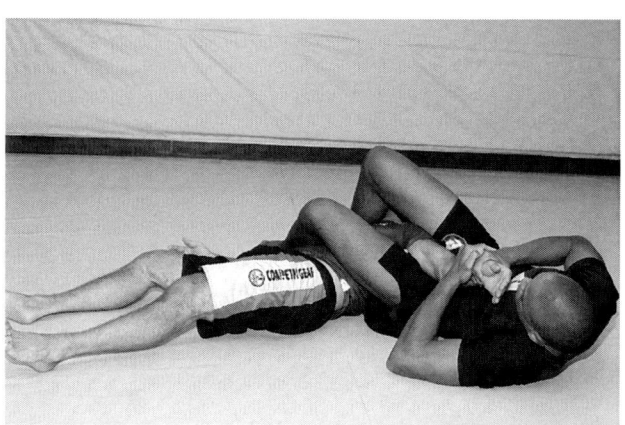

Figure 10-9. Capturing the arm bar.

Figure 10-10. Control your opponent's back by staying tight and by sinking your hooks.

Figure 10-11. Reach across your opponent's neck with your right arm and hold onto his left shoulder.

BACK TOP FOR NHB

Although it is possible to strike an opponent from the back, it is hard to do, and you would risk letting your opponent escape if you try it. For this reason, the rear naked choke is by far the most often used back-attack technique in NHB matches.

Core Technique: Rear Naked Choke

Execute the rear naked choke from back control by following the steps in Figures 10-10 through 10-12.

It can take as much as 30 seconds for a rear naked choke to black an opponent out. Experienced fighters know this and will often hold on to the very last second before tapping. Don't assume that your opponent isn't choking until you've held the choke for a minimum of 30 seconds. Some chokes, such as those that only block one side of the neck, can take much longer to cause blackout.

Figure 10-12. Place your left palm on the inside of your right elbow. Then place your right hand behind your opponent's neck to execute the rear naked choke.

Tactical Options

The power and effectiveness of the rear naked choke can be enhanced by assuming a top position. An example of this is covered below.

Figure 10-13. Rear naked crush.

Figure 10-14. Establish control of your opponent.

Figure 10-15. Taking the arm bar from the back.

Rear Naked Crush

If your opponent turns to his knees, reach under both arms and grab both wrists. Drive your hips down and your weight forward to flatten your opponent's body and crush him to the mat. (Figure 10-13) Then reach under your opponent's neck with your right arm and create the rear naked chokehold as described in the core technique above. Execute the submission.

Take the Arm Bar from the Back

Control your opponent by sinking both hooks and holding with your left arm going over the neck and your right arm under the armpit. (Figure 10-14) When ready, release your left hook and scoot your body to the right. Then swing your right leg over your opponent's head and take the arm bar. (Figure 10-15)

Figure 10-16. Protect your neck by pulling down on your opponent's arms and then looking toward his elbow.

Figure 10-17. Arch backward to the side in which your opponent has least control.

Figure 10-18. Put your shoulders flat on the mat and push yourself away from your opponent.

Figure 10-19. Control your opponent's leg and hips, then go on your knees to assume side control.

BACK BOTTOM WITH THE GI

When an opponent is on your back and has his hooks in place, you have three primary escape options. You can escape by bridging to the weak side, you can escape by bridging to the strong side, or you can escape by turning.

Core Technique: Bridge to the Weak Side

Bridging to the weak side is the preferred method for escaping back control. Follow the steps in Figures 10-16 through 10-19 to escape.

It is always best to go to your opponent's weak side, i.e., away from the arm that is wrapping around your neck. Your odds of escape from the weak side are much greater, as your opponent's leverage will be at its weakest point.

Tactical Option

Of course your opponent will attempt to keep you on his strong side. Your opponent may also switch hands and therefore change strong sides on you during your escape attempt. If you find yourself pulled to your opponent's strong side, you can still escape as shown in the following tactical option.

Bridge to the Strong Side

If you get pulled to your opponent's strong side, you will be at a severe leverage disadvantage. Escape is still possible, however, if you arch your back and place your shoulders flat on the mat. When your shoulders are flat, reach over your opponent's arm and pull upward. Pull your opponent's arm over your head as if you were taking a sweater off. (Figure 10-20) Press your head to the mat as you pull. Once free, turn toward your opponent and control his leg and hips. (10-21) Prevent your opponent from going on top as you scramble. Go to your knees and assume side control or a mounted position.

Figure 10-20. Pull your opponent's arm over your head.

Figure 10-21. Gain control of the leg and hips.

Figure 10-22. Observe that your opponent has crossed his feet.

Figure 10-23. Protect your neck with your right hand and use your left hand to place your left leg over your opponent's ankles.

Figure 10-24. Place your left ankle behind your right knee and arch your back to execute the ankle lock.

BACK BOTTOM WITHOUT THE GI

This counterattack technique will only work if your opponent crosses his ankles. If this happens, proceed quickly with the steps shown in Figures 10-22 through 10-24 to submit your opponent with this opportunistic ankle lock.

Core Technique: Ankle Lock

Even experienced fighters forget sometimes and cross their ankles. Be on the lookout for this mistake and be ready to attack.

Tactical Options

As in gi competitions, the escapes from back control for no-gi and NHB are limited. The no-gi version of the escape to the weak side and escape from the strong side techniques are described next.

Escape to the Weak Side

When your opponent places one arm across your neck, you must defend immediately by pulling down on his arm. Then, without hesitation, arch your back and move your body away from your opponent's leverage. Put your shoulders flat on the mat and continue to arch your hips. Block your opponent's hips as you make your escape and scramble to gain superior position.

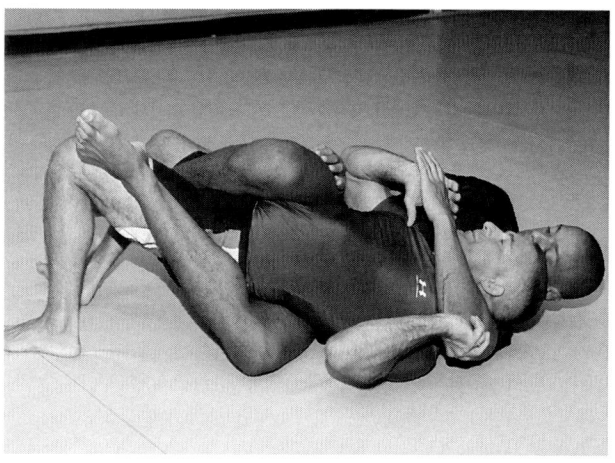

Figure 10-25. Escape to the strong side.

Figure 10-26. Protect your neck by pulling down on your opponent's left arm.

Escape to the Strong Side

If your opponent pulls you to his strong side, you may still be able to escape by lifting your hips and pressing your shoulders to the mat. Then press your opponent's choking arm away and slip your head out to escape. (Figure 10-25) Remember, it is always preferable to go to your opponent's weak side if possible.

BACK BOTTOM FOR NHB

Before you attempt to escape to the weak or strong side in an NHB match, or any match for that matter, you must first protect your neck. If you do not protect your neck first, you will almost certainly be submitted. Do not become complacent about neck protection. Your opponent will be watching for an easy opening.

Figure 10-27. Slip your head under your opponent's left arm.

Core Technique: Escape to the Weak Side

Follow the steps in Figures 10-26 through 10-30 to escape from the weak side when under back control.

Tactical Option

When you escape from back control, you will find that there is almost always a scramble. The fighter with the best scrambling skills often gains control of the fight at this moment.

Figure 10-28. Lift your hips and drop your shoulders onto the mat.

Figure 10-29. Block your opponent's left leg to prevent him from mounting and turn to your left.

Figure 10-30. Keep turning until you face your opponent in a closed guard, top position.

Escape to the Guard

If you follow the procedure described in the core technique above and your opponent stands during the scramble, you can keep your opponent from regaining control by pressing against his hips and using your right leg to hook behind the knee. (Figure 10-31) Keep your opponent away and quickly establish an open guard or closed guard position.

Figure 10-31. Escaping to the guard.

STRATEGIES FOR THE BACK

This section contains strategies for confronting each of the four fighter types—aggressive, deceptive, defensive, and interceptive—in the back-control condition. These are good strategies, but they are not the only strategies. Remember, there is no single best strategy. You must create your own—one that builds on your strengths. Your basic strategy will change slightly depending on the opponent that you face.

Fighting an Aggressive Opponent

When you have an aggressive opponent under back control, you should expect him to use lots of raw power in attempting to escape. For this reason you should firmly establish your position before attempting a submission. Make your aggressive opponent waste his energy trying to escape. Set up your attack following either a deceptive or interceptive strategy.

When you are fighting with an aggressive opponent and you get caught under back control, you are in real trouble. The back is a big favorite for aggressive fighters. You must react quickly and decisively in order to escape. Fake an escape attempt to one side then go hard to get out on the other. Don't wait.

Fighting a Deceptive Opponent

When you get a deceptive-type fighter under back control, you should attack him aggressively. Do not allow this type of fighter time to set up for an escape.

When a deceptive fighter has you under back control, you should watch out for fakes. For example, this kind of fighter is likely to fake the rear naked choke and snatch an arm bar. You can't let him set the agenda. Create an opening using your body weight for leverage and escape without hesitation.

Fighting a Defensive Opponent

Defensive fighters are usually good at squirming out of all sorts of bad situations. When you have a defensive fighter under back control, expect him to twist and turn. Keep him locked down. Then attack in a relentless and systematic way.

If a defensive fighter gets on your back, respond aggressively. Make him uncomfortable by fighting hard and using some power. Remember that defensive fighters are less comfortable in offensive positions. Remind him of that as you bust loose.

Fighting an Interceptive Opponent

When you get onto the back of an interceptive opponent, you can expect him to bait you by leaving something open. When you attack the opening, he will likely go for the escape. Use this to your advantage and attack him in places unexpected. Be deceptive in your approach.

When under back control from an interceptive fighter, you need to be on the lookout for traps and tricks. Remember—this is the fighter who likes to surprise. Watch for openings that lead to traps. Create your own opening and escape in a way that surprises him.

INTERVIEW: FERNANDO GURGEL ON STRATEGY

Alliance black belt Fernando Gurgel is an accomplished competitor and instructor. He is the brother of Fabio Gurgel, who is interviewed in Chapter 7.

Figure 10-32. Fernando Gurgel (right) and Jeff Joslin.

Fernando Gurgel's impressive record includes countless wins in many tournaments in blue and purple belt divisions, best purple belt of the year in 1987; first place Mundial, 1988; second place Pan American black-belt division, 1999; first place three times at the International Masters Tournament; and first place three times at the Brazilian Tournament. His team was team tournament winner in 1998 and 1999.

Question: How old were you when you started training?
Fernando Gurgel: Eighteen.
Q: Jacare was your teacher?
Gurgel: Yes. At his school in Rio de Janeiro.
Q: When did you get your black belt?
Gurgel: In 1994.
Q: You have your own school now?
Gurgel: Yes. My academy is Master Jiu-Jitsu in Rio.
Q: How far in advance should you begin preparing for a big tournament?
Gurgel: Three months.
Q: Do you know who your opponents will be?
Gurgel: Usually you know the guys that you are going to fight. They are always the same, the tough guys, everybody knows. You can make a preparation to focus on these guys, their strong points and how you can beat them. We always put a team together.
Q: How many people are normally on the team?
Gurgel: The more you have the better. At a minimum you have to get at least 10 or 15 guys together.
Q: You were one of the founders of the original Alliance team. How did that come about?
Gurgel: Jacare was the leader. Seven of us black belts decided to make a single team for competition. At this time, each of these black belts had his own team. We were competing one against the other at tournaments. So we decided to make one team, a strong team; we called it the Alliance Team.
Q: How did you prepare for the tournaments as one big team?
Gurgel: We would have special training on the weekends at the Academy in Rio for each division by level.
Q: Did you debrief after each tournament?
Gurgel: We always worked to correct our guys' weak points. For example if a guy lost a fight because he was not able to take his opponent down, we would have him work his takedowns. We did this for all of the students that were competing.
Q: Did you have too many guys for the competitions?
Gurgel: Yes. Sometimes we had internal tournaments to see who would go to the events on the main team. Later we created Alliance team A and Alliance team B. Alliance

B was made up of the guys that did not make the A team.

Q: How many guys were on the teams?

Gurgel: In those days, about 70 or 80 guys.

Q: The Alliance team had a split a few year back. Is it getting stronger again now?

Gurgel: Yes. Alliance is very strong in San Palo under my brother Fabio. We are working to become strong again here in Rio.

Q: Over the years the Alliance team has been a major player. What did you do to make it so successful?

Gurgel: Jacare made several good plans. We were all good friends that worked well together. We had very good relationships between us. We were focused on winning tournaments. We had technique to teach and we were like a family. We worked and trained really hard.

Q: You had many individual champions and you won several major team championships. What did you do differently from the other teams in those early years?

Gurgel: We thought like a team. For example, I was not worried about the other guys on the team that were in my age and weight class. I was not worried to be better than they were. I wanted to be as good as I could be for the team's success.

We used to compete with each other before the Alliance was formed. But after that we didn't mind to share techniques between the guys from the different academies that were in the Alliance Team. We shared the techniques and knowledge with every school in the team. The other teams probably did not do this.

Q: So the really strong teams are made up of several different schools. It must be hard to get those schools to come together and work as a unit.

Gurgel: We had a few problems, but this is the way that I believe works.

Q: What are your plans for the Alliance team?

Gurgel: In San Palo my brother Fabio is working to make a competition team. We are combining it with our guys in Rio. We are building the team back up.

Q: How has the sport of jiu-jitsu changed since you started training?

Gurgel: Nowadays the guys live for jiu-jitsu; they live for the tournaments. Twenty years ago it was only an amateur sport. These days you have a lot of guys that are full-time jiu-jitsu fighters. Their work is jiu-jitsu. They don't need to teach students. They are paid when they win fights. This is a big difference in the physical preparation. The top jiu-jitsu fighters nowadays are all professional athletes.

There was also physical evolution. The jiu-jitsu of today is different from 20 years ago. Twenty years ago you didn't have to know the judo part, the takedown part. Nowadays you have to be good at stand-up, good on bottom, good on top, good at all aspects of the game.

I remember when I was a blue belt. To pull guard worked, it was a very effective position. Very few guys worked the open guard. The open guard was defensive. Nowadays very few guys attack from the closed guard and everyone uses the open guard in an offensive way. This is just one way that jiu-jitsu is different today from 20 years ago.

Q: How would you describe your personal style?

Gurgel: When I started, I used to pull the guy inside my closed guard and attack him all the time. When I was a blue belt, purple, to brown belt I used this game. I had an offensive closed guard. When I became a black belt, I started to work my open guard more. I still pull the guy into my closed guard sometimes but not so frequently these days, because I am now a lot more comfortable fighting on top.

I have some takedowns that work. I use them, but stand-up fighting is not the strong part of my jiu-jitsu.

Q: What weight did you compete at?

Gurgel: 170–180 pounds.

Q: What is your experience with no-gi jiu-jitsu?

Gurgel: We used to do no-gi in the summer because it was too hot to train in the gi.

Q: Is there a big difference in gi and no-gi competition?

Gurgel: There is a big difference because you have more techniques to work with the gi. No-gi you have to work more with power.

Q: What is your experience with coaching no-rules or vale tudo fights?

Gurgel: I worked with my brother Fabio when he fought no rules at the UFC and other fights. Recently I helped coach another fighter for a no-rules match.

Q: What was your strategy to coach him?

Gurgel: I showed him techniques and corrected basic mistakes. He had good takedowns, but when he was inside the guard, he was making some mistakes. He needed to learn how to defend and block the punches when he was on the bottom. He needed to learn how to work his attacks from the bottom. I showed him techniques for fighting on the bottom.

CHAPTER 11

DIAGNOSIS

All warfare is based on deception. Hence, when able to attack, we must seem unable; when using our forces, we must seem inactive; when we are near, we must make the enemy believe we are far away; when far away, we must make him believe we are near.

—**Sun Tzu,** *The Art of War*

CREATING A STRATEGY

Six things are necessary in order for you to create an effective strategy to use against an opponent. You must:

1. Gather intelligence about your opponent
2. Understand your own preferred style of fighting: aggressive, deceptive, interceptive, or defensive
3. Determine your opponent's primary fighting style: aggressive, deceptive, interceptive, or defensive
4. Compare your technical skills with your opponent's
5. Compare your physical attributes with your opponent's
6. Sort through the data and organize it into a strategic plan that is customized to suit this specific opponent

Understand that there is no single strategy that will work for all opponents. Each new opponent whom you face will require a new strategy. Each strategy will operate on two simple rules:

1. Play your strengths against your opponent's weaknesses
2. Do not allow your opponent to play his strengths against your weaknesses

1. Gather Intelligence

In order to create a winning strategy, you must gather intelligence on your prospective opponent. Without proper and accurate intelligence you cannot create a meaningful strategy. The ancient military adviser Sun Tzu put it this way:

If you know the enemy and know yourself, you need not fear the result of a hundred battles. If you know yourself but not the enemy, for every victory gained you will also suffer a defeat. If you know neither the enemy nor yourself, you will succumb in every battle.

You can gain intelligence on your opponent by observing him in competition, viewing videos of his past matches, and by talking to other fighters who have gone up against him. Regardless of how you go about it, you must

Figure 11-1. Professor Cavalcanti (right) coaches NHB fighter Ryan Ellison during a match.

get as much information as you can to maximize your chances for victory.

2. Understand Your Style

In Chapter 1 we said that Dr. Marston's research identified four main personality styles or temperaments: dominance, influence, steadiness, and compliance. We believe these four personality styles present themselves in every aspect of life, including martial contests.

Once a fighter understands the four types he will never look at combat the same way. He will then be able to classify competitors and prepare strategies and cultivate techniques to take advantage of type preference and to overcome these "personality" differences.[1]

To better understand how the four styles manifest themselves in a martial setting, consider this logic: Some fighters are naturally more proactive than others. These fighters are the ones who like to take the fight to their opponent. There are two types of proactive fighters, those who rely on strength and attack constantly, and those who attack continuously but rely on speed, timing, combinations, and fakes to gain the advantage. In boxing lingo, the first type is known as a "slugger" and the second type is known as a "boxer." In jiu-jitsu we call them the aggressive fighter and the deceptive fighter.

Reactive fighters are more defensive, and they come in two types also, those fighters who are more or less purely defensive and those who attack in a calculating way while defending. We call the first type defensive fighters and the second type interceptive fighters. The chart below illustrates how the four styles manifest themselves.

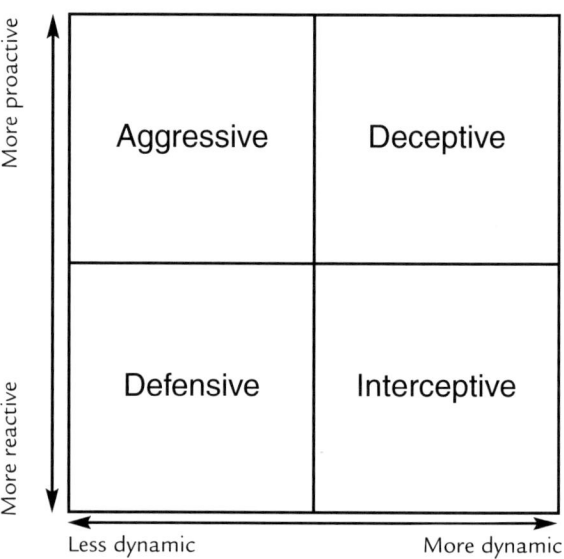

Aggressive fighters are the easiest to recognize because they attack constantly at full power. Deceptive fighters use fakes, combinations, and quick movements assertively to gain advantage. Defensive fighters defend constantly, stall a great deal, avoid submissions, escape from danger, and rarely attack. Interceptive fighters set traps and rely on counterattacks to gain advantage. To be effective in jiu-jitsu, or any martial art for that matter, you must first realize what your own natural style is and then you must be able to identify and adapt to your opponent's style. If, for example, you are a naturally aggressive fighter, you must be able to transform yourself, for a short while at least, into a deceptive, interceptive, or defensive fighter.

Figure 11-2. Alliance Muay Thai fighter and trainer Manu Ntoh, right, with Mark Van Schuyver.

This amounts to your having the ability to adapt your style of fighting in a way that pits your strengths against your opponent's weaknesses. In other words, you must be able to diagnose each opponent and alter your game accordingly.

3. Determine Your Opponent's Style

In the four scenarios that follow, imagine that you will be fighting with four different opponents, one from each of the four fighter types:

- Opponent A is an aggressive fighter
- Opponent B is a deceptive fighter
- Opponent C is a defensive fighter
- Opponent D is an interceptive fighter

Assume that each of these four opponents, A, B, C, and D, weighs about the same as you do, is about the same age as you are, is the same sex as you are, and has trained for about the same amount of time as you have. Also assume that all four of your opponents are ground-fight trained. Pretend, for now, that your own abilities are roughly equal in all four fighting styles, aggressive, deceptive, defensive, and interceptive. (This is hypothetical, of course, as you are almost certainly best in just one of the four styles.)

Strategies for Opponent A

Opponent A is highly aggressive. He is known for charging ahead and relentlessly attempting one submission technique after another. Opponent A is stronger than you are. He has a killer instinct. If Opponent A were a dog, he would be a pit bull, fighting stubbornly to the death while clamping down with jaws of steel. There are four ways that you can play it against Opponent A as shown below. Which strategy, or combination of strategies, will be most effective?

- Aggressive strategy (attack constantly with lots of power)
- Deceptive strategy (Uses timing, fakes, and quick movements assertively to gain advantage)
- Defensive strategy (Defend constantly, stall a lot, avoid submissions, escape danger, and rarely attack)
- Interceptive strategy (set defensive traps and use perfectly timed counterattacks)

Going head-to-head with an aggressive fighter is rarely a good option. Unless you are considerably stronger, you will probably lose. Even if you are stronger and ultimately prevail, you will waste a great deal of energy with this approach.

A defensive strategy usually doesn't work well against an aggressive opponent. Sooner or later your aggressive opponent will break through your defense and you will end up in trouble. An exception to this might be if you were fighting a sport match and you were well ahead on points and just needed to stall a bit to run out the clock. Another exception would be a case in which you play defense for a while and then switch to a different strategy to catch your opponent by surprise.

A deceptive approach can work well against an aggressive opponent. If you are really fast, you can use a deceptive strategy to avoid your opponent's power and take him out. Your goal should be to force the aggressive fighter to go on defense, but this is easier said than done. Defense is his weakest link, but you will need a lot of deception, i.e., fakes, speed, and timing advantages to prevail against superior power.

Fernando Gurgel is a 3rd-degree black belt under Professor Cavalcanti. Gurgel was Rio State Champion many times, Brazilian Champion many times, and was the light heavyweight Master World Champion in 1999 and 2004. Fernando Gurgel is a naturally aggressive fighter, but he uses an interceptive strategy when working against an equally aggressive opponent. He begins with an aggressive response to throw his opponent off balance and then converts to an interceptive style. "I start the fight being just as aggressive as my opponent is. I do this to make him think that the fight will pass this way. Then I slow down the rhythm of the fight and start to counterattack."

You can beat an aggressive opponent with an interceptive style even if he is a lot stronger providing that you have solid counter fighting skills and excellent timing. "I like to let an aggressive opponent feel comfortable in the early part of the match and then suddenly explode into my attack," explained Majid Alkush, an Alliance BJJ and NHB competitor. You always take a risk when you employ an interceptive strategy because you must conduct it from defensive positions. By definition, an interceptive strategy means that you must risk something in order to set up effective counters.

The best-to-worst style strategies to use against an aggressive fighter are shown in order in the chart that follows. This is a general guideline, not an absolute. Use this guideline as a tool but don't forget that a combination of strategies is usually superior to a single strategy. Keep in mind the fact that even fighters with the same style have subtle differences in their delivery. Remember also that your opponent may alter his style during the match because of the point score or other factors.

Strategies for Opponent B

Opponent B is a deceptive fighter. He is known for using a lot of fakes and quick movements to set up effective submission techniques. Opponent B is faster than you are. If Opponent B were a dog, he would be a chihuahua, always darting in and out and running behind you and biting at your heels. There are four ways that you can play it against Opponent B.

Unless you are better at deceptive fighting than your deceptive opponent, you will be wise not to use this same style against him. Speed is one of the key features of the deceptive fighter, so a defensive strategy will only work if you are considerably faster. The same is true with an interceptive approach. You must be one step ahead of your opponent in order to set counterattack traps for him. This means that you must be faster in order to prevail with an interceptive style.

Fernando Gurgel often employs a defensive strategy when faced with a deceptive opponent. "I don't run after him. I wait to grab his gi and I try to keep the fight on the floor. I usually pull him to my guard."

The deceptive fighter's specialty is using speed and timing to take advantage of openings. If you have an excellent defense, you can slow him down and thwart his attacks. This can have the effect of wearing your deceptive opponent out and making him vulnerable to counterattack. Later in the fight you can convert to an aggressive strategy or an interceptive strategy and force him to defend while exhausted.

The best-to-worst style strategies to use against a deceptive fighter are shown in order

Fighter Type A	Best-to-Worst Strategies
Aggressive	Deceptive
	Interceptive
	Aggressive
	Defensive

Figure 11-3. Alliance competitor David Heck goes for a Kimura attack.

in the chart that follows. Use this guideline as a tool, but don't forget that a combination of strategies is generally superior to a single strategy. Keep in mind that even fighters with the same style have subtle differences in their delivery. Remember also that your opponent may alter his style during the match because of the point score or other factors.

Fighter Type B	Best-to-Worst Strategies
Deceptive	Defensive, transforming to interceptive or aggressive
	Interceptive
	Aggressive
	Deceptive

Strategies for Opponent C

Opponent C is a defensive fighter. He is known for defending constantly, stalling a lot, and rarely going on the attack. This opponent considers not losing to be a victory. This opponent is very likely to stall anytime, especially when he is up on points. This opponent is also likely to be very difficult to submit. He is adept at escaping, avoiding, redirecting, and generally surviving the toughest of fights.

Opponent C is more relaxed than you are and very wary. If this fighter were a dog, he would likely be a stray mutt able to evade attacks from much bigger dogs, dodge brooms, shoes, and rocks and able to survive against unlikely odds. The defensive fighter is all about not getting submitted, not losing points, and not giving up position. There are four ways that you can play it against Opponent C.

Opponent's C's game is survival and endurance. He is the quintessential rope-a-doper. If you go after him with an aggressive strategy, you will find him to be exceedingly difficult to submit. If you use a deceptive strategy, you will find the defensive fighter to be really difficult to trick.

To gain a clear victory against a defensive fighter you must somehow force him to attack you. Remember, attack is the weakest part of the defensive fighter's game and therefore his most vulnerable area. According to Fernando Gurgel, you can do this best by using an interceptive strategy. "You have to make him expose himself. You have to draw him into fight."

One way to accomplish this is to feign weakness or injury and offer an easy opening. Use body language that makes you appear to be timid. Open yourself to attack. Pretend to be easy prey so that he will fall into your well-prepared counterattack. With this strategy and a bit of luck, you will have your defensive opponent tapping in no time and with a minimum of energy expended on your part.

The best-to-worst style strategies to use against a defensive fighter are shown in the chart that follows.

Fighter Type C	Best-to-Worst Strategies
Defensive	Interceptive
	Defensive
	Aggressive
	Deceptive

Strategies for Opponent D

Opponent D is an interceptive fighter. He is known for setting defensive traps and using perfectly timed counterattacks. This opponent is extremely dangerous. He thrives on being attacked. This opponent thinks of fighting as if it were chess. The game that this fighter plays is built upon patience and timing. If this fighter were a dog, he would be a chow, waiting quietly by the fence, never barking, seeming very sweet, and then biting you without warning as soon as you walk through the gate.

Opponent D has great timing and is more relaxed than you are. This opponent is willing to risk something in order to win a submission. Some of his favorite techniques are performed during a scramble and from seemingly defensive conditions. There are four ways that you can play it against Opponent D.

Opponent D's game is bait and switch. If you go after him with an aggressive strategy, you will find yourself running into one trap after another. The same is true when you use a deceptive strategy. An opponent strong in interception will watch for patterns in your deceptive attacks and lay traps for you. "When you are up against this kind of fighter, you must be very careful when you attack. You must try not to expose yourself. You have to always be watching for a surprise," according to Fernando Gurgel.

The easiest way to win against an interceptive fighter is to force him to go on the offensive. Use a defensive strategy that causes him to become overconfident and to keep coming after you until you are ready to switch into an interceptive strategy of your own and catch him in a wicked submission trap.

The best-to-worst style strategies to use against an aggressive fighter are shown in the chart that follows. This is a general guideline, not an absolute. Use this guideline as a tool but don't forget that a combination of strategies is generally superior to a single strategy. Keep in mind that even fighters with the same style have subtle differences in their delivery. Remember also that your opponent may alter his style during the match because of the point score or other factors.

Figure 11-4. Alliance competitor Jonathan Tooker attacks from the back.

Fighter Type D	Best-to-Worst Strategies
Interceptive	Defensive, changing to interceptive
	Interceptive
	Deceptive
	Aggressive

Now that you have considered the best approach for taking on a fighter from each of the four different types, you have taken your first step toward victory. To customize a strategy against a particular opponent, however, you must also complete a comprehensive diagnosis of your technical skills and of your opponent's technical skills relative to the 18 ground-fighting conditions.

4. Compare Your Technical Skills

The following assessment tool is designed to give you a way to rate your technical strengths and weaknesses and compare them to your opponent's. First, score yourself on each item below using the following 1–5 scale, with consideration to your rank, age, and sex.

1 = No skill
2 = Below-average skill
3 = Average skill
4 = Above-average skill
5 = Outstanding skills

Place a number 1 through 5 next to each of the 18 ground-fighting conditions shown below.

From this self-assessment you can now see where your game is strongest and where it is weakest. Your first strategy is to train in a way that raises your scores in all areas. You do this by deliberately forcing yourself to spar in conditions that you are weak in. Michael Hanson, winner of a gold medal in his division at the World's Master's International in 2001, put it this way: "When you compete, you fight to win, but when you train, you should train to get better and to improve your game. You spar to learn, not to win."

When it is time to compete, you can use the diagnostic assessment tool to rate your opponent's strengths and weaknesses in the same manner. For this exercise to be meaningful, you must select a single, real opponent.

At this point you are ready to devise a strategy in which you employ an aggressive, interceptive, deceptive, or defensive strategy (or a combination of these) against the areas of your opponent's game in which you are strongest and he is weakest. Rate yourself and your opponent on each of the 18 conditions.

TECHNICAL SKILLS COMPARISON TOOL

Condition	Rate Self	Rate Opponent	Condition	Rate Self	Rate Opponent
Standing Attacks			Standing Counters		
Closed Guard on Top			Closed Guard on Bottom		
Open Guard on Top			Open Guard on Bottom		
Half Guard on Top			Half Guard on Bottom		
Side Control Top			Side Control Bottom		
North-to-South Top			North-to-South Bottom		
Knee-in-the-Belly Top			Knee-in-the-Belly Bottom		
Mount on Top			Mount on Bottom		
Back on Top			Back on Bottom		

To devise a strategy that compensates for the variation in technical skills, first look for any area in which there is a gap of more than one point in your favor. Consider a hypothetical case where your closed guard rates a 4 to your opponent's 1, your open guard on bottom is a 4 to your opponent's 2, your north-to-south top game is 3 to your opponent's 1, your back on bottom skill is 4 and your opponent's is 2.

Now look for any areas in which there is a gap of more than one point in your opponent's favor. In this hypothetical case your opponent's

Figure 11-5. (Left to right) Felipe Neto, Laura Uria, Elaine Rito-Cavalcanti, and Jacare Cavalcanti.

half guard on top is a 4 and yours is 2, your opponent's side control top game is 4 and yours is 1, your opponent's mount on bottom skills are 4 and your mount top skills are 2.

Your best approach against this hypothetical opponent will be to force him to fight you in the areas where your technical abilities are strongest and his are weakest. In this case, you should strive to fight your opponent from your closed guard, open guard, and/or from a north-to-south top position. Avoid attacking this opponent from the top mount position because his mount bottom defensive skills are higher than your mount top offensive skills.

In this hypothetical case your opponent has superior abilities in the half guard top position and the side control position. You must, therefore, avoid getting put into these conditions at all cost. You must stay out of any condition if your opponent has such a superior advantage, even if it means sacrificing an advantage.

Now that you know how to diagnose and accommodate for your opponent's style and technical skill, you are ready for the last stage. You are now ready to look at the strategic value of your opponent's physical attributes in comparison with your own.

In strategy it is important to see distant things as if they were close and to take a distanced view of close things.

—Miyamoto Musashi

5. Compare Your Physical Attributes

Let's continue now to work the diagnostic process with a single, real opponent in mind. At this point you must consider the physical attributes possessed by your opponent. Is he taller, stronger, faster, older, heavier, and so on. On the street you never know what you might face. In the dojo you should train with partners who have a wide variety of attribute variances to stretch your game and learn your limits. Tournaments are designed to level the playing field where attributes are concerned. Even the best-designed tournaments, however, can never totally equal out the attributes formula between fighters.

Use the diagnostic chart that follows to create a comparison between your attributes and those possessed by your opponent. This diagnostic assumes that you are competing with an opponent of the same sex.

Attribute Advantages

Consider the general guidelines on advantages shown below as you construct your strategy for any particular opponent. The percentages shown are approximations based on our experience.

- If you outweigh your opponent by 20 pounds or more, you have an advantage of

20 percent or more (roughly equal to one belt ranking).
- If you are five or more inches taller than your opponent, you have an advantage of approximately 5 percent in the stand-up conditions and in the closed and open guard bottom conditions.
- If your conditioning is high and your opponent's conditioning is low, you have an advantage of 10 percent or more.
- If your strength is high and your opponent's is low, you have an advantage of 20 percent or more.
- If you are fast and your opponent is slow, you will have an advantage of 10 percent or more.
- Given that you have each completed one year of training, you will have an advantage of approximately 15 percent for each additional year of training that exceeds your opponent's (this rule continues up to the point at which each fighter hits his personal best).
- For each belt rank above your opponent, you will have an advantage of 20 percent or more.
- Each time you go to a competition you gain an advantage of approximately 5 percent against an opponent who does not compete.
- If you and your opponent are both between the ages of 18 and 30, neither of you will have any significant age advantage. After 30, your opponent will gain a 5 percent or greater advantage for each 5 years that he is your junior.

Figure 11-6. Alliance competitor Tony Barker (right) wins a no-gi match.

ATTRIBUTES COMPARISON TOOL

Attribute	You	Your Opponent
Weight		
Height		
Age		
Speed (slow, moderate, fast)		
Years of training		
Rank		
Conditioning (poor, fair, good, excellent)		
Strength (low, middle, high)		
Competition experience (none, some, lots)		

The primary attributes of weight, height, conditioning, strength, speed, years of training, rank, competition experience, and age do make a difference. The more attribute advantages that you have going for you the better your chances. It is possible to have a washout in attributes advantages. You might, for example be younger, in better condition, and faster but facing an opponent who is stronger, 20 pounds heaver, and with a bit more competition experience than you. In this case it could be a wash, or some of the remaining attributes could tip the scale in your favor or in your opponent's.

What can you do with this information? In the short term there is little that you can do regarding your weight, height, age, speed, years of training, and rank. You can, however, increase your level of conditioning, your strength, and your competition experience within a short period of time. What was an even match in terms of fighter attributes can be quickly tilted in your favor if you work hard to increase your relative attributes in these three areas.

You have to know your strengths and weaknesses, and you have to know your opponent's strengths and weaknesses. You will try to hide your weaknesses and take advantage of his, and he will do the same. The winner will be the fighter who prepares the best strategy.
—Rodrigo Gracie [2]

6. Organize the Data

As we have discussed, strategy in jiu-jitsu fighting is created from intelligence gathered in advance on three core elements: a fighter's style, technical skills, and physical attributes. The next stage in creating a fight strategy is to combine these data into a comprehensive plan that illuminates the strengths, weaknesses, opportunities, and threats relative to this particular opponent.

Complete your strategic plan by carrying the appropriate data from the three diagnostic tools above and placing them into the strategic planning tool below. If you have a coach, be sure to seek his guidance as you construct your strategic plan.

Congratulations. You have completed a comprehensive diagnosis and developed a strategic plan for taking on this opponent. All that is left to do now is to train hard and practice your strategy.

To practice your strategy you should simulate the conditions that you anticipate in the upcoming fight. Do this by sparring with partners who have traits similar to your opponent's traits and/or by asking your training partner(s) to emulate the traits of your opponent. Apply your strategy in practice with your partner(s). Test your strategy again and again and make revisions as necessary. Include techniques and tactics that fit your strategy and enhance its effectiveness. Ask your training partners and your coach for feedback after every sparring session.

POST-COMPETITION DIAGNOSTIC

You will learn the most about the effectiveness of your strategy when the fight is over. As soon as the match is completed you should conduct an extensive diagnostic of what went well and what did not. Do this as soon as possible after the fight while the memories are fresh in your mind. Use the Post-Competition Diagnostic tool for this purpose.

APPLYING THE LESSONS OF THIS BOOK

If you didn't know before reading this book, you now know that ground-fighting skills are an absolutely essential element of any well-rounded fighter's game. You know the history of the art and you know that Brazilian jiu-jitsu advances a primary strategy based on the well-documented fact that a stand-up-only fighter can be thoroughly neutralized when taken to the ground by a talented ground fighter. You also know how and why Brazilian jiu-jitsu makes sophisticated use of the principles of leverage and of isolation.

Strategic Plan		
Opponent: _____		
My primary fighting style (circle one) Aggressive Deceptive Interceptive Defensive	**My opponent's fighting style** (circle one) Aggressive Deceptive Interceptive Defensive	**Style or styles I will use to defeat this opponent**
My technical skills Strengths Weaknesses	**My opponent's technical skills** Strengths Weaknesses	**Conditions (1–18) that I will use in this fight** **Conditions (1–18) that I will avoid in this fight**
My physical attributes Advantageous to me Disadvantageous to me	**My opponent's physical attributes** Advantageous to him Disadvantageous to him	**Steps I will follow to take advantage of my superior attributes** **Steps I will follow to compensate for my inferior attributes**

From this book you have learned techniques, tactics, and strategies for applying Brazilian jiu-jitsu in various classifications including gi competitions, no-gi competitions, submission matches, and NHB matches. You learned how to attack, counterattack, defend, and outsmart your opponent from each of the 18 ground-fighting conditions.

In this, the last chapter, you learned how to diagnose your opponent's fighting style and how to create a customized strategy based on his style, technical skills, and physical attributes. You learned how to create a comprehensive strategic plan for fighting any opponent. At this point you are ready to tie it all together and make the jump from technician to strategist. Whether you are a beginner, intermediate, or advanced practitioner, your game will never be the same. By reading and studying this book you have taken the first step into a much larger world, a world that only the best fighters know about—the world of the strategic fighter.

We hope that your journey will be victorious and rewarding.

ENDNOTES

1. Pedro Solano Villalobos and Mark Van Schuyver. *Fighting Strategies of Muay Thai: Secrets of Thailand's Boxing Camps.* Boulder, CO: Paladin Press, 2002.

2. Rodrigo Gracie and Kid Peligro. *Brazilian Jiu-Jitsu: No Holds Barred! Fighting Techniques.* Montpelier, VT: Invisible Cities Press. 2005.

Post-Competition Diagnostic			
Strategy	What worked?	What did not work?	What will I do differently next time?
Style Strategy			
Technical Skills Strategy			
Attributes Strategy			

Additional intelligence gained on this opponent:

Notes:

REFERENCES

"Air War College, Gateway to the Internet." United States Air Force. http://www.au.af.mil/au/awc/awcgate/awcgate.htm.

Alliance Martial Arts Center. http://www.alliancebjj.com/index.htm.

"ASME Tools of Discovery." American Society of Mechanical Engineers. http://www.asme.org/education/precollege/discovery/page13.htm (page discontinued).

Beneville, Ed, and Tim Cartmell. *Passing the Guard: Brazilian Jiu-Jitsu Details and Techniques*. Costa Mesa, CA: Grappling Arts Publications, LLC., 2002.

Chen, Jim. "Masahiko Kimura (1917–1993): The Man Who Defeated Helio Gracie." The Original Judo Information Site. http://judoinfo.com/kimura3.htm (accessed 2001).

Cox, Monte. "It's a Styles Thing." Cox's Corner. http://coxscorner.tripod.com/styles.html (accessed 1999).

Ferguson. Robert. *Submission Wrestling: The Martial Arts Guide to Grappling*. Malibu, CA: ABC Publications. 1999.

Gracie, Carlson and Julio Fernandez. *Brazilian Jiu-Jitsu: for Experts Only: Classic Jiu-Jitsu Techniques from the Master*. Montpelier, VT: Invisible Cities Press. 2004.

Gracie, Renzo, Royler Gracie, and John Danaher. Kid Peligro, ed. *Brazilian Jiu-Jitsu, Theory and Technique*, Montpelier, VT: Invisible Cities Press in association with Editora Gracie. 2001.

Gracie, Rodrigo and Kid Peligro. *Brazilian Jiu-Jitsu: No Holds Barred! Fighting Techniques*. Montpelier, VT: Invisible Cities Press. 2005.

Gracie, Royce and Kid Peligro. *Ultimate Fighting Techniques, Volume 1: The Top Game*. Montpelier, VT: Invisible Cities Press. 2005.

Gracie, Royler and Kid Peligro. *Brazilian Jiu-Jitsu: Submission Grappling Techniques*. Montpelier, VT: Invisible Cities Press. 2003.

Gracie.com. Official Domain of Gracie USA. http://www.gracie.com/ (accessed 2005).

Kano, Jigoro. *Kodukan Judo*. Tokyo: Kodansha International Ltd., Bunkyo-ku. 1986.

Kobayashi, Kiyoshi and Harold E. Sharp. *The Sport of Judo as Practiced in Japan*. Rutland, VT, Tokyo: Charles E. Tuttle Company. 1956.

Machado, Jean Jacques and Kid Peligro. *Brazilian Jiu-Jitsu: Black Belt Techniques*. Montpelier, VT: Invisible Cities Press, 2003.

Machado, Jean Jacques and Kid Peligro. *Brazilian Jiu-Jitsu: Championship Techniques*. Montpelier, VT: Invisible Cities Press, 2004.

Machado, Rigan and Jose M. Fraguas. *Encyclopedia of Brazilian Jiu-Jitsu, Volume 1*. Burbank, CA: Unique publications, 2004.

Machado, Rigan. *The Essence of Brazilian Jiu-Jitsu*. Burbank, CA: CFW Enterprises, 2002.

MacKenzie, Brian. "Levers." Sports Coach. http://www.brianmac.demon.co.uk/levers.htm (accessed 2005).

McLaughlin, Brian. "Interviews: Eddie Bravo Interview." BJJFighter.com. http://www.bjjfighter.com/Interview/bravo.html.

Montanha. *The Brazilian Jiu-Jitsu Mind Set: To Submit Your Opponent from Any Position*. Walnut Creek, CA: Montanha Press, 2004.

Official Web Site of the Gracie Jiu-Jitsu Academy. http://www.gracieacademy.com/.

Pedreira, Roberto. A. "Then Came Rorion." Global Training Report: Academy Reports. http://www.geocities.com/global_training_report/rorion.htm (accessed 2000).

Peligro, Kid. *The Gracie Way: An Illustrated History of the Gracie Family*. Montpelier, VT: Invisible Cities Press, 2003.

Personality Assessment Solutions, Ltd. ThePeople@TestsontheNet.com. "The Ubiquitous DISC Test and Lies." http://www.testsonthenet.com/disc/ww-info.htm.

Simco, Gene. *Brazilian Jiu-Jitsu: The Master Text*. Poughkeepsie, NY: Jiu-Jitsu Net, 2001.

Simco, Gene. *Brazilian Jiu-Jitsu: the Student Handbook*. USA: self-published. 1999.

Stockton, R. *Who Was the Greatest?* Phoenix, AZ: Boxing Enterprises, 1977.

Team Resources, Inc. Personal DISCernment Inventory, The DISC Profile System, Atlanta, GA, http://www.teamresources.com. (accessed 2005).

Technology at GCSE. "Mechanisms: Levers & Calculations." http://www.btinternet.com/~hognosesam/gcse/page61.html (accessed 2005).

Tiscali.com Research Machines plc. http://www.tiscali.co.uk/reference/encyclopaedia/hutchinson/m0017416.html (accessed 2005)

Turner, Karyn and Mark Van Schuyver. *Secrets of Championship Karate*. Contemporary Books, 1991.

Tzu, Sun. *The Art of War*. Translated by Lionel Giles. http://classics.mit.edu/Tzu/artwar.html

Various. "Principles of Utilitarianism." Everything2.com. http://www.everything2.com/index.pl?node=Principles%20of%20Utilitarianism.

Villalobos, Pedro Solano and Mark Van Schuyver. *Fighting Strategies of Muay Thai: Secrets of Thailand's Boxing Camps*. Boulder, CO: Paladin Press, 2002.

Yoshinori, Nishi. Yoko Kondo, trans. "Helio Gracie reveals the true story behind his epic battle with Kimura Masahiko." From *Kakutou Striking Spirit*. Global Training Report. http://www.geocities.com/global_training_report/helio.htm (accessed 2002).

About the Authors

Master Romero "Jacare" Cavalcanti is a 6th-degree black belt in Brazilian jiu-jitsu. He is one of only six people in the world to have earned his black belt from legendary jiu-jitsu instructor Rolls Gracie.

When Cavalcanti was 11 years old, he took his first lessons in jiu-jitsu with Jaildo Gomes. At the age of 15 or so he began training at the Gracie School in Rio de Janeiro, at first under Carlson Gracie and later under Rolls Gracie. His classmates at the Gracie School included Carlos Gracie Jr., Crolin Gracie, Fabio Santos, Ricardo Azoury, Lacerda, Talarico, Luis Palhares, Marcio Simas, Marcio Macarrao, Paulo Conde, Nicin Azulay, and Carlos and Rigan Machado.

In 1972 Cavalcanti took a leave from his formal jiu-jitsu training and traveled to the United States to study English and to work. Ironically, it was in New York that he and Rolls Gracie spent a lot of time together and became fast friends. Cavalcanti said, "One day, out of the blue, Rolls showed up at my apartment on the Upper East Side. His mother lived a few blocks away and he was there to visit her. We became very good friends."

Rolls encouraged Cavalcanti to return to the Gracie School, complete his training, and pursue a career in jiu-jitsu. In 1974 Cavalcanti, determined to finish what he started, did return to Brazil. He resumed his formal training at the Gracie Academy under Rolls Gracie and entered one competition after another. "I was part of Rolls' first competition team with Carlos Gracie Jr., Paulo Conde, Nissin, Mauricio Gomes, Ricardo Azoury, Renan Pilanguy, Rodrigo Milanda, Sergio Sucuri, and a few others," he said.

In 1982 Rolls promoted Cavalcanti to the rank of black belt. By then Cavalcanti had competed in many tournaments and had been Rio

Romero "Jacare" Cavalcanti.

de Janeiro State Champion, which was considered the National Championship in those days. "I owe everything to him," Cavalcanti said of Rolls. "He was like a father to me."

Just four months after Cavalcanti's promotion to black belt, Rolls Gracie was killed in a hang-gliding accident. Cavalcanti was so devastated by Rolls' sudden death that for several months he did not train at all. So great was his grief and shock at Rolls' tragic death that for a while he even considered giving up on his dream to build a career for himself in jiu-jitsu.

After much soul searching, Cavalcanti made up his mind to do his part to carry on the legacy of Rolls Gracie. He returned to the Gracie Academy and trained under Helio and Rickson Gracie for three more years. In 1985 Professor Cavalcanti officially launched his professional career in jiu-jitsu by opening his own academy in Rio.

Several years after opening his academy, Cavalcanti partnered with his top students to form the Alliance Team. Today the Alliance Team is enormous, with hundreds of members and professional representation around the globe. The Alliance Team is home to some of the world's top jiu-jitsu competitors and coaches, many of whom were trained by Cavalcanti or his students including Fabio Gurgel, Rodrigo "Comprido" Medeiros, Felipe Neto, Otavio "Ratinho" Couto, Roberto Traven, Ryan Ellison, Leo and Rico Vieira, Marcello Garcia, Chris Moriarty, Fernando Gurgel, Marcelo Mendes, Paulo Sergio Santos, Roger Brooking, Ricardo "Franjinha" Miller, Sarrvco Jamelao, Jeff Joslin, Felipe Costa, Gigi, Bull Shaw, Pat Harvey, Paulo Sergio Santos, Peck Laudier, Toti, Pinduca, Elijah Gardner, Kenny Mclendon, Chad Lebrun, Paul Creighthon, and many others.

In the mid-1990s Cavalcanti left his Rio Academy in the care of Fabio Gurgel and moved to the United States. In 1995 he opened a school in Atlanta, Georgia. Today, Cavalcanti owns and operates the Alliance Martial Arts Centers located at two sites in the Atlanta metro area (http://www.alliancebjj.com/index.htm). He oversees eight satellite schools and many affiliate schools at various locations in the United States, Brazil, Canada, Australia, Finland, Germany, and Venezuela. In addition, Cavalcanti is the hand-to-hand combat consultant/instructor for the U.S. Army Rangers at Fort Benning, Georgia.

Cavalcanti, or Professor Jacare (the Portuguese word for alligator) as he is known to his students, is the founder of the Brazilian Jiu-Jitsu Federation, the president of the Georgia State BJJ/Submission Wrestling Federation, head coach of the international Alliance Team, and a referee for the Brazilian Jiu-Jitsu Federation. In competition he was a three-time winner of the Brazilian Championships and won many Rio de Janeiro State Championships. In 2004 the International Fighting Federation elected him Coach of the Year, and in 2005 he was inducted into the Grappling Hall of Fame. Cavalcanti is widely regarded as one of the top Brazilian jiu-jitsu instructors in the World today. Some highlights from his coaching career are shown below.

2006 NAGA (North American Grappling Society) Georgia: State Champions, Team Champions
2006 Budweiser Jiu-Jitsu World Cup; Charlotte, North Carolina: Team Champions
2005 Arnold Gracie World Submission Championships; Columbus, Ohio: Team Champions
2004 NAGA Georgia: State Champions
2004 Pan American; Los Angeles, California: Team Champions
2004 Arnold Gracie World Submission Championships; Columbus, Ohio: second-place team
2004 Budweiser Jiu-Jitsu World Cup; Charlotte, North Carolina: Champions
2003 Pan American master/seniors; Santa Barbara, California: first-place team
2003 Pan American adult division; Santa Barbara, California: second-place team overall

2003 Pan American; Santa Barbara, California: second-place team overall
2004 Nashville Grappling Championship; Nashville, Tennessee: first-place team
2003 World Championship; Rio de Janeiro, Brazil: second-place team
2003 World Cup; Rio de Janeiro, Brazil: second-place team

2002 NAGA Georgia; Atlanta, Georgia: State Champions

Cavalcanti lives in Atlanta with his wife, Elaine, and their children. See his complete bio online at http://www.alliancebjj.com/index.htm or contact him by e-mail at jacare@alliancebjj.com or via Paladin Press at service@paladin-press.com.

Mark Van Schuyver, PhD, is the author of dozens of martial arts articles. His work has been published in many national magazines including *Black Belt, Inside Kung-Fu, Karate/Kung-Fu Illustrated, Karate Illustrated, Fighter International, MA Training, American Karate, Tae Kwon Do Times, American Handgunner,* and *Inside Karate*. Van Schuyver is also the author of three books, *Fighting Strategies of Muay Thai: Secrets of Thailand's Boxing Camps* (Paladin Press, 2002) written with co-author Pedro Solana Villalobos; *Secrets of Championship Karate* written with co-author Karyn Turner (Contemporary Books, 1991); and this book, *Brazilian Jiu-Jitsu Fighting Strategies,* written with co-author Romero "Jacare" Cavalcanti (Paladin Press, 2006).

Van Schuyver began his study of the martial arts when he was 18 years old. In his early twenties he earned a black belt in the Ching-Yi kung-fu system under Master Her Yue Wong. In the years that followed, he studied a number of different martial art styles. In the spring of 1999, he began training in Brazilian jiu-jitsu under the tutelage of world-renowned jiu-jitsu master and co-author of this book, Romero "Jacare" Cavalcanti. Van Schuyver is a Pan Am medalist and at the time of this writing holds a brown belt in Brazilian jiu-jitsu under Cavalcanti.

With a bachelor's in English Literature, a master's degree in business (MBA), and a master's degree in organization development (MOD), Van Schuyver earned his PhD in human and organizational systems from Fielding Graduate University in Santa Barbara, California (www.fielding.edu). He is a manager at Georgia-Pacific, as well as an adjunct professor rotating between two schools, Mercer University and American InterContinental University. He teaches courses to graduate and undergraduate students in a variety of management-related subjects including leadership and ethics for managers, organization development and change, organizational behavior, leadership and technology, and leadership in the global workplace.

Van Schuyver is the father of three children, Holly, William, and Sarah. He and his wife,

Mark Van Schuyver.

Dessa, live in Lawrenceville, Georgia, a suburb of Atlanta. See his complete bio online at www.vanschuyver.net or contact him by e-mail at vanschuyver@charter.net or via Paladin Press at service@paladin-press.com.